ALLIANCES, NUCLEAR WEAPONS AND ESCALATION

MANAGING DETERRENCE IN THE 21ST CENTURY

ALLIANCES, NUCLEAR WEAPONS AND ESCALATION

MANAGING DETERRENCE IN THE 21ST CENTURY

EDITED BY STEPHAN FRÜHLING
AND ANDREW O'NEIL

Australian
National
University

PRESS

ANU PRESS

Published by ANU Press
The Australian National University
Acton ACT 2601, Australia
Email: anupress@anu.edu.au

Available to download for free at press.anu.edu.au

ISBN (print): 9781760464905
ISBN (online): 9781760464912

WorldCat (print): 1285533360
WorldCat (online): 1285533216

DOI: 10.22459/ANWE.2021

Cover design and layout by ANU Press

Cover photograph: B-2 Spirit operates at Naval Support Facility Diego Garcia. © Tech. Sgt. Heather Salazar. The appearance of U.S. Department of Defense (DoD) visual information does not imply or constitute DoD endorsement.

This book is published under the aegis of the Asia-Pacific Security Studies Editorial Board of ANU Press.

Contents

Part III: Nuclear Weapons and Non-Nuclear Capabilities

Part IV: Bringing the Public Along: Talking about Nuclear Weapons and Deterrence

Conclusions

Acknowledgements

No book, and certainly no edited volume, sees the light of day without the significant support of those behind the scenes. We are very grateful to Dr Emily Robertson for her outstanding research assistance and project management skills that were integral in preparing the volume. We thank all contributors for their sustained commitment to the project during what was for many an exceptionally difficult period navigating the impacts of COVID-19. We would also like to thank Dr Greg Raymond and Emily Tinker at ANU Press for their continuing support for the project and the two anonymous reviewers who provided important suggestions on improvements to the manuscript.

Finally, we gratefully acknowledge the generous financial support for this project provided by Australia's Department of Defence through its Strategic Policy Grants scheme.

Stephan Frühling
Canberra

Andrew O'Neil
Brisbane

Abbreviations

ACM	Alliance Coordination Mechanism
ADF	Australian Defence Force
ANZUS	Australia, New Zealand, United States Security Treaty
APEC	Asia-Pacific Economic Cooperation
ASAT	anti-satellite
ASEAN	Association of Southeast Asian Nations
ASW	anti-submarine warfare
BMD	ballistic missile defence
CCP	Chinese Communist Party
CPGS	conventional prompt global strike
CPS	conventional prompt-strike
CSIS	Centre for Strategic and International Studies
DCA	dual-capable aircraft
DDA	Deterrence and Defence of the Euro-Atlantic Area
DDPR	Deterrence and Defence Posture Review
DSC	Deterrence Strategy Committee
EDSCG	Extended Deterrence Strategy & Consultative Group
EDT	emerging and disruptive technologies
FDO	flexible deterrent options
ICBM	intercontinental ballistic missile
ICRC	International Committee of the Red Cross
INDOPACOM	Indo-Pacific Command
INF	Intermediate-Range Nuclear Forces
LDP	Liberal Democratic Party

MRBM	medium-range ballistic missile
MSDF	Maritime Self-Defense Forces
NATO	North Atlantic Treaty Organization
NDPG	National Defense Program Guidelines
New START	New Strategic Arms Reduction Treaty
NFU	no first use
NPG	Nuclear Planning Group
NPR	Nuclear Posture Review
NPT	Treaty on the Non-Proliferation of Nuclear Weapons
NWS	nuclear weapon states
OPLAN	operational plan
PLA	People's Liberation Army
PRC	People's Republic of China
ROK	Republic of Korea
SACEUR	Supreme Allied Commander Europe
SDF	Self-Defense Forces
SLBM	submarine-launched ballistic missiles
SLCM–N	Sea-Launched Cruise Missile – Nuclear
SSA	Space Situational Awareness
THAAD	Terminal High Altitude Area Defense
TPNW	Treaty on the Prohibition of Nuclear Weapons
UK	United Kingdom
UN	United Nations
US	United States
USFK	US Forces Korea

1

Alliances, Nuclear Weapons and Escalation

Stephan Frühling and Andrew O'Neil

As great power competition once again assumes a central place in international relations, alliances have taken on renewed importance in the security calculations of Australia and other US allies in the Indo-Pacific and Europe. Deterrence of an attack on allies is a core function of US alliances, as are mechanisms through which states seek to manage the risk of escalation—the movement through increasing intensity of conflict up to, in the extreme, global nuclear war.[1] Alliances seek to prevent escalation in the form of an attack on its members through strategies of deterrence and extended deterrence that are themselves predicated on credible threats of escalation. Nuclear weapons are central to deterrence and escalation considerations and form a key component of America's strategic toolkit to reassure Japan, South Korea and Australia in the Indo-Pacific, as well as North Atlantic Treaty Organization (NATO) allies in the Euro-Atlantic.

However, allies cannot afford to be passive actors in their interactions with Washington. They need to prepare for and seek to manage escalation in a broader geostrategic, technological and political context that shapes the ability of alliances to adapt to a new security environment. While the challenge of great power competition is acute at both ends of Eurasia, adversary threats, geography and the institutional context of US

---

1   See Kerry M. Kartchner and Michael S. Gerson, 'Escalation to Limited Nuclear War in the 21st Century', in *On Limited Nuclear War in the 21st Century*, ed. Jeffrey Larsen and Kerry M. Kartchner (Stanford: Stanford University Press, 2014), 144–71.

alliances differ. This volume brings together contributors from Europe, North-East Asia, the United States and Australia to better understand these challenges, identify commonalities and differences across regions, and pinpoint ways to collectively manage nuclear deterrence in twenty-first-century alliances. It focuses on nuclear deterrence in the Indo-Pacific and strategic competition between the US and China; the role of non-nuclear US allies in the Indo-Pacific and Europe in supporting US extended nuclear deterrence; political-military challenges in alliance plans for escalation; allied perspectives on the consequences of new non-nuclear capabilities, including cyber and hypersonic weapons, for deterrence and strategic stability; and lessons on how the US and allied nations can better engage their respective publics on questions relating to nuclear deterrence.

Alliances, Escalation and Nuclear Weapons

How to manage escalation is an inherently political question. The costs and benefits of support in case of attack and of achieving security against specific challenges will differ between allies. The credibility of extended deterrence threats rests on the commitment of certain allies, especially the US, to provide security to other allies who find themselves under more immediate threat. The asymmetric nature of an extended deterrence relationship thus creates anxieties of abandonment on the part of the threatened ally and fears of entrapment by all allies in conflicts in which they have little direct stake. For deterrence to be effective, allies nonetheless have to find ways to agree and credibly commit to what they are willing to do for each other.

Nowhere is this more important than in relation to the role of US nuclear weapons in America's alliances. While some US allies have previously expressed sympathy for the Treaty on the Prohibition of Nuclear Weapons (TPNW), none today is willing to sign it, as their focus has turned to the challenge of managing escalation in potential great power conflicts in Europe and the Indo-Pacific. Moscow's penchant for nuclear sabre-rattling in crises with NATO and Ukraine, Beijing's ambitious nuclear force modernisation, North Korea's development of a thermonuclear and intercontinental range arsenal, and the development of new capabilities—

including hypersonic missiles designed to confer escalation advantage over the US and its allies in regional conflicts—have all roused nuclear strategy from its post–Cold War hibernation. From 2011, the Obama administration established extended deterrence dialogues with North-East Asian treaty allies, Japan and South Korea, in response to growing concerns about North Korea and China. Since 2014, the NATO alliance has paid far greater institutional and political attention to the strategic role of its nuclear forces, and to the possibilities of escalation more generally after the end of the Intermediate-Range Nuclear Forces (INF) Treaty. Under the Trump administration, US nuclear policy was notable for how little controversy it attracted among US allies, despite the administration's decision to introduce the first new (low-yield) warhead variants since the end of the Cold War.

However, the existential dependence of US allies on decisions taken in Washington about US nuclear strategy has been a constant element in the history of US alliances, and key to grasping their inherent tensions: from US Secretary of Defense Robert McNamara's challenge to NATO's nuclear strategy of massive retaliation in the early 1960s, to concerns about US–Soviet arms control undermining the security of Western Europe in the 1970s and the late 1980s, to President Obama's declared commitment to reducing the role of nuclear weapons in US defence posture in the face of rising nuclear threats to North-East Asian allies. Throughout the Cold War, arguments about nuclear strategy were staple fare for official and academic debates, especially regarding the role of nuclear weapons in deterrence. How to interpret and implement the concept of flexible response after its adoption in 1967 was the subject of often acrimonious debate in NATO, as allies sought to balance fears of abandonment, entrapment and a Soviet Union that threatened them all, but in different ways depending on their geographical position. In Asia, forward-based US nuclear forces on the Korean Peninsula were a central element in deterring North Korea until their withdrawal in 1992, and Japan carefully balanced its public aversion to nuclear weapons with practical support for the operation of US nuclear forces as a deterrent against the Soviet Union and China. In Australia, the role of the 'joint facilities' in US nuclear operations was a central element of the alliance in the second half of the Cold War.

Managing Escalation in the Indo-Pacific and Euro-Atlantic Areas

At the 2021 Munich Security Conference, President Biden declared that 'America is back', and that 'the United States is determined … to earn back our position of trusted leadership'.[2] However, while it is clear that public division and disagreement among allies about how to manage escalation and deter threats are undesirable, the US and its allies still have a long way to go in either the Indo-Pacific or the Euro-Atlantic areas to develop viable and commonly accepted political-military strategies for the new era of great power competition.[3] Significant differences remain between the challenges of escalation at either end of Eurasia, but the basic problem—how US allies can achieve political agreement on credible threats of military escalation, including through the use of nuclear weapons, to deter attacks by nuclear-armed powers—remains the same. Hence, the value of exchanging ideas between the Indo-Pacific and Euro-Atlantic areas is also far greater than it has been in the past.

In the 1980s, a US official reportedly observed that exchanges between NATO and Japan throughout the INF negotiations had 'taught the Japanese to speak German'.[4] The Reagan administration's decision to abrogate US obligations towards ANZUS (Australia, New Zealand, United States Security Treaty) ally New Zealand was also in large part motivated by sending signals to Washington's Scandinavian allies, some of whom at the time were flirting with anti-nuclear initiatives.[5] However, the institutional and geostrategic context of US alliances in Europe and the Asia-Pacific was sharply different during the Cold War, as was their manner of engagement on questions of escalation and nuclear strategy.

---

2 'Remarks by President Biden at the 2021 Virtual Munich Security Conference', The White House, 19 February 2021, www.whitehouse.gov/briefing-room/speeches-remarks/2021/02/19/remarks-by-president-biden-at-the-2021-virtual-munich-security-conference/.

3 Brad Roberts, *On Theories of Victory, Red and Blue*, Livermore Papers on Global Security No. 7, Lawrence Livermore National Laboratory Center for Global Security Research, June 2020, cgsr.llnl.gov/content/assets/docs/CGSR-LivermorePaper7.pdf.

4 David Jones, 'Post-INF Treaty Attitudes in East Asia', *Asian Survey* 30(5), 1990, 483, doi.org/10.2307/2644840.

5 Stephan Frühling, '"Key to the Defense of the Free World": The Past, Present and Future Relevance of NATO for US Allies in the Asia-Pacific', *Journal of Transatlantic Studies* 17(4), 2019, 246, doi.org/10.1057/s42738-019-00014-0.

Today, these differences are far less pronounced, and the US, its Indo-Pacific allies and NATO are rediscovering the political-military challenges of escalation management at the same time. In the context of China's rise, North Korea's nuclear tests and the US retirement of its nuclear-armed, submarine-launched cruise missiles in the 2010 Nuclear Posture Review, Japan and South Korea pressed US officials for 'more NATO-like' extended deterrence arrangements.[6] NATO allies, for their part, increasingly recognise the relevance for their alliance of a possible conflict with China.[7] For several years, NATO's institutional architecture has been explicitly drawn on by Japanese security analysts to support proposals to strengthen nuclear deterrence and reassurance in the US–Japan alliance.[8] Even in Australia, former prime minister Kevin Rudd—whose government in 2008 co-sponsored the Australian–Japanese International Commission on Nuclear Non-Proliferation and Disarmament—joined calls in 2021 for an 'Asian Nuclear Planning Group' that would allow the US, Australia, Japan and South Korea 'to discuss specific policies associated with US nuclear forces and conduct war games and exercises, including those involving the highest political-level participation'.[9]

The Challenge for Australia

Of all the countries represented in this book, the challenge of how to manage escalation and the role of nuclear weapons in the US alliance is perhaps the greatest for Australia. This is because its engagement with US nuclear deterrence has diverged significantly from that of other Cold War allies. Canberra and Washington have been content since the late 1960s with keeping a low profile for nuclear weapons in the alliance, and the direct defence of Australia has never been a focal point of the alliance. In addition, Australia was only geographically relevant for US nuclear operations through the joint facilities. Australia, therefore, has little

---

6   See Brad Roberts, *The Case for US Nuclear Weapons in the 21st Century* (Stanford: Stanford University Press, 2015), Chapter 7, doi.org/10.1515/9780804797153.
7   Hans Binnendijk and Sarah Kirchberger, *The China Plan: A Transatlantic Blueprint for Strategic Competition*, Atlantic Council, Scowcroft Center, March 2021, www.atlanticcouncil.org/wp-content/uploads/2021/03/The-China-Plan-A-Transatlantic-Blueprint.pdf.
8   Michito Tsuruoka, *Why the NATO Nuclear Debate is Relevant to Japan and Vice Versa* (Washington: German Marshall Fund of the United States, 2015).
9   *Preventing Nuclear Proliferation and Reassuring America's Allies: Task Force Report*, The Chicago Council on Global Affairs, February 2021, www.thechicagocouncil.org/sites/default/files/2021-02/report_preventing-nuclear-proliferation-reassuring-americas-allies_0.pdf.

experience of how to approach the questions touched on in this book, even as it now faces a region where the possibility of a great power conflict is far more plausible than in the past, and which, in the words of the *2020 Defence Strategic Update*, 'is in the midst of the most consequential strategic realignment since the Second World War'.[10]

Only once did public US–Australian statements in recent years address the operation of the ANZUS Treaty in a 'hypothetical' situation—when Australia and the US agreed in 2011 that a future cyber attack may constitute grounds for invoking its mutual assistance clause. In August 2019, when the US withdrew from the INF Treaty, comments by US Secretary of Defense Mark Esper prior to the 2019 Australia–US ministerial consultations meeting that he would like the US to deploy new land-based, intermediate-range missiles in Asia 'sooner rather than later' took many observers in Australia by surprise.[11] Even though the Biden administration's commitment to once again seek to 'reduce the role of nuclear weapons in [US] national security strategy'[12] speaks to the preferences of many in the Australian policy community, what Australia might have to do to achieve this goal in a new era of great power competition has yet to be fully addressed in Australia's defence debate, a task that this book seeks to help inform.

Outline of the Book

This volume brings together contributors from Europe, North-East Asia, the US and Australia to better understand how to manage the array of political-military challenges confronting European and Indo-Pacific policymakers. The authors are drawn from a wide range of backgrounds, with many having had experience in the policy world addressing the very challenges canvassed in this book.

The first part of the book examines nuclear deterrence and strategic stability with a particular emphasis on the US–China relationship. In the past, Beijing has been hampered by capacity and capability constraints in the

---

10 Department of Defence, *2020 Defence Strategic Update*, www1.defence.gov.au/sites/default/files/2020-11/2020_Defence_Strategic_Update.pdf.
11 Thomas Gibbons-Neff, 'Pentagon Chief in Favor of Deploying US Missiles to Asia', *The New York Times*, 3 August 2019, www.nytimes.com/2019/08/03/world/asia/us-missiles-asia-esper.html.
12 President Joseph Biden, *Interim National Security Strategic Guidance, March 2021*, www.whitehouse.gov/wp-content/uploads/2021/03/NSC-1v2.pdf.

nuclear sphere that have dovetailed with China's overtly defensive nuclear strategy of assured retaliation.[13] Elbridge Colby, in Chapter 2, discusses the prospect of a coalition between the US and its allies in addressing Chinese aspirations for hegemony in the Indo-Pacific. A range of countries in the region have a strong rationale to focus on their own defence in relation to the People's Liberation Army, but Japan and Australia in particular can make decisive contributions to a US-led 'anti-hegemonic' coalition against China. In Chapter 3, Oriana Skylar Mastro examines the role of nuclear deterrence in the US–China relationship and canvasses potential pathways to escalation and conflict. While high-risk scenarios (e.g. a declaration of independence by Taiwan) in which Beijing employs major levels of force cannot be ruled out, escalatory dynamics will be easier to manage if both sides act incrementally. And although China may choose to target a US ally with nuclear weapons, this is unlikely given Beijing's desire to preserve flexible targeting options against the US, the major political costs that would result and China's widening conventional military options in the Indo-Pacific. In Chapter 4, Jeffrey Larsen compares the Indo-Pacific and European models of nuclear weapons cooperation with the US. Although cooperation in the Indo-Pacific is less structured than the formal NATO model, Washington's goal in both theatres remains that of reassuring US allies. In Chapter 5, Heather Williams evaluates the future of arms control and strategic stability in the Indo-Pacific. She argues that reducing the risk of escalation between the US and China should be an overriding objective and that formalising a strategic relationship between Washington and Beijing is key.

---

13 Because China does not practise transparency with respect to its nuclear forces, it is difficult to ascertain the number of warheads in the country's arsenal. However, the most authoritative open-source analysis estimates that:

> China has produced a stockpile of approximately 350 nuclear warheads, of which roughly 272 are for delivery by more than 240 operational land-based ballistic missiles, 48 sea-based ballistic missiles, and 20 nuclear gravity bombs assigned to bombers. The remaining 78 warheads are intended to arm additional land- and sea-based missiles that are in the process of being fielded.

Hans Kristensen and Matt Korda, 'Chinese Nuclear Forces, 2020', *Bulletin of the Atomic Scientists* 76(6), 2020, 443, doi.org/10.1080/00963402.2020.1846432.

Yet, revelations in June and July 2021 that China was constructing a significant number of new nuclear missile silos raised the prospect that Beijing is undertaking a significant expansion of its nuclear weapons force. See William Broad and David Sanger, 'A 2nd New Nuclear Missile Base for China, and Many Questions About Strategy', *The New York Times*, 26 July 2021, www.nytimes.com/2021/07/26/us/politics/china-nuclear-weapons.html.

In Part II, contributors explore how alliances in Europe and across the Indo-Pacific manage the political, financial, and material costs and benefits of peacetime deterrence and wartime strategies. This section focuses on how—or indeed, whether—US allies plan for escalation scenarios. In Chapter 6, Sten Rynning examines how NATO has sought to manage deterrence and escalation strategies. He maintains that military planners have struggled with somewhat incoherent messaging at the political level. Seukhoon Paul Choi, in Chapter 7, investigates the US – Republic of Korea alliance and concludes that it has become increasingly complex due to challenges from an assertive China and growing North Korean capabilities, including in the nuclear domain. Choi argues that Seoul and Washington must focus on how they intend to manage the deterrence challenges from Beijing and Pyongyang within the framework of the alliance. In Chapter 8, Tomohiko Satake considers the state of the US–Japan alliance and argues that, in spite of Japan's growing threat environment, and notwithstanding the Abe government's at times assertive rhetoric, recent Japanese governments have taken their cue from public opinion and have continued to be incremental in their approach to the alliance. Brendan Sargeant, in Chapter 9, discusses the US–Australia alliance with a specific focus on the alliance management challenges Australia confronts, which include how Canberra would respond to a major regional crisis involving the US and China. It is important in this respect for senior political leaders to engage more deeply in strategic-level aspects of the alliance to complement the operational level of military-to-military cooperation.

Part III turns to the role of nuclear weapons as well as the impact of new technologies on alliance cooperation and strategic stability in Europe and the Indo-Pacific. Each alliance is distinctive with respect to nuclear cooperation, but one dimension overdue for analysis is whether there is scope for Indo-Pacific allies to emulate NATO arrangements on nuclear sharing, or at least closer allied support for US nuclear operations in the region. Great power competition and conflict also play out across a host of new technologies including cyber, space, missile defence and hypersonics, which has led to resurgent interest in low-yield warheads and intermediate-range missiles. In Chapter 10, Łukasz Kulesa assesses the continuing impact on NATO of new and emerging technologies and the relationship between these technologies and the alliance's evolving nuclear posture. Kulesa argues that NATO must move quickly to adapt in light of the growing challenge from Russia, including its integration of cutting-edge technologies into its nuclear and conventional forces mix. Alexander Mattelaer, in Chapter 11, examines NATO's nuclear-sharing arrangements and its identity as a nuclear alliance. Mattelaer maintains that the core function of NATO nuclear sharing is to reinforce alliance political cohesion and notes the potential benefits of greater consultation between the US and its Indo-Pacific allies on nuclear matters. In Chapter 12, Michito Tsuruoka considers the role of US nuclear weapons in North-East Asian alliances and pinpoints scope for closer cooperation between the US and its allies. In particular, Tsuruoka focuses on replicating some of the 'physical' characteristics of the NATO model, such as joint training with US strategic bombers and greater allied involvement in missile defence. In Chapter 13, Masashi Murano examines the relationship between new military capabilities and deterrence architecture in North-East Asia. These capabilities present new opportunities for the US and its allies, but there must be a greater effort at joint integration and coordination to counter Chinese and North Korean threats. Andrew Davies, in Chapter 14, provides an analysis of the major new technological challenges confronting Australian strategic planners. Long protected by geographical isolation, Australia can no longer bank on its physical location as a multiplier of security in an era of accelerating cyber and hypersonic missile threats.

The final part of the book examines the public discourse about nuclear weapons and deterrence. In democratic societies, maintaining public support—or, at the very least, tolerance—of the role of nuclear weapons in national defence is crucial for allies and the US alike. Despite decades of support demonstrated by US and allied governments for nuclear weapons in their alliances, the legitimacy of nuclear weapons and deterrence remains under challenge. In Chapter 15, Michael Rühle considers the role of nuclear weapons in NATO and argues that, despite the best efforts of TPNW advocates, the alliance's nuclear arrangements remain as important as ever to alliance solidarity in a period of renewed Russian assertiveness. Tanya Ogilvie-White, in Chapter 16, assesses the 'legitimacy' challenges to Australia posed by its deterrence and disarmament policies. Surging support for the TPNW among non-governmental organisations and sections of the general public has raised questions about the sustainability of Australia's dual commitment to extended nuclear deterrence and nuclear disarmament and requires a more open public debate about the tensions inherent in this commitment. In Chapter 17, Brad Roberts presents the case for a proactive 'campaign' on the part of deterrence advocates aimed at articulating the moral case for nuclear weapons and deterrence. This necessitates greater engagement in dialogue with advocates of disarmament and a more nuanced attempt to shape the discourse over nuclear weapons.

***

As the contributors to this volume illustrate, greater focus on the relationship between nuclear weapons, deterrence and escalation in Europe and the Indo-Pacific alliances is overdue. The risks of armed conflict during periods of intensifying great power competition are well documented throughout history and are higher today than at any time since the end of the Cold War. Major war between the great powers would almost certainly involve threats to employ nuclear weapons and likely witness the actual use of nuclear weapons as a result of deliberate choices, accident or inadvertent escalation. US allies would be central players in any such conflict, and successful deterrence—including through the threat of use of US nuclear weapons—is a shared allied responsibility. Therefore, grasping the challenges surrounding deterrence and escalation is a necessary prerequisite to formulating policy responses that will stand the test of time.

Part I: Alliances, Nuclear Deterrence and Strategic Stability in the Indo-Pacific

2

US Defence Strategy and Alliances in the Indo-Pacific

Elbridge Colby

The central defence problem for the United States and its allies and partners in Asia in the coming years will be a supremely difficult one: how to be ready to defend vulnerable states within an anti-hegemonic coalition against Beijing's best military strategy. This will be exceptionally challenging because of China's enormous strength, and its ability to use its newfound power to simultaneously subject vulnerable states to invasion or searing pain while threatening other sympathetic states with great loss if they come to the target's aid.[1]

This is the military dimension of the broader geopolitical dynamic that now confronts us. China is the largest state to emerge in the international system since the US itself. For a variety of political, economic, geopolitical

---

1   The arguments in this chapter are more fully developed in the author's book, *The Strategy of Denial: American Defense in an Age of Great Power Conflict* (New Haven: Yale University Press, 2021). See also Department of Defense, *Indo-Pacific Strategy Report: Preparedness, Partnerships, and Promoting a Networked Region,* June 2019, media.defense.gov/2019/Jul/01/2002152311/-1/-1/1/DEPARTMENT-OF-DEFENSE-INDO-PACIFIC-STRATEGY-REPORT-2019.PDF.

and, perhaps, ideological reasons, it seeks regional hegemony in the nearer term and, from a position of predominance over the world's largest market, global pre-eminence.[2]

To frustrate Beijing's goal, enough states must come together in a more or less tight coalition to outweigh China in the regional balance of power. While this coalition appears unlikely to result in a formal 'Asian NATO',[3] it will need to be cohesive enough that, linked together, it can bring enough strength to prevent China from dominating. Because of its unique power, only the US can play the role of leader of this anti-hegemonic coalition. Yet it will need to include many other states, especially in Asia, given the limited influence of more distant states in the region. Japan, India and Australia, along with the US—the Quad—are likely to be the pillars of any such coalition, but it will need to include other states if it is to be stronger than China and its own plausible coalition. Thus, states like South Korea, the Philippines, Vietnam and Taiwan are likely to play an important role.

Defending an Anti-Hegemonic Coalition through Favourably Managing Escalation

China's best approach to defeat this coalition will be a focused and sequential strategy designed to short-circuit or pry it apart. Beijing has a powerful incentive to avoid precipitating a large war with such a coalition. Such a conflict would be immensely destructive and China would likely lose against so many powerful states. Instead, Beijing's incentive is to seek to collapse the coalition without exposing itself to a very large war; it can do so by threatening or fighting focused wars against members of this coalition, progressively weakening it until it falls apart.

---

2   'China Seeks Hegemony: America's Pacific Commander Offers a Military Warning', *Wall Street Journal*, 24 February 2016, www.wsj.com/articles/china-seeks-hegemony-1456358971; Ely Ratner, 'Rising to the China Challenge: Prepared Statement Before the House Committee on Armed Services', 15 February 2018, docs.house.gov/meetings/AS/AS00/20180215/106848/HHRG-115-AS00-Wstate-RatnerE-20180215.pdf.
3   Kai He and Huiyun Feng, '"Why Is There No NATO in Asia?" Revisited: Prospect Theory, Balance of Threat, and US Alliance Strategies', *European Journal of International Relations* 18(2), 2012, doi.org/10.1177/1354066110377124.

China can plausibly do this because any anti-hegemonic coalition, whatever form it takes, will rely on its members' confidence in each other—and especially on their confidence in the US, due to its unique and critical role as the cornerstone of any plausible coalition. If Beijing can pry off or subjugate enough coalition members—especially those on which US credibility in Asia turns, namely those with a security commitment from Washington—then the coalition is likely to collapse. Beijing does not need to beat down every state in such a coalition to achieve this goal. If it shows the coalition is hollow, enough remaining states may judge that accommodating Beijing is the more prudent course.

In this case, even if, for example, the US, Japan and Australia remain opposed, the rest of Asia may cut a deal with China. In such conditions, the anti-hegemonic coalition will just be too weak, and China will dominate the region. In such circumstances, Beijing is unlikely to establish direct political control over Asia, but rather exercise a dominant influence over regional countries' economic, security and, quite possibly, political decisions. China will likely use this position to orient the region's trade flows and security relationships to its benefit, fundamentally compromising regional states' autonomy and diminishing its rivals, especially the US.

This frames the military problem for the US and its closest allies, particularly Australia and Japan. China will seek to threaten or wage focused wars, particularly against more vulnerable members of the coalition. Meanwhile, the costs and risks of a massive war with China are too great to be countenanced for such limited stakes; Americans, Japanese and Australians will not support fighting a total war over partial interests. Any defence strategy based on such a response will rightly be seen as a bluff.

Accordingly, the allies need to be able to fight and achieve their goals in *limited wars* defending coalition members, especially members that are beneficiaries of a US security commitment. This means being able to fight in ways that correlate the costs and risks of the struggle with the issues at stake. In other words, because China's incentive will be to narrow the scope and apparent stakes of the war, the US, Australia and others will need to be prepared to fight and prevail within bounds that their populations will be prepared to support.

This points to the central problem of *favourably* bounding any such war with China—and being seen to be able to do so for deterrence's sake. Because any such war will almost certainly be limited, *how* it is limited will be crucial. Equally, how well the allies are prepared to fight within such bounds will be critical, if not determinative. If China can set the bounds of such a war, it can make them work to its own advantages. And if China can fight better within whatever bounds constrain the war, it is likely to win.

This reality frames the role of nuclear weapons in US and allied strategy vis-a-vis China. For all intents and purposes, China has now developed a secure second-strike capability against the US, and it is highly likely that Beijing will be able to deliver far more damage against the US than in the past. Because the stakes for Americans in Asia are grave but not existential, because of China's incentive to limit any conflict with the coalition and because of the enormous burden of escalation associated with resorting to nuclear weapons first (especially at scale), allied strategies against China that rely too much on nuclear weapons for deterring and defeating China will not be sufficiently credible, let alone sensible. US nuclear weapons will therefore play an important role in Asia, but ideally should be reserved to deter China from escalating its way out of conventional defeat. The overwhelming focus of coalition strategy should be to ensure an effective conventional defence.[4] That said, the US should reserve the right to use nuclear weapons first, but any such employment—to be credible and sensible—would almost certainly need to be integrated within a robust conventional posture and as localised and limited as possible.

The Importance of Preparing for a Fight over Taiwan

Which war should the US, Australia and other coalition members prepare for? China would be best off trying its focused war strategy (or the credible threat thereof) against Taiwan, followed in attractiveness by the Philippines or Vietnam.

---

4   For a landmark study laying out a likeminded analysis, see Ashley Townshend, Brendan Thomas-Noone and Matilda Steward, 'Averting Crisis: American Strategy, Military Spending and Collective Defence in the Indo-Pacific', United States Studies Centre, 19 August 2019, www.ussc.edu.au/analysis/averting-crisis-american-strategy-military-spending-and-collective-defence-in-the-indo-pacific.

Taiwan is Beijing's best target for a variety of reasons. It is near China and the People's Liberation Army (PLA) has focused its development on bringing Taiwan to heel. Taiwan is also located right in the middle of the first island chain; its subordination would allow China nearly uninhibited military power projection into the Western and Central Pacific.[5] Further, Taiwan's ambiguous international political status and intrication with China may appear to give Beijing firmer standing to assault it. Finally, and critically, the widespread perception that Taiwan is the beneficiary of a real, if qualified, security commitment from the US means that Washington's credibility would be on the line. Rather than being a bug, this would more likely be a feature for Beijing in attacking Taiwan. Subordinating Taiwan would cut right at the heart of that critical confidence, especially in Washington's reliability, within the anti-hegemonic coalition.

Beijing might also target the Philippines or Vietnam. The Philippines is a US ally and has limited military strength, but it is difficult for China to get at, especially without first subordinating Taiwan. Vietnam, meanwhile, is China's neighbour and Beijing could attack it without crossing water, which is where the US military is at its strongest; however, Vietnam's reputation for strength and resolve, as well as its lack of a US security commitment, might make it less appealing for Beijing.

Over time, the immense growing reach and potency of the PLA will make additional Asian states more plausible targets for China.[6] South Korea is separated from China only by the Yellow Sea, not much more than what separates the mainland from Taiwan, and South Korea is a US ally. Thailand, whose 'alliance' with the US is considerably more ambiguous than other US allies, is separated from China only by a weakened Laos. This is not to say that Beijing will seek to rampage across the Asian continent. Rather, it means that China will have more and more opportunities to target weak and material links in the anti-hegemonic coalition, especially those that are beneficiaries of a US security commitment.

---

5   Elbridge Colby and Jim Mitre, 'Why the Pentagon Should Focus on Taiwan', *War on the Rocks*, 7 October 2020, warontherocks.com/2020/10/why-the-pentagon-should-focus-on-taiwan/.

6   Eric Heginbotham et al., *The US–China Military Scorecard: Forces, Geography, and the Evolving Balance of Power 1996–2017* (Santa Monica: RAND Corporation, 2015), 343, www.rand.org/content/dam/rand/pubs/research_reports/RR300/RR392/RAND_RR392.pdf.

In the nearer term, however, this means that the prime scenario that the US and, by extension, the anti-hegemonic coalition as a whole need to be concerned about is Taiwan. While Taiwan's fall would not necessarily doom the coalition, it would seriously damage it.

But while the whole anti-hegemonic coalition must be concerned about Taiwan, this does not mean that all states within it should focus on preparing to defend the vulnerable island. This is for several reasons. First, most states in the region (or for that matter, beyond it) do not have the capacity to meaningfully contribute to Taiwan's defence. Defending Taiwan, while practicable, would be immensely challenging for even the most sophisticated militaries, including the US. States in South-East Asia, for instance, lack the technological capacity and wealth to develop militaries that could project power to the Taiwan area and be relevant against the mighty PLA. States in Europe, meanwhile, lack the power projection capacity to make a meaningful difference in a Taiwan contingency.

Second, most states—even those with more wealth and technological development—need to focus on their own defence against the PLA. States like Vietnam, Thailand or Malaysia will need to focus their efforts simply on ensuring their own territorial defence against a PLA that will boast not only major land and anti-access/area denial prowess but also power projection forces such as carrier battle groups, nuclear-powered submarines and a large and sophisticated space architecture. Even wealthy but (compared with China) small South Korea will need to focus its efforts on its own territorial defence. Major power India, meanwhile, will be better off concentrating on its territorial defence and on dealing with China in South Asia, not trying to develop the capability to project power into the Western Pacific to contend with the PLA.

Japan's and Australia's Roles in Coalition Defence

In addition to the US, this leaves Japan and Australia as the two states with the ability and reason to prepare to pursue collective defence of threatened anti-hegemonic coalition members, especially those on which US credibility turns. These two states have the capacity to both develop and field high-end power projection forces, and could prudently turn some of those forces to the defence of threatened coalition members.

Japan is the foremost regional pillar of the anti-hegemonic coalition. It is the fourth largest economy in the world by the purchasing power parity metric (third by market exchange rates) and at the forefront of technology development.[7] Moreover, it could and indeed must dedicate a much larger fraction of its national wealth to defence spending as China continues to grow. It therefore clearly has the capacity to help Taiwan's defence. At the same time, while Japan is a 'frontline state' vis-a-vis China and therefore must pay primary attention to its own territorial defence of the far-flung Japanese archipelago, it also is likely to have enough military capacity to contribute to other contingencies—especially those that are nearby and directly relate to the defence of Japan itself. Taiwan certainly falls into this category. Taiwan is at the end of the chain of islands that form the Japanese archipelago, so is proximate to the main area of Japanese defence focus— the Southwest Islands. And Taiwan's defence is directly relevant to the defence of the Japanese archipelago itself. Given its location, Taiwan's fall would dramatically weaken Japan's defence. Accordingly, Tokyo should be able to play an important role in Taiwan's defence, alongside the US.

This leaves Australia. Australia is, of course, a smaller economy than Japan. But it is very advanced, with a sophisticated and capable military experienced at expeditionary warfare. It therefore can contribute to defending other threatened members of an anti-hegemonic coalition. Strategically, Australia's fate will clearly be determined far from its own shores. If China is able to dominate the Asian mainland and its periphery, Australia will have no chance of an independent future. Such a hegemonic China would present an overwhelmingly powerful challenge to Australia, even one closely allied with the US. The costs and risks of such a war over such distant stakes could very well be too great to countenance for Americans, leaving Australia 'high and dry'.

Nor would an independent nuclear arsenal solve Australia's problems. First of all, it is not clear that Australia will be able to develop a nuclear arsenal that could survive and penetrate to deliver sufficiently devastating effects to deter China from coercing it. China is developing a tremendously capable suite of precision missiles, including ones capped with nuclear warheads, as well as bombers, submarines and other potential launch platforms; a space and aerial architecture for targeting; and air and missile

---

7   For purchasing power parity and market exchange, see the most recent World Bank data: data.worldbank.org/indicator/NY.GDP.MKTP.PP.CD?most_recent_value_desc=true; databank.worldbank.org/data/download/GDP.pdf.

defences to blunt and even deny an adversary's ability to penetrate and hit valuable targets in China. These integrated capabilities will challenge even the US to deliver devastating effects against China. Much smaller Australia, then, would face a very real challenge in ensuring the delivery of a meaningful number of nuclear weapons against valued targets in China in the face of such a robust Chinese military.[8]

Moreover, even if Australia were confident it could deliver such a level of nuclear devastation, it is by no means clear that it could use the threat of such devastation to deter China from anything other than total conquest and annexation of Australia. In such conditions, Beijing would have the ability to retaliate with far greater force than whatever Australia could deliver. Consequently, any use of nuclear weapons against China under such circumstances would be, if not pulling the temple down over one's head, inviting enormous destruction. Perhaps such a risk could be countenanced for preventing Beijing from destroying or colonising Australia. But that is not what Beijing would likely try—or need—to do. Rather, Beijing would almost certainly be demanding that Canberra accede to its hegemonic position over Australia—that is, that Canberra, like other nations already under Beijing's predominance, would hew to its line over key security, political and economic questions. Would Australians be prepared to commit mass suicide over this? It seems unlikely.

Accordingly, Australia's fate will be settled with that of the anti-hegemonic coalition as a whole, which is to say, farther forward in Asia. If the struggle gets beyond that, it will probably be too late for Australia. This means that Canberra has a very direct interest in ensuring a war in the Western Pacific or South-East Asia goes well for the coalition. Thus, rather than fielding a military optimised purely for, or even significantly oriented on, territorial defence of Australia or expeditionary operations in the Middle East, Australia would be best off focusing on developing forces that can help the US and Japan achieve their joint objectives in key scenarios in the Western Pacific (which, of course, likely will include some capability for territorial defence of Australia, such as air and missile defences).

---

8   For debates about Australia acquiring a nuclear arsenal, see Christine Leah, *Australia and the Bomb* (New York: Palgrave Macmillan, 2014), 131–45; Hugh White, *How to Defend Australia* (Carlton: La Trobe University Press, 2019); Stephan Frühling, 'Never Say Never: Considerations about the Possibility of Australia Acquiring Nuclear Weapons', *Asian Security* 6(2), 2010, 146–69, doi.org/10.1080/14799851003756618.

Implications for Australian Defence Planning

How, then, might Australia think about contributing to these scenarios? And which ones? And in what balance or relationship? This is important because Australia will need to use its significant but, in the grand balance, relatively limited resources carefully and strategically to generate maximum effect.

As indicated previously, because Taiwan is China's best target for its focused strategy, the top priority for the coalition is its defence. Given the difficulties of defending Taiwan, only the US's active effort can make the island defendable. The primary focus for the US, then, must be preparing an effective defence of Taiwan, alongside redoubled and better focused self-defence efforts by Taiwan itself.[9] Such efforts must address two primary routes by which Beijing might plausibly seek to subjugate Taiwan: an invasion, especially a fait accompli attempt, or an effort to bring the island to heel through the imposition of pain—for instance, through blockade, bombardment and other such measures short of direct assault. Japan is likely to need to play an important role in both scenarios, both indirectly through the provision of basing and logistics support, and directly through the commitment of forces.

Australia might also play a useful, albeit limited, role. Canberra might contribute forces to the direct defence of Taiwan from a PLA invasion. But the fact is that a defence of Taiwan would take place a great distance from Australia; moreover, the central military effort would require either operating relatively near to China's coasts, which would necessitate highly survivable platforms, or striking from longer distances with a highly sophisticated and resilient command, control, communications, computers, intelligence, surveillance and reconnaissance (C4ISR) architecture. In this context, Australia's forces might be better focused on other tasks important to the favourable resolution of such a conflict, such as striking at or holding at risk China's forces in other areas—for instance,

---

9   Valerie Insinna, 'A US Air Force War Game Shows What the Service Needs to Hold Off—Or Win Against—China in 2030', *DefenceNews*, 30 April 2021, www.defensenews.com/training-sim/2021/04/12/a-us-air-force-war-game-shows-what-the-service-needs-to-hold-off-or-win-against-china-in-2030/.

the South China Sea and South Pacific. Such forces might not even need to become engaged but will need to present a credible prospect to Beijing of an unfavourable outcome if it seeks to expand the war.

This is critical because the US and the coalition's optimal outcome is a focused 'denial defence' of Taiwan. This would involve defeating China's attempted invasion or bludgeoning of Taiwan into surrender while limiting the war as much as possible, keeping the burden of escalation on Beijing. This requires not only defeating China's focused attack on Taiwan—necessarily the main line of effort—but also demonstrating to Beijing that trying to escalate its way out of defeat by expanding the war to the South China Sea or beyond would also have unfavourable results for China. For this it will be critical to have sufficient credible forces prepared to make that threat a reality. US and Japanese forces—and the forces of other supportive powers like India and Vietnam, as well as possibly the United Kingdom, France, and other North Atlantic Treaty Organization (NATO) allies—would play an important role in this effort. But Australia's might be especially suited to the task. This is not to say that Australian forces should be excluded from the direct defence of Taiwan, but simply that they may be, at least on the whole, better allocated to other critical missions.

But the coalition must also consider scenarios beyond Taiwan. This is because China might seek to circumvent the island or succeed in subjugating it despite the US and others' efforts. While the coalition should not countenance the latter, it is only prudent to prepare for failure in such a difficult and uncertain contingency. Moreover, if Taiwan were to fall to Beijing, the pressures on the coalition would be far more intense; it would be critical to avert any further losses to avoid the coalition being hollowed out—or even falling apart.

In lieu of, or after, subjugating Taiwan, Beijing would probably look to either the Philippines or Vietnam. The Philippines, however, would need to command the US and Australia's attention. Manila is a US ally, and therefore implicates Washington's credibility, while Hanoi is not the recipient of such a commitment and therefore does not. Further, the Philippines's geographical position as a lengthy segment of the first island chain is critical. If the Philippines were to fall under China's hegemony, military access to South-East Asia (including Vietnam) would become much more difficult, if not impossible. Thus, while the coalition would suffer from Vietnam's subordination to Chinese hegemony, the loss of the Philippines would be far graver. Accordingly, the coalition should prioritise defence of the Philippines after Taiwan.

Australia could likely play a much more significant role in the defence of the Philippines, both due to its closer position as well as the reality that a contest over the Philippines would probably be more permissive for coalition forces than one over Taiwan, given the archipelago's greater distance from mainland China. In such circumstances, Australian forces could make significant contributions to blunting or defeating an attempted Chinese invasion of the Philippine main islands (such as Luzon) or an attempt to bludgeon Manila into submission.

It likely makes sense for Australia to focus on these two scenarios. If the coalition were to fail to effectively defend both Taiwan and the Philippines, it might already be too late to prevent China from dominating Asia. And even if it were not, the coalition could then regroup, albeit in this much worse position, to focus on defence of Japan itself and likely Indonesia.

***

In conclusion, Australia and the US (as well as Japan) will need to play special roles in any anti-hegemonic coalition. Critical to its success will be the ability to defeat any Chinese theory of victory against a US ally within the coalition. And the reality is that while such a contingency sounds extreme, it is far from implausible. Indeed, the very fact that such a coalition already appears to be forming, and that Beijing is likely finding its attempt to use non-military instruments of coercion unsatisfying, increases the allure of the military option. This both frames the requirements and provides the urgency for Washington and Canberra to work together, lest lassitude result in failure and the loss of autonomy and national freedom for Australia.

3

Nuclear Deterrence and the US–China Strategic Relationship

Oriana Skylar Mastro

Ever since the United States dropped the first atomic bomb on Japan in 1945, countries have had to consider the impact of nuclear weapons on their security and stability more broadly. Nuclear weapons were central to the great power competition between the United States and the Soviet Union. The US–Soviet nuclear balance relied on 'a very high degree of mutual vulnerability',[1] in which peace was maintained through both sides' belief that the other could inflict widespread destruction. In the late 1960s, the nuclear stockpiles of both powers numbered in the tens of thousands, but mutual reductions were gradually achieved through a series of arms control agreements and initiatives.

But there are several reasons to suspect that the nuclear dynamics between the US and China are different from those that existed between the Soviet Union and the US during the Cold War. For one, China's approach to nuclear weapons is fundamentally different from the US and Soviet approaches of assured destruction capability.[2] Instead, China's policy of

---

1   Elbridge Colby, 'The Role of Nuclear Weapons in the US–Russian Relationship', Carnegie Endowment for International Peace, 26 February 2016, carnegieendowment.org/2016/02/26/role-of-nuclear-weapons-in-US-russian-relationship-pub-62901.
2   M. Taylor Fravel and Evan S. Medeiros, 'China's Search for Assured Retaliation: The Evolution of Chinese Nuclear Strategy and Force Structure', *Quarterly Journal: International Security* 35(2), 2010, 48–87. doi.org/10.1162/ISEC_a_00016.

assured retaliation with a no-first-use pledge, designed to deter nuclear attack and coercion, reduces the strategic importance of nuclear weapons in the bilateral relationship.[3]

The great power nuclear relationship also impacts US allies differently. European countries are committed to collective defence, but no North Atlantic Treaty Organization – style construct exists between US allies in Asia. Additionally, key US European allies such as France and the United Kingdom have their own nuclear capabilities while Asian allies rely exclusively on the US to deter nuclear attack against their countries.

This chapter evaluates the role that nuclear deterrence plays in the US–China strategic relationship. It lays out the pathways to conflict and the implications for nuclear use, evaluates how allies influence nuclear dynamics (the conditions under which nuclear weapons would most likely be used and how) and explores how escalation to nuclear conflict may affect US allies in the region depending on their level of involvement in the contingency. In doing so, it highlights that, when it comes to nuclear use, there is a sizeable difference between what is possible (the operational realities) and what is plausible (the strategic logic behind potential use).

Pathways to Conflict and Implications for Nuclear Deterrence

In the near term, the most likely situation that could spark a US–China war is a contingency over Taiwan. This is also the most plausible scenario for nuclear use because of Taiwan's importance to both China and the US, and US commitments for involvement. The Chinese Communist Party (CCP) is primarily concerned about maintaining power. If the US shifted strategies to proactively undermine the regime by arming and training separatists or protestors in Xinjiang, Tibet, Hong Kong or Taiwan, for example, this could lead to protracted war between the two sides. Additionally, if a war occurred and the US refused to negotiate a peace unless the Communist Party gave up power, such a scenario would almost

---

3   Fiona S. Cunningham and M. Taylor Fravel, 'Dangerous Confidence? Chinese Views on Nuclear Escalation', *International Security* 44(2), 1 October 2019, 61–109, doi.org/10.1162/isec_a_00359; M. Taylor Fravel and Fiona Stephanie Cunningham, 'Assuring Assured Retaliation: China's Nuclear Posture and US–China Strategic Stability', *International Security*, Fall 2015, hdl.handle.net/1721.1/101390.

certainly escalate to the nuclear level even if Taiwan were not directly involved. China could theoretically also change its nuclear doctrine to threaten nuclear use even at low levels of conventional war to make up for conventional shortcomings, or to strengthen its deterrent against US nuclear use.

However, a comprehensive analysis of Chinese military writings by Fiona Cunningham and M. Taylor Fravel suggests that China is not motivated to shift to an offensive posture for several reasons, including its confidence that nuclear deterrence will hold. In their words:

> China's strategists believe that the interests at stake would be too low in any US–China scenario for either side to create risks of nuclear escalation. Moreover, China's no-first-use policy means that only the United States would escalate to the nuclear level, which is unlikely, given its conventional military superiority over China.[4]

Because it is generally uncontroversial that a US attempt to overthrow the communist regime or a Chinese shift to an offensive nuclear doctrine would increase the likelihood of nuclear use, this chapter develops a typology to help understand the relative risks of nuclear war in more plausible conflict scenarios.

Reactive versus Proactive Pathway to Conflict

Since 1996, analysts have mainly been concerned with a pathway to conflict in which Beijing perceives a need to *respond* to a situation. In this scenario, Taipei or Washington crosses a red line that precipitates conflict, such as a declaration of independence from Taiwan. For example, the Third Taiwan Strait Crisis originated in part with an explicitly political speech given by Taiwanese President Lee Tung-hui at his alma mater, Cornell University. The speech and the Taiwanese president's visit to the US angered the Chinese leadership and led to the People's Republic of China (PRC) conducting threatening missile tests in and near the Taiwan Strait. Similarly, China passed the Anti-Secession Law in 2005 in response to the rise of a Taiwanese separatist movement. The law declared Taiwan

---

4   Fravel and Cunningham, 'Assuring Assured Retaliation', 10.

a part of China and indicated that the CCP supported unification by force. As the Chinese Ministry of Defence clearly stated on 28 January 2021: 'Taiwan independence means war'.[5]

China's red lines on Taiwan are ambiguous; therefore, analysts also worry that policies designed to strengthen cross-strait deterrence could push Beijing over the brink. For example, Bonnie Glaser argues that 'a US security guarantee for Taipei … might even provoke a Chinese attack'.[6] If strategic ambiguity was abandoned, Beijing might choose to act immediately, believing that the US is least likely in the short term to mount a credible defence. Alternatively, Taipei could be emboldened to risk military conflict if it had no doubt that the US would come to its defence. A credible, but not unconditional, security guarantee is therefore the gold standard for deterrence. Critics of US arms sales to Taiwan apply a similar logic: arms sales run the risk of either provoking China or giving Taiwan dangerous confidence.[7] However, while recent high-level visits between US and Taiwanese officials undoubtedly triggered Chinese ire, they stopped short of being destabilising.

Impressive Chinese military modernisation, the US's failure to build robust coalitions to counter Chinese regional aggression and Xi Jinping's personal ambition coalesce to create a situation in which Chinese leaders may see some aggregate benefit to using force. Therefore, an equally, if not more, plausible pathway to conflict is that Beijing will launch a military operation to force 'reunification', irrespective of Washington's or Taipei's policies or actions.[8] In this scenario, Xi Jinping will use force to compel Taiwan to unite with the mainland once he is confident of the Chinese military's ability to succeed in relevant joint operations, especially an amphibious attack.

---

5   Wang Feng, ed., 'Transcript of the Regular Press Conference of the Ministry of National Defence in January 2021', Department of Defence Network, 28 January 2021, www.mod.gov.cn/shouye/2021-01/28/content_4878245.htm [in Chinese].
6   Bonnie S. Glaser et al., 'Dire Straits: Should American Support for Taiwan Be Ambiguous?', *Foreign Affairs*, 24 September 2020, www.foreignaffairs.com/articles/united-states/2020-09-24/dire-straits.
7   A. Trevor Thrall and Jordan Cohen, 'Time to Rethink Arms Sales to Taiwan', Cato Institute, 2 November 2020, www.cato.org/commentary/time-rethink-arms-sales-taiwan.
8   Oriana Skylar Mastro, 'The Taiwan Temptation', *Foreign Affairs* (July/August 2021), 1–10.

While military balances and outcomes of military operations are notoriously hard to assess and predict, China's military has made significant strides in its ability to conduct joint operations in recent years. China's massive military reform program, which Xi launched shortly after coming to power in 2012, aims to transform China's military into a 'fully modern' force by 2027.[9] Senior Colonel Ren Guoqiang, a spokesperson for China's Ministry of National Defence, has claimed:

> China has basically completed the national defence and military reform of the leadership and command systems, scale, structure and force composition, which promoted the joint operations of the Chinese military to a new stage.[10]

On 7 November 2020, the People's Liberation Army (PLA) revised its strategic guidelines, for only the fifth time in its history, to incorporate this new focus on joint operations.[11]

Because of these reforms and the modernisation of Chinese equipment, platforms and weapons, China may now be able to prevail in cross-strait contingencies even if the US intervenes in Taiwan's defence. China's improved anti-access/area denial capabilities and its strides in cyber and artificial intelligence also contribute to the weakening of cross-strait deterrence. In the words of Michèle Flournoy: 'In the event that conflict starts, the United States can no longer expect to quickly achieve air, space, or maritime superiority'.[12] As Beijing hones its spoofing and jamming technologies, it may be able to interfere with US early warning systems and thereby keep US forces in the dark. Worryingly, other analysts have concluded that Chinese interference with satellite signals is only likely to grow more frequent and sophisticated.[13] China also possesses offensive

---

9   Liu Caiyu, 'China's Centennial Goal of Building a Modern Military by 2021 in Alignment with National Strength: Experts', *Global Times*, 31 October 2020, www.globaltimes.cn/content/1205238.shtml.
10   Li Wei, ed., 'Guidelines on PLA Joint Operations (Trial) Aim for Future Warfare: Defense Spokesperson', *China Military Online*, 26 November 2020, eng.chinamil.com.cn/view/2020-11/26/content_9943059.htm.
11   Qiao Nannan, ed., 'With the Approval of the Chairman of the Central Military Commission Xi Jinping, the Central Military Commission Issued the "Outline of Joint Operations of the Chinese People's Liberation Army (Trial)"', *Xinhua News Agency*, 13 November 2020, www.mod.gov.cn/topnews/2020-11/13/content_4874081.htm [in Chinese].
12   Michèle A. Flournoy, 'How to Prevent a War in Asia: The Erosion of American Deterrence Raises the Risk of Chinese Miscalculation', *Foreign Affairs*, 18 June 2020, www.foreignaffairs.com/articles/united-states/2020-06-18/how-prevent-war-asia.
13   Todd Harrison et al., 'Space Threat Assessment 2020', Center for Strategic and International Studies, 30 March 2020, www.csis.org/analysis/space-threat-assessment-2020.

weaponry, including ballistic and cruise missiles, which, if deployed, could destroy US bases in the Western Pacific in days.[14] Finally, the US intelligence community warns:

> China has the ability to launch cyber attacks that cause localised, temporary disruptive effects on critical infrastructure—such as disruption of a natural gas pipeline for days to weeks—in the United States.[15]

Gradual versus Rapid Approaches

In addition to the reactive/proactive dichotomy, China has a variety of military options in forcing Taiwan's unification with the mainland. According to an authoritative Chinese text,[16] there are four main campaigns for which China is preparing:

1. joint firepower strike operations against Taiwan (大型岛屿联合火力突击作战)
2. joint blockade operations against Taiwan (大型岛屿联合封锁作战)
3. joint attack operations against Taiwan (大型岛屿联合进攻作战)
4. joint anti–air raid operations (联合反空袭作战).[17]

The first scenario would consist of the PLA employing missile and air strikes to disarm Taiwanese targets. The second scenario would consist of the PLA employing tactics ranging from cyber attacks to naval surface raids to cut Taiwan off from the outside world. The third scenario would presumably follow the successful completion of the first two scenarios and would involve an amphibious assault on the island. The last scenario is specifically designed to counter American forces deployed in the region.

---

14   Renanah M. Joyce and Brian Blankenship, 'Access Denied? The Future of US Basing in a Contested World', *War on the Rocks*, 1 February 2021, warontherocks.com/2021/02/access-denied-the-future-of-u-s-basing-in-a-contested-world/.

15   Daniel R. Coats, 'Statement for the Record: Worldwide Threat Assessment of the US Intelligence Community', Office of the Director of National Intelligence, 29 January 2019, www.dni.gov/files/ODNI/documents/2019-ATA-SFR---SSCI.pdf.

16   '战役学' [The Science of Campaigns], 国防大学 [National Defence University], 2006, michalthim.files.wordpress.com/2015/12/the-science-of-campaigns-e68898e5bdb9e5ada6-2006.pdf.

17   Ian Easton, 'China's Top Five War Plans', Project 2049 Institute, accessed 14 September 2021, project2049.net/wp-content/uploads/2019/01/Chinas-Top-Five-War-Plans_Ian_Easton_Project2049.pdf.

Many analysts think that the most likely scenario is one of graduated escalation, in which China starts with lower-level coercive options, only escalating if Taiwan does not capitulate.[18] This strategy reduces the likelihood of US and allied involvement, but is risky. PLA strategists understand that if the US has time to amass forces in the region, the likelihood of victory drops considerably. If prevailing in spite of US intervention is the main consideration, China is more likely to move quickly to the highest level of violence that the scenario requires to force Taiwan's capitulation to Beijing's demands before the US can intervene.[19] If China's objective in the scenario is unification (versus punishing Taiwan or compelling a reversion to the status quo) and it expects US intervention, it could even pre-emptively hit US bases in the region to cripple Washington's ability to respond.

Because of the aforementioned capabilities, many US experts are concerned with a fait accompli—a scenario in which China takes Taiwan before even the most resolved US could act decisively. Recent war games jointly conducted by the Pentagon and RAND Corporation have shown that a military clash between the US and China over Taiwan could result in a US defeat, with China completing an all-out invasion in a matter of days.[20]

A Typology of Nuclear Deterrence

The impetus and nature of the war from China's perspective will greatly determine whether the countries involved will move up the escalation ladder and the options for de-escalation. These scenarios focus on the conditions under which Beijing would consider using nuclear weapons and assume that China would only consider nuclear use if it was unable to achieve its goals through conventional means.[21]

---

18   Linda Jakobson, 'Why Should Australia Be Concerned About … Rising Tensions in the Taiwan Straits?', China Matters Explores, *China Matters*, February 2021, chinamatters.org.au/policy-brief/policy-brief-february-2021/.

19   Samson Ellis, 'Here's What Could Happen If China Invaded Taiwan', *Bloomberg*, 7 October 2020, www.bloomberg.com/news/features/2020-10-07/here-s-what-could-happen-if-china-invaded-taiwan.

20   Daniel L. Davis, 'Can America Successfully Repel a Chinese Invasion of Taiwan?', *National Interest*, 6 August 2020, nationalinterest.org/blog/skeptics/can-america-successfully-repel-chinese-invasion-taiwan-166350.

21   This is for analytical purposes, and not meant to suggest that the US will prevail in all contingencies against the modernised PLA.

Table 3.1: Typology of Nuclear Deterrence

	Reactive	Proactive
Gradual escalation	High cost of peace—MODERATE risk	Maximum flexibility—LOW risk
Rapid escalation	Point of no return—HIGH risk	High cost of peace—MODERATE risk

Escalatory dynamics will be harder to manage if Beijing feels like it is reacting to unfavourable changes in the status quo. For example, if Taiwan declares independence, Beijing will fight until Taiwan renounces independence. If a successful US intervention threatens this goal, Chinese leadership may consider escalating to the nuclear level to avoid losing Taiwan. The US could do a number of things to create this impression: for example, effectively destroying Chinese military capability so that, at a certain point, Beijing will not be able to continue fighting; or successfully implementing a compellence campaign, such as strangling Beijing economically, so that the leadership feels like its options are capitulation or escalation.[22]

Escalatory dynamics will also be harder to manage if Beijing pursues a rapid escalation of military force. There are two reasons for this. First, there are fewer rungs on the escalatory ladder between the current level of force being used and nuclear use. This constrains the options available to leaders short of nuclear use. Second, China has more deniability regarding objectives with coercive campaigns than an amphibious assault. In the former scenario, if things do not go as planned, the Chinese leadership could argue that its goal was to 'teach Taipei a lesson'; in other words, use of force itself is enough to demonstrate success to the Chinese people. However, the visual of hundreds of ships making their way across the strait suggests an attempt at unification by Beijing, especially in the case of an ongoing crisis.

---

22 A point of emphasis: US strategists have articulated the concern that miscalculation and misunderstanding about US intentions towards China's nuclear capability in particular could provoke a nuclear war. Caitlin Talmadge, 'Would China Go Nuclear? Assessing the Risk of Chinese Nuclear Escalation in a Conventional War with the United States', *International Security* 41(4), Spring 2017, 50–92, doi.org/10.1162/ISEC_a_00274. But there is nothing in Chinese nuclear strategy, doctrine, training or modernisation that suggests Beijing would use tactical nuclear weapons tactically (it has none) or do so pre-emptively, even if it feared a US attack on its strategic capabilities.

Even with an amphibious assault, Chinese leaders have some off-ramps if they want to avoid escalation. Xi would likely be cautious about what he publicly promises in order to give himself flexibility. As long as the US does not push for Taiwan's independence as part of the war termination agreement, Beijing can accept half-measures. One option, for example, is to seize some Taiwanese-controlled islands that China also claims, such as Matsu, Pratas, Itu Aba or Quemoy/Kinmen. But the point here is that there are more drivers of escalation than of de-escalation if Beijing skips some low-level options to a high-intensity option early on.

In this proactive scenario, the US is less likely to offer enticing off-ramps. There will be the sense in Washington that China needs to be punished for taking offensive action, and for the war to be worthwhile, the US needs to be in a better overall position at the end of it. US leaders may want a war termination settlement that sufficiently punishes Beijing for this action and reinstates deterrence—likely by demanding concessions on Taiwan's political status that Beijing will not make. In this scenario, Beijing's tendency for disproportionate escalation will come to the fore, bringing about an end to the war on its terms.[23] China would start by increasing the costs on US military forces in the region; if that did not work, they would consider civilian targets in the US. However, due to range limitations (China has limited conventional options for hitting the US homeland),[24] this is more likely through non-traditional means like cyber or counterspace attacks. This is one of the few scenarios in which the leadership may consider using nuclear weapons, although in the author's view they would not do so.[25]

Thus, nuclear deterrence is most likely to hold if Beijing choses a gradual escalation approach in an attempt to revert to a more favourable status quo. The most dangerous scenario is one in which Beijing is compelled to respond to an action taken by Taipei or Washington and does so by implementing the highest-intensity military option.

---

23   Oriana Skylar Mastro, 'How China Ends Wars: Implications for East Asia and US Security', *Washington Quarterly* 41(1), 2018, doi.org/10.1080/0163660X.2018.1445358.

24   David C. Gompert, Astrid Stuth Cevallos and Cristina L. Garafola, *War with China: Thinking Through the Unthinkable* (Santa Monica: RAND Corporation, 2016), www.rand.org/content/dam/rand/pubs/research_reports/RR1100/RR1140/RAND_RR1140.pdf.

25   Oriana Skylar Mastro, 'The United States Must Avoid a Nuclear Arms Race with China', Cato Institute, 21 September 2020, www.cato-unbound.org/2020/09/21/oriana-skylar-mastro/united-states-must-avoid-nuclear-arms-race-china.

Allied Contributions in a Taiwan Scenario and Implications for Nuclear Deterrence

The degree and nature of allied and partner contributions in a Taiwan contingency are of great debate in Washington as well as in capitals around the region. Countries in the region may directly contribute forces to engage with Chinese forces or varying degrees of base access, with most analysts thinking Australia and Japan are likely to contribute the most in both categories.[26]

It is beyond the scope of this chapter to articulate the conditions under which allies and partners are likely to contribute to the war effort. Based on the author's conversations with allied government officials— in particular, detailed discussions in Canberra in December 2019 and March 2021—allies are most likely to contribute if Beijing has proactively used force and at a high-intensity level. There are several reasons for this logic. First, the level of violence determines the degree to which Beijing attacks the US. It will be difficult for allies to remain neutral if Beijing attacks US bases or regional assets, especially if the surprise attack occurs before the US has declared war on China. Second, such a move on the part of Beijing may heighten threat perceptions within these countries, inspiring a domestic political cry to punish and constrain such dangerous behaviour in the region. Third, if Beijing takes this proactive, high-intensity approach, it will be more difficult for politicians in the region to argue that the scenario is another US 'war of choice' in which they can avoid entanglement without threatening their alliance relationships with the US and the future role of the US in the region.

The main question of this contribution is: how will allied contributions influence nuclear deterrence and escalation? First and foremost, the prospect of allied involvement is the greatest deterrent against a proactive Chinese use of force. China's grand strategic goal of rejuvenation is most at risk if a long-term countervailing coalition forms against it. Avoiding actions that could spark such a coalition has been the central feature of Chinese competitive strategy. If deterrence fails, allied involvement still increases the costs of escalation to both Beijing and the US, thereby decreasing the likelihood of escalation to the nuclear level.

---

26 Sheena Greitens and Zack Cooper, 'What to Expect from Japan and Korea in a Taiwan Contingency', Nonproliferation Policy Education Center, February 2021, t.co/bfQSKZRaYE?amp=1.

For the allies, there is a trade-off. Their involvement will reduce the likelihood that the conflict will escalate to the nuclear level. But allied involvement, in the form of base access or contributing military forces, increases the likelihood that they will become a military target. Indeed, there is little doubt that Beijing would target US bases hosted in other countries or allied military forces directly involved in a contingency. What exactly allies are contributing, and the impact these contributions may have on the US-led military effort, could influence the Chinese strategic calculus. For example, if a country contributes both bases and forces, China may attack forces first; the ally might then retreat from the conflict, before China escalates to attacking bases within the allied country itself. On the other hand, US base access may have more of an operational impact on its ability to fight and prevail than the direct military engagement of allies. If military trends are not going in China's favour, its leadership may prioritise bases as the target to limit the US's ability to operate from those sites and coerce host countries to retract their permissions. But, even in terms of bases, the US would rely on certain bases more than others given functional and geographic constraints. For example, the US has three air force bases, three army bases and five naval facilities in Japan, all of which are located in geographic proximity to the Taiwan Strait.[27]

Could Beijing target US allies supporting US operations with nuclear weapons? It is operationally possible but strategically highly implausible that Beijing would target US allies with nuclear weapons.

Technically, China could attack any regional actor with nuclear weapons. Over the past 20 years, China has been industriously modernising its nuclear forces. Currently, Beijing's nuclear arsenal is estimated to number in the two-hundreds, and the Pentagon anticipates that the stockpile will double over the next 10 years.[28] China also added a sea leg to its nuclear deterrent in 2016 with the introduction of submarine-launched ballistic

---

27 'US Military Bases in Japan', Military Bases (blog), accessed 12 February 2021, militarybases.com/overseas/japan/.

28 Office of the Secretary of Defense, 'Military and Security Developments Involving the People's Republic of China 2020', United States Department of Defense, 2020.

missiles (JL-2) on its *Jin*-class ballistic missile submarine. China reportedly recently completed the final leg of the triad with the H-GN bomber, which is nuclear-capable and able to be refuelled in midair.[29]

Additionally, China is producing ballistic missile systems with multiple independently targetable re-entry vehicle and manoeuvrable re-entry vehicle technologies that enhance missiles' effectiveness. To this end, China launched more ballistic missiles for testing and training in 2019 than the rest of the world combined.[30] The Chinese military has increased the number of ballistic missile brigades by around a third in the past three years to enhance its nuclear strike capabilities amid escalating tensions with the US and to prepare for a possible war against Taiwan.[31] Meanwhile, the PLA's new hypersonic cruise missiles are supposedly capable of piercing existing missile defence systems.[32] One Beijing-based military source reported that the PLA deployed its most advanced hypersonic missile, the DF-17, to the area.[33]

China's Possible Use of Nuclear Weapons

Chinese use of nuclear weapons against US allies is operationally possible. However, such a move makes little strategic sense. If China does use nuclear weapons, there are a number of reasons the US, not its allies, would be the target.

First, China pledges no nuclear use against non-nuclear states (such as US allies in Asia). Authoritative Chinese writings on nuclear doctrine are vague about targeting, listing adversary cities, infrastructure and soft military targets without any specific target countries.[34] They describe

---

29 Joe Gould, 'China Plans to Double Nuclear Arsenal, Pentagon Says', *DefenseNews*, 1 September 2020, www.defensenews.com/congress/2020/09/01/china-planning-to-double-nuclear-arsenal-pentagon-says/.
30 Office of the Secretary of Defense, '2019 Missile Defense Review', United States Department of Defense, 19 January 2019, www.defense.gov/Portals/1/Interactive/2018/11-2019-Missile-Defense-Review/The%202019%20MDR_Executive%20Summary.pdf.
31 Minnie Chan, 'China Boosts Nuclear Strike Capability in Face of Growing Rivalry with US, Report Says', *South China Morning Post*, 11 December 2020, www.scmp.com/news/china/military/article/3113639/china-boosts-nuclear-strike-capability-face-growing-rivalry-us.
32 Richard Stone, '"National Pride Is at Stake": Russia, China, United States Race to Build Hypersonic Weapons', *Science*, 8 January 2020, www.sciencemag.org/news/2020/01/national-pride-stake-russia-china-united-states-race-build-hypersonic-weapons.
33 Chan, 'Chinese Military Beefs Up Coastal Forces'.
34 I would like to thank Fiona Cunningham for this point.

only one campaign for the use of China's nuclear forces: the 'nuclear counterstrike campaign' (核反击战役). The main component of this campaign corresponds to China's no-first-use doctrine—in other words, China would only execute a nuclear strike after it had been attacked with nuclear weapons. The posture of China's forces (which includes relatively small numbers of intercontinental ballistic missiles and the separate storage of warheads) and its training to launch on attack and not on warning, are consistent with a singular campaign intended to launch only a retaliatory strike.[35]

Developments in 2019 indicate that China intends to increase its peacetime readiness nuclear posture from launch on attack to launch on warning, casting doubt upon the no-first-use policy.[36] However, there are no indications that its commitment not to use nuclear weapons against non-nuclear states is in question.[37] In other words, if China is going to use nuclear weapons, its doctrine encourages use against the US homeland, not the territory of its allies.

Second, there are operational trade-offs between targets.[38] The US and China do not have a mutually assured destruction relationship. Their nuclear relationship is highly asymmetric. The US has 5,800 nuclear warheads; it is estimated China will have 200 only after a significant building program. China also has limited delivery options (approximately 30 launchers), possessing only a few intercontinental ballistic missiles that can reach the US.[39]

Using nuclear weapons against US allies would be less influential in terms of the US's willingness and ability to continue fighting than using them against the US homeland. But such a move could precipitate the use of nuclear weapons against the Chinese homeland. The US provides a nuclear umbrella for allies through an extended deterrence guarantee—or the

---

35 Fravel and Cunningham, 'Assuring Assured Retaliation'.

36 Office of the Secretary of Defense, 'Military and Security Developments'.

37 吴莼思 [Wu Chunsi, Researcher at Shanghai Research Institute of Global Issues], '核安全峰会、全球核秩序建设与中国角色' [Nuclear Security Summit, Global Nuclear Order and the Role of China], *International Security Research* 33(02), 2015, 56–57; Xuequan Mu, 'Nuclear Deterrence Targeting Non-Nuclear States a Sign of Hegemonism: Chinese Ambassador', *Xinhua*, 16 May 2019, www.xinhuanet.com/english/2019-05/16/c_138061422.htm.

38 The author would like to thank Fiona Cunningham for highlighting this factor.

39 The silo-based CSS-4 Mod 2 (DF-5A) and MIRV-equipped Mod 3 (DF-5B); the solid-fuelled, road-mobile CSS-10-class (DF-31, DF-31A and DF-31AG); and the DF-41, which is still in production. See, 'DF-5', Missile Threat, last modified 2 August 2021, missilethreat.csis.org/missile/df-5-ab/.

reassurance that nuclear action against allies would trigger a US response. Additionally, given the PRC's current operational warhead stockpile and launchers, there would be a numbers trade-off with inflicting unacceptable retaliation on the US and attacking US allies. For example, the Chinese nuclear-tipped missiles that could strike Australia (DF-31, 31A, 41, JL-2 and perhaps DF-4) are the same as those that bring US territory into range. Using its nuclear weapons against allies would thus undermine its deterrent against the US.

As Beijing increases its arsenal, the trade-off may decrease in severity, but it will still significantly discourage nuclear use against US allies given that asymmetry in US nuclear dominance will remain. If the PRC has already absorbed a damage-limiting US strike, the opportunity cost of striking an allied versus a US target would be particularly high. There is also an opportunity cost in the training and targeting realm. China is focused on deterring US nuclear use, and for a nuclear counterstrike campaign, it is unclear how flexible the strategic rocket force can be to change approaches and targets.

Third, China's ability to threaten the US and its allies with conventional weapons in the region is significant. After three decades of focused military modernisation, China now has one of the most advanced and largest militaries in the world. China has many options to inflict massive harm on regional countries through non-nuclear means: through employment of traditional air, naval or sea power; through having the most advanced cruise and ballistic missile program in the world; through grey-zone activities that leverage militias and law enforcement forces such as the coastguard; or through cyber, space or electronic warfare.

This means that China has many options for military coercion short of nuclear use. The potential economic costs alone have caused many leaders in the region to question the degree to which they would support the US. Manila, for example, has considered ending its Visiting Forces Agreement with Washington as a result of deepening economic ties between the Philippines and China, largely fuelled by Belt and Road Initiative investments from the latter. While the agreement with the US was ultimately maintained, this incident demonstrates that Beijing clearly has increasing influence. In short, Beijing can likely convince countries to withdraw their support with conventional threats and means alone. Chinese actions also suggest that its military is not thinking about nuclear weapons as a coercive, signalling tool—indeed, Chinese nuclear operational doctrine lacks any clear plans for limited nuclear use and the strategic rocket force lacks tactical nuclear weapons.[40]

***

In most contingencies, even over Taiwan, the prospects for nuclear use are extremely low, with the highest risk being a situation in which Beijing chooses to respond with a high level of force to a perceived attack on its interests. Allied involvement would further decrease the likelihood that either side will cross the nuclear threshold. Admittedly, the more involved and critical allied support is, the more likely it is those countries' military forces and territory could become a target for military attack. But Chinese doctrine and force posture all point to the US as the target for a 'nuclear counterattack' campaign. A nuclear attack on allied forces or territory makes little sense from a strategic perspective.

There are many factors that allies would have to consider when deciding how much to support the US in a contingency against Taiwan. How would the choice impact the relationship with the US? What is the likelihood that the US would prevail without support? What are the most operationally effective (political) and feasible (demanded) forms of support? How is Beijing likely to respond both in wartime and after the conflict is over? What will the region look like after these decisions have been made and the conflict plays out? While these factors create a complex decision space, this chapter suggests that there is little need to fear nuclear retaliation as one of the primary considerations.

---

40 Cunningham and Fravel, 'Dangerous Confidence?'.

4

US Allies and Nuclear Weapons Cooperation

Jeffrey Larsen

The United States maintains a national security strategy that recognises the distinctions between different regions of the world and appreciates the allies with whom it shares common values and worldviews. For many of America's allies, this commitment includes US nuclear deterrence guarantees. US national security strategy highlights the importance of maintaining peace and security in the regions, ensuring the defence of close allies and partners, and negating the efforts of regional or global adversaries. This chapter examines and compares the extended deterrence arrangements in Europe with those in the Indo-Pacific. While there remain important differences between the two regions—most notably the degree of formal structure underpinning nuclear sharing in the North Atlantic Treaty Organization (NATO)—both sets of arrangements fulfill the key purpose of reassuring US allies that Washington would come to their assistance if their security was threatened.

The US has particularly longstanding linkages with the states of Europe. However, in the Indo-Pacific, it also has close relations with a number of democratic nations, including economic, political, trade and military partnerships. As one analyst has written, 'the grave obligations associated with the US nuclear guarantees to Seoul and Tokyo are consistent with the high stakes the United States has in their safety from aggression'.[1] The same could be said regarding the member states of NATO, as well as additional allies in Europe, the Middle East and the Indo-Pacific.

Recent presidents have reiterated America's commitment to its allies. President Barack Obama's 2015 National Security Strategy defined America's regional strategies as having a long-term affirmative agenda in each region, rather than focusing on immediate threats.[2] His administration pursued this agenda with the help of reinvigorated alliances with longstanding friends. In the Indo-Pacific, for example, this meant modernising the alliances with Japan, South Korea, Australia, the Philippines and Thailand, and using such regional institutions as the Association of Southeast Asian Nations (ASEAN), the East Asia Summit and the forum for Asia-Pacific Economic Cooperation (APEC). While recognising the rise of China and the need to be competitive, the Obama strategy rejected 'the inevitability of confrontation' with Beijing.[3]

Two years later, President Donald Trump's administration published a new National Security Strategy that accepted many of these principles, but with a more assertive tone. In what is now called the Indo-Pacific, the US declared China to be an aggressive challenger to peace and security in the region. The strategy highlighted the importance of regional allies and promised to increase quadrilateral cooperation with Japan, Australia and India. It also highlighted the Philippines and Thailand as important allies; recognised the growing security and economic partnerships with Vietnam, Indonesia, Malaysia and Singapore; emphasised the importance of ASEAN and APEC; and stated that the US would maintain its close ties with Taiwan.[4]

The 2017 National Security Strategy also emphasised how closely the US and Europe were bound together, as exemplified in NATO. It stated that the US remained fully committed to NATO's Article 5 commitment that an attack on one was an attack on all. The strategy highlighted threats to

---

1   Keith Payne, *US Extended Deterrence and Assurance for Allies in Northeast Asia* (Washington: National Institute Press, 2010), 39, nipp.org/wp-content/uploads/2021/05/US-Extend-Deter-for-print.pdf.
2   *National Security Strategy* (Washington: The White House, September 2015), 23, obamawhite house.archives.gov/sites/default/files/docs/2015_national_security_strategy_2.pdf.
3   Ibid.
4   *National Security Strategy of the United States of America* (Washington: The White House, December 2017), 46, acqnotes.com/wp-content/uploads/2014/09/National-Security-Strategy-Dec-2017.pdf.

Europe that included a resurgent Russia, terrorism and growing Chinese influence in European affairs, and committed the US to retaining the necessary military capabilities in Europe to deal with such challenges.[5]

The 2018 Nuclear Posture Review (NPR) affirmed America's commitment to the security of its allies and partners, tailored to the differing requirements of the two regions of greatest importance to the US. In the Asia-Pacific, the North Korean nuclear program and China's more aggressive behaviour threaten key allies. Dealing with these threats includes extended deterrence and the assurance of America's friends.[6] While all America's key allies in East Asia strongly supported the 2018 NPR, NATO allies accepted its premises with some uncertainty. Further, while they were pleased to see in its words a strong rebuttal of Russia, they were concerned about the continuing reliability of the US commitment given statements by President Trump.

Bilateral security arrangements are embedded in larger diplomatic, political and economic dealings with Asia. Traditionally, Washington had pushed for greater economic cooperation in the region, such as the Trans-Pacific Partnership. The US withdrew from this treaty in 2017. However, despite this withdrawal, the Trump administration supported the concept of 'a free and open Indo-Pacific'—a proposal originated by Japanese Prime Minister Shinzo Abe. In late 2017 Abe also proposed a 'democratic security diamond', which led to meetings and cooperation among the so-called Quad.[7]

In his first round of telephone calls to allied leaders in late 2020, President-elect Joseph Biden confirmed that the US wanted to retain and enhance these linkages. He expressed his desire to strengthen alliances with South Korea and Japan—two countries he called the 'cornerstones of a prosperous and secure Indo-Pacific region'.[8]

---

5   Ibid., 48.

6   *Nuclear Posture Review* (Washington: Office of the Secretary of Defense, February 2018), 34–35, media.defense.gov/2018/Feb/02/2001872886/-1/-1/1/2018-NUCLEAR-POSTURE-REVIEW-FINAL-REPORT.PDF.

7   Atman Trivedi, 'Analysis: US Allies Are Stepping in to Ensure Asian Regional Order', *The Wire*, 21 April 2018, thewire.In/diplomacy/US-allies-are-stepping-in-to-ensure-asian-regional-order.

8   Kim Tong-hyung, Rod McGuirk and Mari Yamaguchi, 'Leaders of America's Asian Allies Call President-Elect Biden', *The Diplomat*, 13 November 2020, thediplomat.com/220/11/leaders-of-americas-asian-allies-call-president-elect-biden/.

Tailored Extended Deterrence

As a sovereign, independent nation-state, the US's primary national security goal is the protection of its own people, territory and interests. But it has also promised to protect many of its friends and allies around the world. This guarantee is accomplished by extending its nuclear and conventional umbrella over some 40 allies, nearly all of them non-nuclear weapon states.[9]

The concept of extended deterrence means that one state will provide security for another state through the threat of punishment against a third party that may wish to attack or coerce the second state. In short, extended deterrence commits the US to the possibility of going to war with another great power in order to protect a more vulnerable ally.[10] This logical extrapolation of deterrence theory is a commitment that is not made lightly or offered to everyone.

Very different models of extended deterrence are found in different regions of the world.[11] Yet the US's extended deterrence umbrella faces the same challenges in both Europe and Asia: it is invaluable for assuring allies of American support and commitment, but worrisome to allies who may doubt the credibility of a president actually committing those weapons to use when necessary. Credibility is enhanced by the visible presence of US service personnel and their families in allied countries, conventional weapon and missile defence deployments, and allies developing indigenous capabilities for self-defence and deterrence by denial.

---

9   The specific nations covered by the US nuclear umbrella are not specified in official documents. Brad Roberts has written that 'the United States continues to provide security guarantees to more than 40 allies in three regions (Europe, Northeast Asia, and the Middle East)'. Brad Roberts, *The Case for US Nuclear Weapons in the 21st Century* (Stanford: Stanford University Press, 2015), 7, doi.org/10.1515/9780804797153.

10   On extended deterrence, see Austin Long, *Deterrence from Cold War to Long War: Lessons from Six Decades of RAND Research* (Santa Monica: RAND Corporation, 2008); Steven Pifer et al., 'US Nuclear and Extended Deterrence: Considerations and Challenges', The Brookings Institute, May 2010; and Robert Legvold and Christopher Chyba, eds, 'Meeting the Challenges of a New Nuclear Age', Special Edition of *Daedalus* 149(2), Spring 2020, www.amacad.org/daedalus/meeting-challenges-new-nuclear-age.

11   On models of extended deterrence, see Richard C. Bush, 'The US Policy of Extended Deterrence in Asia: History, Current Views, and Implications', The Brookings Institute, February 2011; Hillary Clinton, 'America's Pacific Century', *Foreign Policy*, November 2011, 56–63; and Jeffrey Larsen, 'US Extended Deterrence in Europe: Time to Consider Alternative Structures?', in *The Future of Extended Deterrence: The United States, NATO, and Beyond*, ed. Stefanie von Hlatky and Andreas Wenger (Washington: Georgetown University Press, 2015), Chapter 2.

Extended deterrence has served a number of additional purposes. For example, it has created caution among the nuclear players on the world stage and it may prevent nuclear proliferation by America's allies. The nuclear umbrella has also served to reinforce the commitment of NATO states to the Nuclear Non-Proliferation Treaty—one example being West Germany, which was often touted as a potential nuclear weapon state during the 1950s and 1960s.[12] In return for a US security guarantee, NATO allies agreed not to pursue their own nuclear capabilities. A similar understanding was in place in North-East Asia for the purpose of containing proliferation pressures in Japan and South Korea.

In Asia, the US has longstanding security commitments to Japan through the US–Japan Security Pact.[13] Both sides have always assumed that this means the possible use of US nuclear weapons to protect Japanese territorial sovereignty against potential aggression, Japan's anti-nuclear stance notwithstanding. In 2009, the US secretary of state travelled to Japan to proclaim publicly that this solemn commitment to defend Japan was intact in the face of North Korean military threats.[14]

South Korea is also the recipient of the US nuclear security guarantee. The US and South Korea have maintained a mutual security arrangement since 1954, and US nuclear weapons were stationed in South Korea until 1992.[15] Australia also assumes that the US nuclear umbrella extends

12 Alexander Lanoszka, *Atomic Assurance: The Alliance Politics of Nuclear Proliferation* (Ithaca: Cornell University Press, 2018), Chapter 3.
13 Officially the 'Treaty of Mutual Cooperation and Security between Japan and the United States of America', signed January 1960, www.mofa.go.jp/region/n-america/US/q&a/ref/1.html. See also Margaret Williams, 'The 2018 Nuclear Posture Review: Perception by US Allies in the Asia-Pacific', CSIS Nuclear Network, 23 May 2018, nuclearnetwork.csis.org/2018-nuclear-posture-review-reception-u-s-allies-asia-pacific/.
14 Jim Garamone, 'Clinton Meets Japanese Leaders on First Leg of Asian Tour', Defense Visual Information Distribution Service, 18 February 2009, www.dvidshub.net/news/30164/clinton-meets-japanese-leaders-first-leg-asian-tour.
15 'The Withdrawal of US Nuclear Weapons from South Korea', The Nuclear Information Project, 28 September 2005, www.nukestrat.com/korea/withdrawal.htm.

over its territory, as part of the 1951 Australia, New Zealand, United States Security Treaty (ANZUS). Canberra has reiterated this belief in a succession of defence white papers.[16]

Nuclear weapons are likely to continue to play a central role in US security policy. The US has determined that providing security guarantees for its allies remains in its vital interests. Unlike the situation in Europe, where dual-capable aircraft stand ready to deliver American nuclear weapons in case of a crisis, North-East Asia benefits from American security guarantees without having any US nuclear weapons in the region. Deterrence, after all, is essentially psychological, working on the perceptions of the potential adversary.

Debates about allies developing their own nuclear weapons have occasionally risen to the surface. While many of the NATO allies have put such thoughts behind them, the concept has been raised relatively recently by the US itself, with President Trump musing about Japan and South Korea developing their own nuclear weapons to reduce US commitments and costs. Subsequently, and in response to concerns that the US might withdraw its extended deterrence umbrella, interest in developing nuclear programs gained some limited traction in those two countries.[17] South Korea and Japan both worry about North Korea and its nuclear program, but Japan's long-term concern is China and its growing military capability. Seoul and Tokyo are developing improved conventional strike capabilities and missile defence systems to supplement US forces and provide options below the nuclear threshold in case of conflict. These could simultaneously enhance deterrence while reducing reliance on the US nuclear guarantee.[18] Some analysts even suggest that

16 Although New Zealand and the US no longer share defence commitments under the treaty (since 1984), it remains in effect between Australia and the US. There is no specific commitment to extend nuclear deterrence over the signatories, but Australian governments believe that is implied in the agreement. *Defence White Paper 2013: Defending Australia and Its National Interests* (Australian Department of Defence, 3 May 2013), www.defence.gov.au/whitepaper/2013/docs/WP_2013_web.pdf (site discontinued). See also Richard Tanter, 'Rethinking Extended Nuclear Deterrence in the Defence of Australia', *Japan Focus: The Asia-Pacific Journal*, 14 December 2009, www.japanfocus.org/-richard-tanter/3269.
17 See, for example: 'Who Will Go Nuclear Next?', *The Economist*, 30 January 2021, 9; Jesse Johnson, 'South Korea Developing its Own Nukes One Solution to US Cost-Sharing Demands, Ex-Top Diplomat Says', *Japan Times*, 12 November 2019, www.japantimes.co.jp/news/2019/11/12/asia-pacific/nuclear-weapons-cost-sharing-south-korea/; Mark Fitzpatrick, 'How Japan Could Go Nuclear', *Foreign Affairs*, 3 October 2019, www.foreignaffairs.com/articles/asia/2019-10-03/how-japan-could-go-nuclear.
18 Eric Gomez, 'Revisiting the Value of the US Nuclear Umbrella in East Asia', *War on the Rocks*, 6 March 2018, warontherocks.com/2018/03/revisiting-value-u-s-nuclear-umbrella-east-asia/.

the US should allow 'friendly proliferation' of nuclear weapons to reduce its burden and enhance the credibility of such threats when they are brandished by those states most affected by neighbouring adversaries.[19]

However, as Brad Roberts has written:

> The benefits of remaining a non-nuclear ally of the United States are high relative to the benefits of the available options, while the costs are relatively low. Thus, it is hardly surprising that no US ally has determined to have nuclear weapons of its own since the very earliest days of the Cold War.[20]

The same calculation is in play in those states not explicitly under the guarantee of US extended nuclear deterrence. They see no better option than teaming with the US.

What do America's non-nuclear allies want in return for their commitment to the US as their protector?[21] In today's world, many allies seek greater assurance from the US, given security trends and the rise of potentially adversarial powers in their region. Anxious allies favour a balanced approach, such as that posited by President Obama in his 2009 Prague speech, which called for reduced emphasis on nuclear weapons and doctrine while still accepting the need for an arsenal that was second to none.[22] That said, some allies are also concerned by the possibility of further reductions in weapons by the US, given the need for Washington to deter both China and Russia.

The European Model: NATO and Formalised Risk and Burden Sharing

The US's extended deterrence and assurance arrangements for NATO are well established. The US agreed to guarantee the security of the other members as long as all contributed to the general defence—a process

---

19 Examples of such thinking can be found in Doug Bandow, 'America's Asian Allies Need their Own Nukes', *Foreign Policy*, 30 December 2020, foreignpolicy.com/2020/12/30/nuclear-weapons-china-great-power-competition-asia/; Se Young Jang, 'Will America's Asian Allies Go Nuclear?', *National Interest*, 4 May 2018, nationalinterest.org/feature/will-americas-asian-allies-go-nuclear-16055.
20 Roberts, *The Case for US Nuclear Weapons*, 220.
21 Ibid., 214–16.
22 'Remarks by President Barack Obama', The White House, President Barack Obama, 5 April 2009, obamawhitehouse.archives.gov/the-press-office/remarks-president-barack-obama-prague-delivered.

called risk and burden sharing. This included the full weight of America's military capabilities, including forward-deployed conventional forces and nuclear weapons; the creation of a nuclear planning group for the alliance, which meets regularly to discuss issues related to nuclear deterrence in a collaborative environment; and the sharing of nuclear missions and tasks with allies.[23] All members except France participate in the Nuclear Planning Group.

While acknowledging that the US defence posture in Europe has changed significantly since the end of the Cold War, the US recognises the regional and global importance of keeping significant military forces on the continent. This rationale includes maintaining a robust US military presence in Europe to deter the political intimidation of allies and partners, promote stability, demonstrate America's commitment to NATO allies, build trust and goodwill among host nations, and facilitate multilateral operations in support of mutual security interests.[24]

The presence of US nuclear weapons—combined with NATO's nuclear-sharing arrangements under which some non-nuclear members possess specially configured aircraft capable of delivering nuclear weapons—contributes to alliance cohesion and provides reassurance to allies and partners who feel exposed to regional threats. The US has affirmed that it will not make unilateral decisions as to the future of those weapons or their basing in Europe, stating: 'Any changes in NATO's nuclear posture should only be taken after a thorough review within and decision by the Alliance'.[25] NATO's 2012 Deterrence and Defence Posture Review determined that the alliance's nuclear risk and burden-sharing arrangements were sufficient for NATO deterrence

23   The history of NATO nuclear policy is well documented, but perhaps no longer so well known. For recent reminders of the background and value of this relationship, see Ivo Daalder, 'Does the US Nuclear Umbrella Still Protect America's Allies?', *Foreign Policy*, 27 October 2020, foreignpolicy. com/202010/27/u-s-nuclear-umbrella-proliferation/; Jeffrey Larsen, 'NATO Nuclear Adaptation since 2014: The Return of Deterrence and Renewed Alliance Discomfort', *Journal of Transatlantic Studies* 17(2), 2019, 174–93, doi.org/10.1057/s42738-019-00016-y.
24   *Quadrennial Defense Review Report* (Washington: Office of the Secretary of Defense, February 2010), 65, dod.defense.gov/Portals/1/features/defenseReviews/QDR/QDR_as_of_29JAN10_1600.pdf.
25   *Nuclear Posture Review Report* (Washington: Office of the Secretary of Defense, April 2010), xii, dod.defense.gov/Portals/1/features/defenseReviews/NPR/2010_Nuclear_Posture_Review_Report.pdf.

'under current circumstances'.[26] Given changes in the European threat environment since 2012, parts of that document are out of date, but its conclusions are still followed by the alliance.

The 2018 NPR listed specific steps that the US would undertake in cooperation with NATO allies to strengthen nuclear deterrence in Europe. These included enhancing the readiness, survivability and operational effectiveness of dual-capable aircraft, as well as modernisation programs to update existing aircraft and weapons; promoting the broadest possible participation in nuclear risk and burden-sharing efforts; enhancing training and education about the deterrence mission; and ensuring NATO's nuclear command, control and communications systems were updated.[27]

US policy under the Biden administration will focus on restoring close ties to America's allies and NATO. After years of relations based on transactional and often vituperative demands, America's allies in Europe, with few exceptions, are pleased to return to a more normal relationship with Washington.

The non-nuclear states of the alliance will play a role in all decisions on how to best respond to the multitude of security challenges facing Europe today, through their shared membership in the North Atlantic Council, the Nuclear Planning Group and the various bodies of the European Union as it develops a common defence and security policy for Europe. On the other hand, the alliance will face challenges keeping some member states in the non-nuclear fold. The US may have to enhance its extended deterrence guarantees to assure those allies of American security promises.

The Asian Model: Bilateral Defence Agreements

Allies in the Indo-Pacific lack a region-wide alliance structure akin to NATO in Europe. Extended deterrence in East Asia is a particularly complicated topic. A combination of differing cultures, divergent regional interests, historical animosities and the tyranny of geography prevents the creation of a pan-Pacific defence coalition. Evolving relationships and

---

26 'Deterrence and Defence Posture Review', NATO Press Release, 20 May 2012, www.nato.int/cps/en/natolive/official_texts_87597.htm.
27 *Nuclear Posture Review* (2018), 36.

changing threat perceptions within the region, and different outlooks on US extended deterrence guarantees, make even a trilateral defence relationship between the US, Japan and South Korea an unlikely prospect. Assuring Indo-Pacific allies and partners holding disparate perspectives on national security requirements, and deterring regional adversaries, depends on the credibility of the US commitment and confidence on the part of both allies and adversaries that it will abide by those commitments. Working with the US to address common threats represents an important common denominator across the national security strategies of these disparate states.

Despite facing serious threats in the immediate neighbourhood, at least two of these states may have been prevented from developing their own nuclear weapons because of US extended deterrence. Japan and South Korea have dabbled with the idea of developing their own strategic deterrent weapons whenever they began to have doubts about the US guarantee.[28] Some analysts in those countries have called for even greater participation in plans, forces, deployments and exercises, similar to the involvement that US allies in NATO have via the alliance's existing institutions.

The 2010 NPR stated:

> In Asia and the Middle East—where there are no multilateral alliance structures analogous to NATO—the United States has maintained extended deterrence through bilateral alliances and security relationships and through its forward military presence and security guarantees.[29]

This position remains unchanged. The US withdrew its forward-deployed nuclear weapons from the Pacific region at the end of the Cold War. Since then, it has relied on 'its central strategic forces and the capacity to redeploy non-strategic nuclear systems in East Asia, if needed, in times of crisis'.[30]

---

28 Payne, *US Extended Deterrence and Assurance*, 39–40; Zack Cooper, 'Pacific Power: America's Asian Alliances beyond Burden-Sharing', *War on the Rocks*, 14 December 2016, warontherocks.com/2016/12/pacific-power-americas-asian-alliances-beyond-burden-sharing/; 'Who Will Go Nuclear Next?'.
29 *Nuclear Posture Review* (2010), 32.
30 Ibid.

The Trump administration reiterated that 'the US commitment to our allies and partners in the Asia-Pacific region is unwavering'. The alliance system in the region continues to be 'a series of bilateral relationships with varying degrees of multilateral cooperation across different missions'.[31] To ensure credible extended deterrence in the region, the US committed to maintaining integrated, flexible and adaptable nuclear and non-nuclear capabilities; investing in regional missile defences; demonstrating joint commitment through multinational exercises; and working together to ensure shared understandings of common threats and resulting deterrence requirements.

The strategy of maintaining a 'continuous presence' of US aircraft in the Indo-Pacific ensures that potential adversaries are always aware that the US has nuclear-capable forces in-theatre. This strategy, however, faces challenges from both allies and adversaries. Some politicians and commentators in Japan and South Korea, for example, have either argued for their own countries to develop an independent nuclear deterrent or called for the US to permanently station nuclear forces on their territory.[32] These calls represent an implicit challenge to the assurance value of the continuous presence strategy and its reliance on nuclear-capable forces that are geographically distant from the countries they are intended to protect.

Japan faces a number of regional security challenges and turns to the US for assurance as its most important ally. The two governments agreed in 2011 to establish the Extended Deterrence Dialogue as a bilateral extended deterrence consultative mechanism to address a range of matters, such as Japan's inclusion in the US nuclear umbrella.[33] The US–Japan Defence Cooperation Guidelines were revised in 2015 to reflect greater Japanese contributions to its own defence.[34]

The US has maintained close defence ties with the Republic of Korea (ROK) since the Korean War. The 1953 ROK–US Mutual Defence Treaty pledges that any attack on either party will be met by a joint response to

---

31 *Nuclear Posture Review* (2018), 37.
32 See 'Who Will Go Nuclear Next?'; Joseph Hincks, 'Calls to Bring Nuclear Weapons Back to South Korea Are Getting Louder', *TIME*, 19 October 2017, time.com/4988994/south-korea-nuclear-weapons/.
33 US State Department, 'Joint Statement of the US–Japan Security Consultative Committee', 21 June 2011.
34 Nidhi Prada, 'Japan's Nuclear Insurance against North Korea', *East Asia Forum*, 12 October 2016, www.eastasiaforum.org/2016/10/12/japans-nuclear-insurance-against-north-korea.

'meet the common danger'. In 2010, the US and South Korea established an Extended Deterrence Policy Committee as a formal mechanism for discussing deterrence matters.[35]

In the case of Australia, the continued close engagement with the Indo-Pacific by the US is viewed as vital to both its national security and regional stability.[36] Under Article IV of the ANZUS Treaty, the US and Australia pledged:

> That an armed attack in the Pacific Area on any of the Parties would be dangerous to its own peace and safety and declares that it would act to meet the common danger.

De facto, the US includes Australia under its nuclear umbrella. The Australian Government views US extended nuclear deterrence as a guarantee that has allowed the country to enjoy protection from nuclear attack without having to develop its own independent deterrent capability. It also believes that nuclear deterrence will become more relevant to Australia's defence as the Chinese threat grows in coming years.[37]

* * *

The increasing demand on American military might in both Europe and the Indo-Pacific serves to highlight the continued need for close allies that represent strength in numbers and can provide conventional forces and missile defences that synergistically enhance the defence of these alliances. In both Europe and East Asia, the US welcomes inputs from allies into its extended deterrence strategies, including nuclear planning and policy. While this input is codified in longstanding institutions in NATO, it is conducted on a bilateral basis with allies in Asia. The objective in both regions, however, is the same: to assure America's closest friends of the depth of its commitment to their security, and of the sense of obligation felt by the US to come to their aid in a crisis.

---

35 Shane Smith, *Implications for US Extended Deterrence and Assurance in East Asia* (Washington: US–Korea Institute at SAIS, 2015), 16, www.38north.org/wp-content/uploads/2015/11/NKNF-Smith-Extended-Deterrence-Assurance.pdf.
36 Commonwealth of Australia, *Australia in the Asian Century*, October 2012, 3, www.defence.gov.au/whitepaper/2013/docs/australia_in_the_asian_century_white_paper.pdf.
37 Stephan Frühling, Andrew O'Neil and David Santoro, 'Nuclear Deterrence and the US–Australia Alliance', *Strategist*, Australian Strategic Policy Institute, 15 November 2019, www.aspistrategist.org.au/nuclear-deterrence-and-the-US-australia-alliance/.

5

The Future of Arms Control and Strategic Stability in the Indo-Pacific

Heather Williams

One of the final policy initiatives of the Trump administration included an effort to incorporate China into strategic arms control. According to a senior (unnamed) United States defence official: 'Getting China involved in some sort of an arms control framework is what's needed today in order to stave off a potential three-way arms race in the future'.[1] Chinese officials such as Ambassador Fu Cong, director-general of the Department of Arms Control, repeatedly rebuffed these efforts, stating:

> Given the huge disparity between the Chinese nuclear arsenal and that of the US and the Russian Federation, we simply do not believe that there is any fair and equitable basis for China to join the US and the Russian Federation in a nuclear arms control negotiation.[2]

Nonetheless, the rise of geopolitical competition in Asia, emerging technologies and anxiety on the part of US allies in the region suggest the need for renewed attempts to pursue arms control to strengthen strategic stability. The Trump administration's goal of incorporating China into arms control was not wholly unreasonable; rather, their way of going

1   Jack Detsch, 'Trump Wants China on Board with New Arms Control Pact', *Foreign Policy*, 23 July 2020, foreignpolicy.com/2020/07/23/trump-china-russia-new-arms-control-agreement-start/.
2   Fu Cong, 'Director-General FU Cong's Interview with Kommersant', Ministry of Foreign Affairs of the People's Republic of China, 16 October 2020, www.fmprc.gov.cn/mfa_eng/wjbxw/t1824545.shtml.

about it was short-sighted. Any arms control that strengthens strategic stability in the region will have to account for Chinese interests while also tailoring to regional security and stability issues. Rather than trying to replicate US–Soviet arms control or fitting China into existing arms control structures, a more practical approach to strategic stability and arms control in the region would be to focus on crisis management as a means of promoting transparency and dialogue, which could lay the groundwork for more significant progress in the future.

While strategic stability and arms control are familiar concepts developed during Cold War superpower competition, they are less familiar in the contemporary context of Asia.[3] China's seeming interest in becoming a regional hegemon, along with growing reliance on new technologies, such as cyber and artificial intelligence, present challenges to strategic stability and arms control in both theory and practice. Arms control has historically sought to establish balance between nuclear peer competitors and achieve quantitative and/or qualitative parity in nuclear forces. Given the disparity in China's nuclear arsenal, with approximately 300 warheads compared with 1,323 deployed strategic warheads held by the US,[4] Beijing has limited incentives to join traditional cooperative reduction agreements, such as a follow-on to the 2010 New Strategic Arms Reduction Treaty (New START). Why, then, would China participate in arms control? How can the US use arms control vis-a-vis China to strengthen strategic stability in Asia? And what should be the priorities of arms control tailored to the Indo-Pacific region?

These questions are particularly timely, not only because of increasing geopolitical and technological uncertainty, but also because of shifts in US policies towards allies in recent years. At the end of 2020, views of the US were at a record low in the United Kingdom, Canada, Australia and Japan.[5] After years of tension in America's relationship with its allies in both Europe and Asia, rebuilding its credibility as a partner and security guarantor may be a long-term effort. Numerous allies are hoping the

---

3   Important exceptions to this include work by Fiona Cunningham, Taylor Fravel, David Logan, Brad Roberts, David Santoro, Tong Zhao and others cited elsewhere in this chapter.

4   As of March 2020. This figure does not include non-deployed or reserve warheads, which the Arms Control Association assesses to contribute to an overall total of 5,800.

5   Richard Wike, Janell Fetterolf and Mara Mordecai, 'US Image Plummets Internationally as Most Say Country Has Handled Coronavirus Badly', Pew Research Center, 15 September 2020, www.pewresearch.org/global/2020/09/15/us-image-plummets-internationally-as-most-say-country-has-handled-coronavirus-badly/.

Biden administration will not only repair relations to the levels of the pre-Trump era, but also offer stronger support in the form of extended nuclear deterrence. Recent polls in South Korea, for example, suggest that most people support the redeployment of US tactical nuclear weapons there.[6] Reassuring allies while also pursuing arms control with China may be a difficult balance for the US.

This chapter begins by defining strategic stability, with a focus on broadening the nature of the concept to include non-nuclear capabilities and the increasingly asymmetric nature of stability. It then examines challenges to strategic stability in Asia—namely, geopolitical competition, emerging technologies, China's lack of interest in arms control and concerns of US allies. Finally, it offers three options for US–China arms control with a focus on strengthening crisis stability: trilateral arms control to include Russia; using the 'P5 process'—a series of meetings among the five nuclear weapon states under the Treaty on the Non-Proliferation of Nuclear Weapons (NPT)—to demonstrate commitment to their NPT obligations, facilitate confidence-building measures and lay the groundwork for progress on disarmament; and crisis communication agreements. These recommendations may seem modest, particularly in comparison with some of the ideas floated by the Trump administration; however, they may ultimately contribute to a longer process of cooperation working towards more ambitious arms control between Washington and Beijing.[7]

Strategic Stability is Increasingly Asymmetric

Strategic stability was developed as a concept during the Cold War to describe a relationship in which two adversaries had sufficient nuclear forces to survive a first strike and maintain the ability to retaliate, thus

---

6   Toby Dalton, 'Between Seoul and Sole Purpose: How the Biden Administration Could Assure South Korea and Adapt Nuclear Posture', *War on the Rocks*, 9 February 2021, warontherocks.com/2021/02/between-seoul-and-sole-purpose-how-the-biden-administration-could-assure-south-korea-and-adapt-nuclear-posture/.
7   While this chapter is focused on strategic stability and arms control in the US–Russia context, there are numerous other strategic stability concerns in the Indo-Pacific region that are also worthy of attention by scholars and policymakers. See, for example: Dmitri Trenin, 'Strategic Stability in the Changing World', Carnegie Moscow Center, 21 March 2019, carnegie.ru/2019/03/21/strategic-stability-in-changing-world-pub-78650.

establishing a balance of mutual deterrence. In the 1960s, arms control scholars Thomas Schelling and Morton Halperin refined this concept to define strategic stability as dependent on arms race stability and crisis stability.[8] In arms race stability, neither side has incentives to pursue capabilities that would undermine the survivability of the other's nuclear forces. In crisis stability, neither side has incentives to escalate a crisis in the hope of achieving strategic gains or launching a surprise attack.

Cold War definitions of strategic stability largely focused on the balance of nuclear forces, as experts and policymakers believed that as long as neither side had the capability or incentive to attempt a disarming first strike, deterrence would hold and a nuclear exchange would be avoided. But new research has demonstrated that while this definition dominated discussions in Washington, it was not universal. The Soviet Union, for example, conceptualised strategic stability much more broadly to focus on psychological factors in decision-making.[9] Recent scholarship by Kristin ven Bruusgaard further demonstrates that conventional capabilities are a primary consideration in Russia's nuclear posture and calculations of nuclear balancing.[10] China, like Russia, views America's missile defence and advanced conventional weapons as a threat to deterrence; however, its approach to strategic stability and how it might respond to US strategic developments is complex. At present, Beijing subscribes to a nuclear strategy of assured retaliation, largely achieved through a minimum deterrent and mobile missiles that could survive a first strike. But experts disagree as to whether China will maintain its commitment to no first use or gradually seek an offensive nuclear capability.[11] From Washington's perspective, this uncertainty around Chinese strategy further complicates decision-making and could exacerbate the 'fog of war'.

The primary objective of arms control is to strengthen strategic stability and prevent nuclear war. While arms control may include numerical reductions, this is not its primary goal and occasionally arms control

---

8   Thomas C. Schelling and Morton H. Halperin, *Strategy and Arms Control* (Washington: Pergamon-Brassey, 1985 [1961]).

9   For the classic analysis, see Richard Pipes, 'Why the Soviet Union Thinks it Could Fight and Win a Nuclear War', *Commentary*, July 1977, www.commentary.org/articles/richard-pipes-2/why-the-soviet-union-thinks-it-could-fight-win-a-nuclear-war/.

10   Kristin ven Bruusgaard, 'Russian Nuclear Strategy and Conventional Inferiority', *Journal of Strategic Studies* 44(1), 2020, 1–33, doi.org/10.1080/01402390.2020.1818070.

11   See Fiona S. Cunningham and M. Taylor Fravel, 'Assuring Assured Retaliation: China's Nuclear Posture and US–China Strategic Stability', *International Security* 40(2), Fall 2015, 7–50, doi.org/10.1162/ISEC_a_00215.

allows for the build-up of nuclear forces. For example, Russia actually increased its number of nuclear delivery vehicles under New START.[12] Arms control can contribute to security and stability by limiting the destabilising effects of weapons[13] and pursuing areas of mutual interest with adversaries in limiting the risks of conflict.[14] Schelling and Halperin offer one example of how arms control might strengthen arms race stability through 'cooperative measures to improve intelligence and warning facilities, or cooperative measures with respect to weapons themselves designed to facilitate warning'.[15] Arms control can cover a spectrum of formality, ranging from legally binding treaties, such as New START, to more informal communication measures, such as the 'hotline' established between Washington and Moscow in 1963 following the Cuban Missile Crisis, or the 1973 Agreement on the Prevention of Nuclear War. These examples demonstrate not only the diversity of arms control mechanisms, but also the political nature of arms control as a tool in international security. Economic and ethical concerns might also be drivers of arms control, but improving the security environment is typically the main driver and a mutual interest for all parties.[16] Ultimately, the form and content of arms control depend on the relationship between the parties involved and their unique interests, and the agreement must be tailored to both political and technical realities.

As the concept of strategic stability has broadened to include non-nuclear strategic capabilities (such as cyber), arms control will also have to adapt. States will have to pursue asymmetric arms control to account for quantitative and qualitative imbalances not only in their nuclear forces but also in their reliance on new technologies that can impact the strategic equation.[17] Rather than thinking of strategic stability purely in terms of the number of nuclear weapons, states should think of stability as promoting both *equilibrium*, whereby a relationship is relatively balanced so there are no incentives by either side to launch a pre-emptive attack, and *equanimity*, which means actors would be able to de-escalate tensions

---

12 See, for example: Heather Williams, 'Asymmetric Arms Control and Strategic Stability: Scenarios for Limiting Hypersonic Glide Vehicles', *Journal of Strategic Studies* 42(6), 2019, 802, doi.org/10.1080/01402390.2019.1627521.
13 Hedley Bull, *The Control of the Arms Race* (London: Institute for Strategic Studies, 1961), 3.
14 Schelling and Halperin, *Strategy and Arms Control*, 1.
15 Ibid., 12.
16 Bull, *The Control of the Arms Race*, Chapter 1.
17 Williams, 'Asymmetric Arms Control'.

to restabilise or rebalance the relationship relatively quickly.[18] This broader approach to strategic stability will require more dynamism and flexibility in arms control than in the past. This might mean developing agreements rather than treaties, which can be static and take years to conclude, or by including non–like-for-like exchanges, such as agreeing to limits on missile defence deployments in exchange for a cap on non-strategic nuclear weapons. Ultimately, arms control is about managing uncertainty, which means it is both desperately needed and woefully challenging in the Indo-Pacific.

Challenges for Strategic Stability and Arms Control in Asia

The 2020 Australian *Defence Strategic Update* described a 'more competitive and contested region' with 'greater potential for military miscalculation'.[19] Conflict over Taiwan is a particular concern and was listed as a top 'Conflict to Watch in 2021' by the Council on Foreign Relations.[20] In 2020, the Chinese leadership increasingly talked about 'unification by force' with regard to Taiwan, escalated its military posturing and embarked on activities to influence partners such as Sri Lanka,[21] while also conducting influence operations in Australia, Japan, New Zealand, Singapore and elsewhere.[22] Also in 2020, the US defence leadership identified China as the number one long-term challenge and talked about shifting troops and capabilities from the Middle East to Asia.[23] This competition, particularly as both sides continue to develop novel technologies with military applications, threatens to incentivise arms racing and increase the risks of misperception during a crisis.

---

18 Ibid. See also Aaron Miles, 'The Dynamics of Strategic Stability and Instability', *Contemporary Security Policy* 35(5), 2016, 423–37, doi.org/10.1080/01495933.2016.1241005.

19 Department of Defence, *2020 Defence Strategic Update*, www1.defence.gov.au/sites/default/files/2020-11/2020_Defence_Strategic_Update.pdf, 6.

20 Yun Sun, 'Top Conflicts to Watch in 2021: The Danger of US–China Confrontation Over Taiwan', Council on Foreign Relations, 22 January 2021, www.cfr.org/blog/top-conflicts-watch-2021-danger-us-china-confrontation-over-taiwan.

21 Jacob Stokes, 'Does China Really Respect Sovereignty?', *The Diplomat*, 23 May 2019, thediplomat.com/2019/05/does-china-really-respect-sovereignty/.

22 Larry Diamond and Orville Schell, eds, *China's Influence & American Interests: Constructing Vigilance* (Palo Alto: Hoover Institution Press, 29 November 2018).

23 Bonnie Kristian, 'Esper's Dark Vision for US–China Conflict Makes War More Likely', *DefenseNews*, 19 March 2020.

Arguably, China and the US are already in an arms race; however, neither side is obviously seeking to acquire a capability that might undermine the other's nuclear retaliatory capability. Additionally, both the US and China are still developing many novel technologies, so it is not yet clear whether they might undermine strategic stability. From a practical perspective, neither side is likely to be willing to limit them under an arms control agreement in the meantime.[24] This is not to suggest complacency in terms of arms race stability, rather to suggest that this may not be the primary concern for strategic stability in the Indo-Pacific at present.

Yet, as indicated by the Australian *Defence Strategic Update*, crisis stability and miscalculation are major concerns. China's entanglement of conventional and nuclear forces is particularly worrying and could lead to inadvertent escalation.[25] Building on work by Barry Posen during the Cold War, David Logan identifies various inadvertent escalation pathways with regards to China—such as heightened vulnerability, target ambiguity and warhead ambiguity—that are exacerbated by misperceptions and missed signals between various actors in the region.[26] According to Logan, 'strategic signalling and perception management will be key to controlling escalation risks stemming from nuclear–conventional entanglement in China'.[27] Cunningham and Fravel similarly argue that China's limited ambiguity in its nuclear posture might *increase* escalation risks, both because China is optimistic about crisis stability and does not believe its actions could be mistaken for preparation for first use and because it could 'increase US suspicions that in a crisis China might abandon its no first use policy altogether'.[28]

An additional challenge from Washington's perspective with regards to strategic stability is its regional allies. Historically, some allies in the region have been strongly opposed to any reduction in US capabilities, such as the 2010 decision to retire the nuclear-armed Tomahawk cruise missiles, which raised concern among many allies about America's commitment to

---

24 Christopher S. Chiba, 'New Technologies and Strategic Stability', *Daedalus* 149(2), Spring 2020, 150–70, doi.org/10.1162/daed_a_01795.

25 James M. Acton, 'Escalation through Entanglement: How the Vulnerability of Command-and-Control Systems Raises the Risks of Inadvertent Nuclear War', *International Security* 43(1), Summer 2018, 56–99, doi.org/10.1162/isec_a_00320.

26 David C. Logan, 'Are They Reading Schelling in Beijing? The Dimensions, Drivers, and Risks of Nuclear–Conventional Entanglement in China', *Journal of Strategic Studies* 11, 2020, 5, doi.org/10.1080/01402390.2020.1844671.

27 Ibid., 1.

28 Cunningham and Fravel, 'Assuring Assured Retaliation', 11. The authors also point to risks of arms racing.

their security.[29] Any arms control efforts with Beijing, therefore, will have to be preceded by close consultation with Tokyo, Seoul, Canberra and elsewhere to ensure that, in the process of cooperating with China, the US is not simultaneously undermining its own credibility. A complicating factor will be the diversity of allies' views not only about the US and China, but also about the role of nuclear weapons in regional security. Some US allies in the region, such as Pacific Island nations, experienced damaging consequences from nuclear testing and advocate for reducing reliance on nuclear weapons and moving away from strategies of deterrence. Palau, for example, is in a Compact of Free Association with the US (which guarantees its security) while also being a member of the Treaty on the Prohibition of Nuclear Weapons.

Arms control has the potential to strengthen strategic stability and reduce some of these risks, particularly around crisis instability, but China has a mixed record with arms control. It has been active in numerous multilateral efforts, such as the NPT, and helped revive the 'P5 process', which involves the five nuclear weapon states (NWS) recognised by the NPT, in 2019. China was also active in negotiating the Comprehensive Test Ban Treaty and participates in the Conference on Disarmament. Nonetheless, Beijing has refused invitations to join arms control talks with the US and Russia and refrained from participation in confidence and transparency-building activities, such as the International Partnership for Nuclear Disarmament Verification. This reluctance is understandable given the numerical disparity in nuclear forces, as previously discussed; however, as competition with Washington increases, so will the incentives for China to participate in more ambitious arms control projects.

Options for Arms Control with China

Although China will likely continue for the foreseeable future to avoid arms control agreements that require transparency or reductions, there are at least three reasons China might be open to other types of arms control. First, China's continued rise hinges on regional stability and arms control provides one means for promoting security through cooperation with the US and its allies. Second, China wants to avoid a costly arms race for economic reasons. According to Tong Zhao, 'China will probably be

---

29 William A. Chambers, Caroline R. Milne, Rhiannon T. Hutton and Heather W. Williams, 'No-First Use of Nuclear Weapons: A Policy Assessment', Institute for Defense Analyses, January 2021.

unable to increase defence spending at its prior rate without undermining its population's key socioeconomic interests'. Arms control is a promising cost-saving mechanism.[30] And, finally, while China is less concerned about its nuclear ambiguity being mistaken as aggression,[31] the risk of this misperception would be exacerbated by a crisis and it would be in China's interest to ensure Washington and its allies are equally assured. A focus on crisis stability, while still leaving open the possibility of contributing to arms race stability and other political and security benefits, points to three options for arms control to incorporate China. These recommendations are meant to reflect a balance of the ideal and the possible.

First, the Biden administration might revise the Trump administration's proposal to pursue some form of trilateral strategic arms limitation agreement with Moscow and Beijing. Tong Zhao has suggested that the US and China set an equal ceiling for the combined stockpile of intermediate-range nuclear missiles, whether land or air-launched, with flexibility in how they mix their systems.[32] Russia might also be included in such an agreement. Another option would be a ratio agreement, similar to the Washington Naval Treaty, establishing a 4:4:1 ratio in strategic launchers and a 1:1:1 ratio in tactical launchers between the US, Russia and China, again allowing for flexibility in how each party mixes their own forces. The benefits of a trilateral agreement would be to promote transparency between the three largest nuclear actors, such as verification mechanisms and a consultative commission, to provide assurances that none of the parties is seeking a break-out capability that would incentivise a nuclear first strike or crisis escalation. But this option is ambitious and is more likely a mid to long-term option over the next decade. Getting to such an agreement would require building transparency with China through more informal mechanisms, and further US–Russian reductions in the meantime.

A second, more modest option would be to use the 'P5 process' to develop crisis stability mechanisms. This might include incorporating concerns about emerging technologies and gradually working collaboratively on bigger questions around strategic stability.[33] While numerous recent

---

30 Tong Zhao, 'Opportunities for Nuclear Arms Control Engagement with China', *Arms Control Today*, January/February 2020, 10.

31 Cunningham and Fravel, 'Assuring Assured Retaliation', 10.

32 Zhao, 'Opportunities for Nuclear Arms Control', 10.

33 Shata Shetty and Heather Williams, *The P5 Process: Opportunities for Success in the NPT Review Conference*, King's College London Centre for Science and Security Studies Occasional Paper, June 2020, www.europeanleadershipnetwork.org/report/the-p5-process-opportunities-for-success/.

studies have called for adding strategic stability and other issues to P5 dialogues, if done too quickly, this would be dangerous for two reasons.[34] First, the United Kingdom and France have not indicated a willingness to participate in arms control dialogues or to reduce their arsenals. Putting this issue in the P5 process might exacerbate existing tensions around the issue. Second, the P5 process remains tied to the NPT and as a vehicle for the NWS to work towards progress in fulfilling their Article VI commitments of 'general and complete disarmament'.[35] Expanding the mandate would risk overloading it, leading to inertia, while also potentially undermining its contribution to the NPT. This option, therefore, would require the NWS to jointly agree to one or two additional items in their program of work, of limited scope, to be discussed during the next NPT review cycle, with the goal of agreeing to new crisis communication channels by the 2025 NPT Review Conference. For example, they might add discussions on the risks to nuclear command and control to the existing dialogue on transparency of doctrine, working towards a 'cyber no first use' agreement.[36] Of all the options offered here, cooperation in the P5 process is probably the most feasible; however, it would be at risk of being held hostage to NPT politics and may still require significant time and effort to socialise China and other NWS to the necessary transparency measures.

A final option is to develop a suite of dynamic confidence-building measures with a focus on crisis de-escalation. A Washington–Beijing hotline already exists and includes a 'space hotline' and a 'cyber hotline', but this might be expanded to incorporate China into the Nuclear Risk Reduction Centre system, which includes Russia and members of the Organization for Security and Co-operation in Europe. They might also establish regular strategic stability dialogues with an explicit focus on crisis avoidance and crisis communication. Other agreements might resemble the 1972 Incidents at Sea Agreements, which included joint commitments to avoid collisions, non-interference, surveillance and information exchanges. Another example is the 1973 Agreement on the Prevention of

---

34 See, for example: The Chicago Council on Global Affairs, *Task Force Report: Preventing Nuclear Proliferation and Reassuring America's Allies*, 2021.

35 Article VI of the NPT reads:

> Each of the Parties to the Treaty undertakes to pursue negotiations in good faith on effective measures relating to cessation of the nuclear arms race at an early date and to nuclear disarmament, and on a treaty on general and complete disarmament under strict and effective international control.

36 Jacquelyn Schneider, 'A Strategic Cyber No-First-Use Policy? Addressing the US Cyber Strategy Problem', *Washington Quarterly* 32(2), 2020, 159–75, doi.org/10.1080/0163660X.2020.1770970.

Nuclear War established between the US and the Soviet Union; a similar agreement between the US and China (and also potentially Russia) could restate their commitment to practise nuclear restraint towards each other and promote strategic stability in their nuclear postures. This option is potentially feasible but does not readily align with China's current thinking about the risks of crisis escalation; therefore, it would also require engaging China in transparency-building measures and socialisation with arms control practices. There is also, of course, the possibility that China will continue to insist on further reductions in American and Russian arsenals before participating in *any* arms control dialogues, even those aimed at de-escalating crises.

***

Arms control in the Indo-Pacific should focus on reducing the risks of escalation, particularly with regard to new technologies that are creating strategic asymmetries. This would address the most pressing challenges to regional and international security, particularly rising competition between the US and China, and growing concerns about China's regional ambitions and nuclear posture. But this approach is not without its drawbacks. Cooperation of any kind between Washington and Beijing tends to make Moscow nervous; therefore, the US will have to engage in parallel discussions with Russia for a New START follow-on. Additionally, US overtures to China might prompt fears of abandonment among US allies in the region, and therefore arms control must be part of a multi-pronged strategy including deterrence and assurance. Any progress towards arms control or disarmament with China may require a counterbalancing effort for allies, such as increased conventional presence in the region, basing sites or cruise missile defences.[37]

This crisis-driven approach to arms control may be modest in the short term but has longer-term ambitions for strengthening strategic stability. The Strategic Arms Limitation Talks in the 1960s and 1970s grew out of relatively modest arms control efforts following the Cuban Missile Crisis, such as hotlines, yet it initiated unprecedented cooperation and transparency between the superpowers. A similar trend might prove possible in Asia, but hopefully it will not take a crisis to prompt interest among the key actors.

---

37 Christopher Dougherty, 'Short-Term Action Items for Austin's Pentagon', *War on the Rocks*, 15 February 2021.

Part II: Political-Military Challenges in Alliance Planning for Escalation

6

NATO: Ambiguity about Escalation in a Multinational Alliance

Sten Rynning

Following Russia's 2014 annexation of Crimea and stoking of civil war in Eastern Ukraine, managing the escalation of conflict between great powers has once again become a central challenge for the North Atlantic Treaty Organization (NATO). Confronted with a great power threat both to their borders and to the continental political order, the allies have reconsidered their powers of denial at the border, as well as their powers of punishment, should the adversary, Russia, breach the border. In this, NATO has the advantage of being able to draw on a long Cold War history of strategising discussion on its concept of 'flexible response', but conditions change: NATO has grown to an alliance of 30 nations, events outside the European theatre pull allies in diverse directions, technology has leapt into a fourth industrial revolution, nuclear weapons remain an object of strong normative concern and Russia's skilful information warfare generates friction in allied threat assessments.

Consequently, the politics of managing escalation have grown more complex, and NATO is therefore explicit on defence and deterrence posture and principle but deliberately vague on escalation. As part of its 'overall posture', the alliance now has an enhanced 'forward presence' along the eastern borders of NATO allies (albeit by rotating troop deployments and exercises, not the permanent stationing of troops) reinforced by a layered force structure of reaction, ready and mobilisable conventional forces.[1] Three of NATO's allies maintain nuclear forces. NATO's principle remains that the purpose of strategic and nuclear forces is to 'preserve peace, prevent coercion, and deter aggression'. It considers any circumstance in which the alliance may be forced to use such weapons 'extremely remote' and that their use would 'fundamentally alter the nature of a conflict'.[2]

NATO's ladder of escalation thus lies between its forward ability to defend its borders and its deterrent capacity to inflict nuclear punishment. It is explicit about the involved conventional–nuclear threshold—that is, the altered nature of a conflict—but not about its political red lines or the steps it will take to manage escalation up to this threshold. To understand why NATO is so committed to a policy of escalatory ambiguity, we must dig into the particular politics of multinational and multilateral deterrence.

The Evolving Challenge of Escalation

There is a strong undercurrent of continuity in NATO's wrestle with issues of deterrence and escalation that concerns transatlantic geography and exposure to threat. As a rule, European allies seek to minimise the prospect of Europe turning into a theatre of protracted warfare and thus prefer threats of rapid escalation. Inversely, the United States, worried that threats of rapid escalation lack credibility, has tended to favour more paced escalatory options.

When the US prodded NATO in the early 1960s to move away from a strategy of massive retaliation to flexible response, it was effectively seeking to slow the threatened pace of escalation. Prolonged tension in the alliance followed. France's decision to stick to its own strategy of massive retaliation and to step outside NATO's integrated command enabled a wider compromise. NATO adopted a flexible response strategy (MC 14/3) with three escalatory steps: a) direct defence, b) deliberate escalation

---

1   For the rationale of NATO's enhanced forward presence, see NATO, *Warsaw Summit Communiqué*, 8–9 July 2016, paragraph 40, www.nato.int/cps/en/natohq/official_texts_133169.htm.
2   NATO, *Brussels Summit Declaration*, 11–12 July 2018, paragraph 36, www.nato.int/cps/en/natohq/official_texts_156624.htm.

controlled in scope and intensity, and c) general nuclear response.[3] The assurance offered to allies by the US consisted of several measures: that the rationale of 'the threat of escalation' was deterrence; that, should deterrence fail, escalation would be guided by the 'concept of forward defence'; and, finally, that allies gained special access to (US) nuclear plans and policies in a new NATO Nuclear Planning Group.

If striking a balance, as a staff officer of NATO's Supreme Allied Commander Europe (SACEUR) General Norstad put it, between a 'technical plan for limited warfare' and 'a spirit of unity in NATO' was difficult in the 1960s, such a balancing act is even harder today.[4] NATO's post–Cold War enlargement has not only introduced the challenge of decision-making by 30 (allies), but also moved NATO territory closer to the border of Russia (principally in the Baltics but also in the Black Sea). The effect is to compress and intensify the process of escalation. Because the confrontation would initially be confined to the Central European space, a Cold War armed confrontation would conceivably not have involved early strikes on US and Soviet territory. In the past, this gave the key decision-making centres, Washington and Moscow, a semblance of opportunity to control escalation by managing both its geographical and its nuclear confines. Today, however, geography has disappeared from this equation: in the case of aggression, NATO would immediately be faced with the decision of whether to retaliate against Russian forces or support infrastructure inside Russia.[5]

Moreover, the presence of Russian minorities in allied countries on Russia's borders defines an opportunity for Russia to wrap limited military action—such as a land grab operation—in political uncertainty. Minority unrest, politico-legal objections and claims of systematic abuse form part of the information or hybrid warfare toolbox that Russia has explored and continues to develop primarily in Ukraine but also in Georgia and elsewhere, along with measures to disrupt the functioning of targeted government and society.

---

3   NATO, *Final Decision on MC 14/3: A Report by the Military Committee to the Defense Planning Committee on Overall Strategic Concept for the Defense of the North Atlantic Treaty Organization Area*, 16 January 1968, www.nato.int/docu/stratdoc/eng/a680116a.pdf.
4   Timothy Andrews Sayle, *Enduring Alliance: A History of NATO and the Postwar Global Order* (Ithaca: Cornell University Press, 2019), 83.
5   See Hans Binnendijk and David Gompert, 'Decisive Response: A New Nuclear Strategy for NATO', *Survival* 61(5), 2019, 113–28, doi.org/10.1080/00396338.2019.1662119.

Finally, Russia benefits from Europe's political geography in the sense that it is capable both of mobilising significant military force in a short time and of choosing the time and place of their operation. Inversely, NATO is constrained by its commitment dating back to 1997 to carry out collective defence by 'interoperability, integration, and capability for reinforcement' rather than 'by additional stationing of substantial combat forces' on the territory of post–Cold War NATO allies.[6]

In summary, escalation involves two dilemmas for NATO. One is the classical dilemma between European and American interests in fast versus paced escalation. Another is a new dilemma between, on the one hand, the need for a posture of decisive and rapid military action to deny Russia opportunities for limited aggression, and, on the other, a need to maintain strict measures of political control to prevent a local crisis from escalating inadvertently to general war.

Political Guidance

To navigate these dilemmas, NATO should settle on political principles to guide military planning. However, in practice, NATO has addressed such principles in a piecemeal and evolving fashion and is only now, in 2021, preparing for a revision of its overarching strategic concept.

NATO has primarily relied on summitry to calibrate its political message— in Wales (2014), Warsaw (2016) and Brussels (2018)—which is primarily one of condemnation: Russia's actions are labelled 'aggressive' (Wales), 'provocative', 'destabilising' and 'illegal and illegitimate' (Warsaw and Brussels). However, it is also one of restraint: NATO remains attached to the old framework of partnership (entered into in 1997 and updated in 2002) and believes its own actions to enhance defence and deterrence take place in respect of this framework, whereas Russia is violating it.

While NATO officialdom defends the wisdom of this balancing act with reference to a dual-track framework of both 'defence' and 'dialogue'—a heralded balancing act in NATO dating back to its 1967 Harmel doctrine—the fact is that NATO has struggled to reach agreement on its assessment of the Russian threat. The Trump presidency

---

6 NATO and Russia, *Founding Act*, 27 May 1997, www.nato.int/cps/en/natohq/official_texts _25468.htm.

proved to be debilitating: for as long as the alliance leader was unable to define its own Russia policy, partly out of President Trump's anxiety that it could question the legitimacy of his 2016 presidential election, NATO was stuck. In Europe, the allies geographically close to Russia sought a hard line, but Mediterranean allies sought a balanced East–South policy, and Western allies such as Germany and France sought a balanced defence-and-dialogue policy. A number of Western allies, including Canada, the United Kingdom and the Netherlands, supported a tough policy but lacked the military hardware that Eastern allies requested as evidence of a firm policy.

In consequence, NATO has politically been unable to define the desired effects for which military planners are supposed to plan. Its 2010 Strategic Concept, which is still in force, puts collective defence on par with crisis management operations and cooperative security. While NATO quickly agreed in a post-2014 setting that it needed to think differently about Russia, gaining substantial political agreement has been a challenge. NATO has sought a defence-and-dialogue balance, as mentioned, and it has also—in its 2019 political guidance issued to military authorities—enhanced its level of ambition to a 'major joint operation plus', meaning a significant conventional armed confrontation with Russia. However, while this upgrade addresses the level of threat—which is to say that military capability requirements increase—it did not address the nature of the threat: that is, how Russia is expected to act, and what NATO should be capable of doing in order to deter it.

It remains an open question whether a revised 2022 Strategic Concept will enable the identification of such desired military effects. The secretary general's 'Food for Thought' paper, which kicked off high-level NATO deliberations in February 2021, mentions Russia just once, and this in conjunction with China as part of an 'authoritarian pushback against the rules-based international order'.[7] From the point of view of managing escalation, it is a start, but only just.

---

7   NATO Secretary General, *Food for Thought Paper: NATO 2030—A Transatlantic Agenda for the Future*, Document PO (2021) 0053, 11 February 2021, NATO Unclassified.

Conventional Force

While the political level is struggling to interpret Russia, the military level has advanced beyond this point. Naturally, NATO military planning is guided by political considerations and does not exceed political boundaries, but NATO military authorities have had to confront the meaning of Russia's military challenge or threat in a markedly direct way.

The search for 'coherence'—an often-invoked keyword when NATO military officials speak on background—began in the wake of the 2014 Wales summit, which directed military authorities to deliver on both 'assurance measures' (rotational military presence to assure exposed allies) and 'adaptation measures' (force and command structure reforms to ensure future defence and deterrence capability).[8] Through a long and winding road marked in part by the aforementioned absence of politically defined 'desired effects', NATO's military authorities produced first a new NATO Military Strategy (MC400/4), approved by the Military Committee in May 2019, and then a concept for Deterrence and Defence of the Euro-Atlantic Area (DDA), approved by defence ministers in June 2020.[9]

The outcome is a markedly improved deterrence posture comprising forward-deployed troops (again, rotational and not permanently deployed), enhanced reaction forces and follow-on forces. NATO's command structure has also been revamped, gaining a third Joint Force Command in Norfolk, USA, to assure transatlantic links, as well as a Joint Support and Enabling Command in Ulm, Germany, principally to connect NATO's Western European seaboard to the frontiers of Eastern allies.[10]

In terms of escalation, the posture is deliberately ambiguous. To counter Russian advantages in speed and choice of location, NATO is best off approaching the European theatre as one integrated theatre of (potential) conflict and to offer its supreme commander, SACEUR, the authority and means of rapid reaction. And this is precisely the direction in which the 2020 DDA concept is moving: it is a 'theatre-wide' approach meant to deter Russia by the robustness and unpredictability of NATO's response.

---

8 'Wales Summit Declaration', Press Release, NATO, 5 September 2014, paragraphs 5–13, www. nato.int/cps/en/natohq/official_texts_112964.htm.

9 These meetings are followed by press conferences, not communiqués or declarations. For the Military Committee meeting, see '181st Military Committee in Chiefs of Defence Session', NATO, 22 May 2019, www.nato.int/cps/en/natohq/events_166141.htm?selectedLocale=en. For the Defence Ministerial, see 'Meetings of NATO Ministers of Defence', NATO, 17 June 2020, www.nato.int/cps/en/natohq/events_176298.htm?selectedLocale=en.

10 The two other Joint Force Commands are in Brunssum, the Netherlands, and Naples, Italy.

If NATO is not going all-out in implementing a theatre-wide escalatory policy, it is because of issues of political control. First, allies are not in agreement on how far to go in building up a 'heavy metal' response to Russia. Eastern allies are alarmed and seek the build-up of significant armoured projection capability from West to East; other allies seek a lighter touch. For as long as this tension remains, NATO military authorities will have to labour on a middle ground of enhancing the readiness and mobility of sizeable but not overwhelming conventional forces.[11]

Second, most allies are reluctant to give up on the geographically compartmentalised response plans that NATO introduced in 2015 (so-called Graduated Response Plans). While allies recognise the need to deter Russia through strategic agility and SACEUR command options, they also, and each in their own way, worry that SACEUR, were he to be liberated to act flexibly within the full theatre, might de-emphasise deterrence in their particular neighbourhood. Relatedly, SACEUR flexibility could introduce the type of paced or 'horizontal' escalation European allies tend to abhor because it could prolong a conventional war in Europe. Hence, they insist that theatre-wide planning must proceed on the basis of geographically narrow response plans. It remains for NATO to work out a political framework for deciding on and managing such horizontal escalation without entirely inhibiting it.[12]

Finally, Mediterranean allies worry that all the talk about Russia implies decreased attention and resources to 'southern' threats—which, in NATO-speak, are 'international terrorist groups'. At the insistence of these allies, NATO's 2019 Military Strategy has to equally address Russia and the consequences of instability in NATO's south. The alliance's concept for DDA and other plans and policies are therefore embedded in references to '360 degree' thinking and approaches that disguise sometimes deep political disagreement. Thus, in the year spanning 2019–20, Turkey blocked the political approval of NATO's Graduated Response Plans as a measure to force NATO to recognise Kurdish groups in Syria as terrorist entities.[13]

---

11 In part the enhancement of NATO's Response Force; in part the improved readiness of 30 mechanised battalions, 30 air squadrons and 30 combat vessels—ready to go in 30 days or less (hence, a 4 x 30 readiness initiative).
12 See Sten Rynning, 'Deterrence Rediscovered: NATO and Russia', in *Deterrence in the 21st Century: Insights from Theory and Practice*, ed. Frans Osinga and Tim Sweijs (The Hague: Asser Press, 2020), 29–46, doi.org/10.1007/978-94-6265-419-8_3.
13 Robin Emmott and John Irish, 'Turkey Still Blocking Defence Plan for Poland, Baltics, NATO Envoys Say', *Reuters*, 17 June 2020.

Political control, therefore, concerns a multitude of sensitive issues at the highest level of NATO: the nature of the Russian threat, options for horizontal escalation within theatre and the relative merits of other threats and theatres of concern. It is safe to predict that NATO can improve upon some of these issues but not overcome them, and the policy of escalatory ambiguity will thus remain in one shape or another.

Nuclear Force

Unlike its conventional posture, NATO is not seeking to change its nuclear posture. It maintains a number of principles that have emerged out of years, if not decades, of careful diplomatic adjustment: for example, that nuclear weapons are unique and for the preservation of peace, not war; that as long as nuclear weapons exist, NATO will remain a nuclear alliance; that NATO will defend and deter with an appropriate mix of nuclear, conventional and missile defence capabilities; and that UK and French nuclear forces contribute to alliance deterrence while US nuclear forces, some of them forward deployed in Europe, remain central to deterrence.[14]

Continuity in the nuclear posture was questioned in 2017–18 when experts established that Russia's ground-launched cruise missile SSC8 was fully developed, deployed and in violation of the Intermediate-Range Nuclear Forces (INF) Treaty.[15] In the course of 2018, the US Nuclear Posture Review called for investment in US intermediary nuclear capabilities (mainly sea-based), and the US withdrew from the INF Treaty. For NATO and, in particular, the European allies, the question was whether these developments implied a lowered threshold for nuclear conflict and, by implication, eroding trust in Washington in strategic nuclear deterrence.

NATO contained these potentially disruptive questions in a posture of continuity.[16] The countermove to Russia's SSC8 is thus not the forward deployment of more US nuclear weapons—unlike the dual-track decision

---

14   See NATO, *Brussels Summit Declaration,* paragraphs 33–36.

15   Russia did not share the assessment and countered that the US violated the INF Treaty with its Aegis Ashore missile defence system.

16   For more on the disruptive potential, see Michael Rühle's chapter in this volume as well as Stephan Frühling, 'Managing Escalation: Missile Defence, Strategy and US Alliances', *International Affairs* 92(1), 2016, 81–95, doi.org/10.1111/1468-2346.12501.

of 1979—but further investment in the 'safety, security, and effectiveness' of NATO's existing nuclear option. In practice, this means enhanced surveillance and reconnaissance as well as air defence capabilities, and intensified training of the nuclear chain of command from the North Atlantic Council to military units. Finally, it means continuity in terms of the upgrading of nuclear-sharing arrangements between the US on the one hand and Belgium, Netherlands, Germany, Italy and Turkey on the other.[17]

Moreover, NATO's nuclear deterrence posture is defined by the principle of strategic deterrence: any use of nuclear weapons would change the nature of the conflict. This posture sends a strong message to Russia and allows NATO to divert normative and political controversy at home. The fact that the most vocal proponent of a massive retaliation deterrence posture, France, now has troops at Russia's border as part of the alliance's enhanced forward presence and inside an alliance posture that remains, at heart, one of flexible response, raises interesting questions for a meeting of nuclear minds in NATO. However, this meeting of minds takes place outside NATO's Nuclear Planning Group, where France continues not to take part, and in the informal corridors of high-level US, British and French consultations.

***

NATO is dedicated to strengthening deterrence through pursuing a robust posture and escalatory ambiguity. Robustness and ambiguity follow from the full-spectrum political imperative in NATO of countering Russia, assuring geographically exposed allies and catering to a complex and diverse range of sensitivities that 30 allies bring to the table. NATO's 2022 Strategic Concept will likely advance and deepen the alliance's appreciation of the threat posed by Russia as well as the military robustness with which NATO must respond. With careful preparation, the outcome will be an improved posture. On the subject of escalation, NATO may succeed in clarifying its approach to theatre-wide conventional defence and deterrence, but the basic need for escalatory ambiguity will remain, certainly where it concerns the conventional-nuclear threshold.

---

17 Nuclear sharing refers to the stationing of US gravity bombs (B61) and allied means of delivery (F15, F16 or Tornado aircraft) as well as secure base facilities. For an outline of NATO's posture, see 'Press Conference by NATO Secretary General Jens Stoltenberg Following the Meetings of NATO Defence Ministers', NATO, 17 June 2020, www.nato.int/cps/en/natohq/opinions_176520.htm?selectedLocale=en.

7

South Korea: The Limits of Operational Integration

Seukhoon Paul Choi

'Forged in the crucible of war', the alliance between the Republic of Korea (ROK) and the United States has two mottos: 'we go together' and ready to 'fight tonight'. Beyond mere rhetoric, the alliance consists of a deeply integrated defence posture with a combined warfighting headquarters, bilaterally agreed-upon operational plans (OPLANs) and a 28,000-strong forward-deployed US military presence working side-by-side with half a million active-duty ROK service members.

Despite this close military cooperation, the alliance finds itself in crisis. 'The fight' for which the alliance must prepare has changed. The return of great power competition and the dawn of the second nuclear age have transformed the strategic environment. Escalation dynamics are shifting both below and above the traditional threshold of war and with greater integration of other instruments of national power. These developments present complex political-military challenges, complicating alliance coordination in defending ROK and US collective interests.

This chapter will examine ROK and US management of political-military tensions in their preparations for common defence from a South Korean perspective. It will do so in the context of the alliance's two major challenges: the rise of China and advances in North Korea's asymmetric military capabilities. It will also identify shortcomings in alliance efforts to realise strategic agreement on effective management of escalation across the spectrum of competition, crisis and conflict, and highlight alliance political-military mechanisms that, if refitted, could be used to address these gaps.

From an increasingly tense Sino-US rivalry to a North Korean nuclear threat with intercontinental reach, the environment in which the ROK–US alliance operates has become more dangerous and complex. China and North Korea have advanced strategies and fielded capabilities to offset traditional US and alliance advantages. They are exploiting asymmetries in the stakes involved and thresholds of risk not only with, but also between, South Korea and the US. This context raises the importance of cooperation but makes alliance cohesion more difficult. In particular, several political-military challenges constrain the alliance's ability to plan for three important escalatory pathways to and in war: 1) China's intervention in a Korean Peninsula contingency; 2) a regional Sino-US conflict that draws in the alliance; and 3) ROK, US and Japanese responses to North Korea's increasingly sophisticated nuclear and missile force posture.

The China Challenge

From Beijing's perspective, North Korea's nuclear sites along its border, weapons proliferation, the potential mass inflow of refugees, the forward-deployed presence of US forces and the ROK–US alliance all pose strategic risks, especially in the context of crisis or active war on the Korean Peninsula.[1] Given China's national interests, there are a range of assessments on the likely role of China in numerous contingencies. These include cooperative involvement to interference or intervention that has China in direct military conflict with South Korea or the alliance. This variance poses political-military challenges to alliance planning. For example, some in the US with a non-proliferation focus and concern about ROK nuclear ambitions, may prefer to cooperate with China, as a permanent member of the United Nations (UN) Security Council and recognised nuclear power under the Treaty on the Non-Proliferation of Nuclear Weapons (NPT), in securing nuclear sites—especially those just south of its border. Despite South Korean concern over 'loose nukes',

---

1   Currently the Korean Peninsula is in a state of 'suspended war'; the 1950–53 conflict ended in an armistice rather than a declaration of peace.

many, particularly in the ROK military, would not welcome infiltration of the peninsula by the People's Republic of China (PRC). Respective ROK and US priorities, as they influence whether each ally's interests converge or diverge with those of China, thereby complicate alliance efforts to forge a collective approach to the escalation of a peninsular scenario to involve PRC intervention.

Ambition for regional hegemony and Korea's geostrategic importance also incentivise Beijing to project its power and influence in peacetime through various means and escalatory tactics. These include ongoing information operations and economic coercion to the threat of force. China demonstrated such behaviour in its escalatory, albeit non-military, response to the 2016 US deployment of a Terminal High Altitude Area Defense (THAAD) system to South Korea. Despite this deployment having been an alliance decision to strengthen deterrence and defence against North Korea's nuclear and missile threat, China argued that the system's AN/TPY-2 radar threatened its own nuclear deterrent capability vis-a-vis the US.[2] Thus, it proactively reframed the issue as one between China and the US, inspiring debate in South Korea and challenging the alliance. Further, in addition to conducting cyber attacks and applying diplomatic pressure on South Korea, China most notably exacted costs on the ROK economy estimated at US$7.5 billion.[3]

While the ROK decided to host the THAAD battery against PRC protests, South Koreans were nevertheless traumatised by the significant costs China imposed on the country in retaliation. This worsened ROK perceptions of China, catalysing ROK efforts to reduce its economic dependency on China and to build relations with other countries. However, it also inspired perceptions of US abandonment, as the US response to PRC retaliation seemed limited to diplomatic statements and absent actions to counter such coercion or mitigate the economic damage.[4] Scarred and uncertain of concrete US support, South Koreans have subsequently

2   Ethan Meick and Nargiza Salidjanova, 'China's Response to US – South Korean Missile Defense System Deployment and its Implications', US–China Economic and Security Review Commission Staff Research Report, 26 July 2017, 5, www.uscc.gov/research/chinas-response-us-south-korean-missile-defense-system-deployment-and-its-implications.
3   Victoria Kim, 'When China and US Spar, It's South Korea that Gets Punched', *Los Angeles Times*, 19 November 2020, www.latimes.com/world-nation/story/2020-11-19/south-korea-china-beijing-economy-thaad-missile-interceptor; Meick and Salidjanova, 'China's Response to US – South Korean Missile Defense System', 7–8.
4   Brad Glosserman, 'Seoul Draws Wrong THAAD Lessons', *Japan Times*, 27 January 2020, www.japantimes.co.jp/opinion/2020/01/27/commentary/japan-commentary/seoul-draws-wrong-thaad-lessons/.

felt an increased need to, diplomatically at least, accommodate if not appease China's position. This was reflected in Seoul's 2017 messaging to Beijing: a policy of no additional THAAD battery deployments, no ROK integration into a US-led regional missile defence system and no trilateral alliance with the US and Japan. Although none of these options was the subject of alliance discussions or even realistic at the time, this policy inspired US concern that South Korea was conceding too much and drawing too close to Beijing.[5]

Not only does Sino-US strategic competition increase the likelihood of PRC intervention on the Korean Peninsula, but also it raises the risk that regional conflict may escalate horizontally, thus impacting the alliance, if not directly involving US and ROK forces. Despite North Korea being the dominant focus of US Forces Korea (USFK), both permanently and rotationally stationed US forces on the peninsula support the US doctrine of 'strategic flexibility' and could be employed to support regional crisis or war. This makes USFK and South Korea a target during such contingencies.

It is not only critical that the alliance plan for such scenarios, but also coordination is needed between the two allies to address the second-order effects of ongoing US preparations for conflict with China. As the US continues adapting its defence strategy, forces and doctrine to address China in scenarios beyond the peninsula, it is unclear in South Korea what impact this will have for the combined ROK–US alliance's deterrence and defence posture. From the US discontinuing its Continuous Bomber Presence and operationalising its Dynamic Force Employment concept to revising its Unified Command Plan and redesigning its Global Force Management strategy, these changes that impact South Korea and alliance planning are often only explained after completion.[6]

---

5   Troy Stangarone, 'Did South Korea's Three Noes Matter? Not So Much', *The Diplomat*, 30 October 2019, thediplomat.com/2019/10/did-south-koreas-three-noes-matter-not-so-much/.

6   For ROK perceptions of, and initial angst about, the US transition from Continuous Bomber Presence to Dynamic Force Employment, see S. Paul Choi, 'Deterring North Korea: The Need for Collective Resolve and Alliance Transformation', *38 North*, 23 July 2020, www.38north.org/2020/07/spchoi072320/. For reporting on Unified Common Plan and ongoing US defence reform, see Theresa Hitchens, 'Exclusive: Milley to OK New Unified Command Plan; Defines SPACECOM's Roles', *Breaking Defense*, 26 August 2020, breakingdefense.com/2020/08/exclusive-milley-to-sign-new-unified-command-plan-defines-spacecoms-roles/.

In South Korea, like in the US, China is increasingly perceived as a challenge to ROK interests. In both 2018 and 2019, polling conducted by the Seoul National University Institute for Peace and Unification Studies revealed South Koreans considered China the most threatening country to peace on the Korean Peninsula.[7] Relatedly, in October 2020, a Pew Research Center survey found that 75 per cent of South Koreans had an unfavourable opinion of China and 83 per cent had 'no confidence in Chinese President Xi Jinping to do the right thing regarding world affairs'.[8]

These public attitudes are reflected in changes to ROK defence policy and force development, which are now aimed not only at North Korea, but also at South Korea's 'omnidirectional threats'.[9] ROK military strategists are designing concepts that leverage conventional capabilities with strategic effects. South Korea, incorporating the reality of its limitations, is implementing force improvement measures aimed at employing increasingly advanced means in asymmetric ways to counter China.[10] Despite these tangible defence preparations, successive ROK administrations have preferred a diplomatic strategy that hedges and aims to balance cooperation with its sole treaty ally and its increasingly powerful neighbour. With China's geopolitical significance and unique influence over North Korea, South Korea—while unwavering in its commitment to its US alliance—maintains a less confrontational approach to Beijing than the US. Paradoxically, South Korea's 'strategic ambiguity' on issues that

---

7   '통일의식조사' [Tongil Euisik Josah or A Survey of Attitudes towards Unification] (Seoul: Seoul National University Institute for Peace and Unification Studies, 2019), 154.
8   Laura Silver, Kat Delvin and Christine Huang, 'Unfavourable Views of China Reach Historic Highs in Many Countries', *Global Attitudes & Trends*, Pew Research Center, 6 October 2020, www.pewresearch.org/global/2020/10/06/unfavorable-views-of-china-reach-historic-highs-in-many-countries/.
9   *2018 Defence White Paper* (Seoul: Ministry of National Defence, 2019); Brad Glosserman and S. Paul Choi, 'Don't Lose Sight of Under-the-Hood Changes to South Korea's Defense Posture', *The Diplomat*, 13 November 2019, thediplomat.com/2019/11/dont-lose-sight-of-under-the-hood-changes-to-south-koreas-defense-posture/. It is important to note that, while the focus of 'omnidirectional threat' may be China, the scope of ROK perceived challenges also includes Japan and potential US abandonment.
10   Glosserman and Choi, 'Don't Lose Sight'; Chung Min Lee, 'South Korea is Caught Between China and the United States', Carnegie Endowment for International Peace, 21 October 2020; Ian Bowers and Henrik Stalhane Hiim, 'Conventional Counterforce Dilemmas: South Korea's Deterrence Strategy and Stability on the Korean Peninsula', *International Security* 45(3), 2021, doi.org/10.1162/isec_x_00403.

antagonise China is, in part, a reflection of ROK perceptions and fears of US abandonment; it is also inspiring US suspicions and criticism that pose political challenges to necessary alliance planning.

The North Korean Challenge

Advancing North Korean military capabilities and adaptations to its doctrine also present formidable political-military challenges to ROK–US alliance cooperation. The Kim Jong-un regime has explicitly messaged a desire to develop and field tactical nuclear weapons that portends a shift of nuclear strategy from one of deterrence to warfighting.[11] This is in addition to North Korean efforts to strengthen its option for massive retaliation against the US with solid-fuelled intercontinental ballistic missiles and a survivable second-strike submarine-launched capability.

Even before such developments, then US Secretary of Defense Robert Gates described North Korea in 2009 as posing 'a direct threat to the United States'.[12] Not only did an outgoing Obama administration subsequently identify North Korea as the top national security priority for the Trump administration, but also, in 2021, the commander of US Indo-Pacific Command, Admiral Phil Davidson, considered it the most immediate threat.[13] This emphasis highlights North Korea as both an extended and a central deterrence priority challenge for the US, shifting escalation dynamics and requiring adjustments to how the alliance addresses this transformed threat.

Adding to the situation's complexity is North Korea's ability to manipulate the degree of risk it poses to not only South Korea and the US, but also Japan. This allows North Korea to exploit differences in preferred approaches to deterrence between the two US allies, potentially placing the US in a dilemma, which in turn introduces further tensions into its alliances. South Korea, the US and Japan have all adjusted their force

---

11 Joshua Berlinger and Yoonjung Seo, 'Kim Jong Un Says North Korea Is Developing Tactical Nukes, New Warheads and a Nuclear-Powered Submarine', *CNN*, 9 January 2021, edition.cnn.com/2021/01/09/asia/north-korea-nuclear-development-intl-hnk/index.html.
12 Robert M. Gates, *Duty: Memoirs of a Secretary at War* (New York: Random House, 2015), 525.
13 Gerald F. Seib, Jay Solomon and Carol E. Lee, 'Barack Obama Warns Donald Trump on North Korea Threat', *Wall Street Journal*, 22 November 2016; Byun Duk-kun, 'N. Korea Poses "Most Immediate Threat" to US: Indo-Pacific Commander', *Yonhap News Agency*, 4 March 2021, en.yna.co.kr/view/AEN20210304000600325.

postures. The US has also collectively advanced its deterrence cooperation with its two North-East Asian allies, but with disturbingly limited progress made in ROK–US and ROK–US–Japan strategic alignment.

North Korea's ability to threaten nuclear escalation and hold the continental US at risk exacerbates ROK concerns of alliance decoupling. For South Korea, past crises and US responses to North Korean challenges in 2010, 2015 and 2017 are assessed in this context. The 2010 sinking of the ROK navy corvette *Cheonan* and shelling of Yeonpyong Island are considered examples of an emboldened nuclear North Korea more confident in its ability to manage escalation to war and conduct lower-level conventional provocations without triggering major alliance responses. This has led to South Korea's pursuit of several defence reforms, including a shift in its approach to deterrence from one based on passive reactive counterforce options to active countervalue-redefined responses tailored to target the North Korean regime's decision-making calculus.

This shift manifested itself in South Korea's adoption of a 'proactive deterrence' policy and changes in its rules of engagement from 'controlled response' to 'manifold retaliation'.[14] To be clear, this approach called for neither pre-emptive strikes, attacks on North Korean cities and civilians nor unlimited military responses. Rather, it aimed at responding to North Korean provocations with updated conceptions of 'in kind', 'proportionality' and 'value'—interpreted within the context of North Korea's leadership and an emphasis on what it considered of equal value or utility instead of a general definition based on equal quantity and identical means. Thus, it supported a tailored deterrence strategy aimed at altering escalation dynamics and breaking the cycle of attacks below the threshold of war under the cover of North Korea's nuclear shadow.

This South Korean approach, designed and implemented in the conservative administrations of Lee Myung-bak and Park Geun-hye, has been maintained by the progressive administration of Moon Jae-in. However, it remains a source of alliance tension, with US concern that its authorisation of 'disproportionate' responses, in the general and more traditional conceptualisation of the term, may lead to uncontrolled escalation.

---

14 Michael McDevitt, 'Deterring North Korean Provocations', Brookings, 7 February 2011, www.brookings.edu/research/deterring-north-korean-provocations/.

Similarly, the two allies seemingly lacked a shared understanding of escalation dynamics and preferred responses when, in 2015, North Korea planted landmines near a known ROK border patrol path that maimed two ROK soldiers. In response, South Korea signalled resolve and capabilities to target the Kim regime's valued control of information. The ROK military set up speakers along the inter-Korea border and resumed broadcasts that promoted democracy, capitalism and life in South Korea, as well as commented on corruption and state mismanagement in North Korea.[15] This was arguably a form of cross-domain countervalue-redefined activity, based on the ROK belief that information penetration would be more threatening to the Kim regime than other military options. Ironically, while both Koreas assessed this action as escalatory, some US defence officials (dismissing the utility of this soft response) initially underestimated its efficacy.

Finally, in 2017, as Kim Jong-un and then US President Donald Trump traded threats of nuclear strikes, tensions between Seoul and Washington were evident with President Moon ruling out another war on the Korean Peninsula.[16] Admittedly, senior US officials denied a 'bloody nose' plan for a preventive strike on North Korea.[17] Further, in emphasising the centrality of allies in US decision-making, US Joint Chiefs Chairman General Joseph Dunford stated there was 'no question' South Korea would be consulted before any military action on North Korea.[18] Still, concerns remain that US 'consultation' will more closely resemble mere 'notification' as the threat North Korea poses to the US increases. Such fears are exacerbated not only by the understandable US order to 'develop credible viable military options', but also by the then commander in chief's statements about the military being 'locked and loaded', and

---

15 Simeon Paterson, 'Korean Loudspeakers: What are the North and South Shouting About?', *BBC News*, 12 January 2016, www.bbc.com/news/world-asia-35278451.

16 Anna Fifield, 'No American Strike on North Korea without My Consent, Says South's President', *The Washington Post*, 17 August 2017, www.washingtonpost.com/world/asia_pacific/no-american-strike-on-north-korea-without-my-consent-says-souths-president/2017/08/17/775290e8-8332-11e7-82a4-920da1aeb507_story.html.

17 David Brunnstrom, 'No "Bloody Nose" Plan for North Korea: US Official, Senators', *Reuters*, 16 February 2018, www.reuters.com/article/us-northkorea-missiles-usa-bloodynose-idUSKCN1FZ2KK.

18 'US to Consult Seoul before Acting Against North Korea', *Straits Times*, 18 August 2017.

Senate leader Lindsey Graham stating that the damage and deaths from a war with North Korea 'would be worth it in terms of long-term stability and national security'.[19]

Beyond this political messaging, changes to American and Japanese capabilities also inspire ROK concerns of escalation and highlight the need for heightened cooperation in strategy design and planning integration. US development of boost-phase and left-of-launch missile defence systems, as well as new low-yield nuclear options on Trident submarine-launched ballistic missiles and future sea-launched nuclear cruise missiles, addresses some ROK concerns about potential gaps in US extended deterrence, but also requires greater shared understanding of escalation dynamics and operational implications for planned alliance operations. Similarly, Japan's stated need for a first-strike capability, accompanied by its acquisition of joint strike missiles for its F-35A stealth fighters, as well as long-range anti-ship missiles and extended-range joint-air-to-surface stand-off missiles for its F-15Js, further complicates ROK–US alliance defence preparation. This is especially the case given the real threat North Korea poses to Japan, but the deficit of trust and political constraints in South Korea and Japan limit trilateral cooperation.

Like the tension in the ROK–US alliance regarding China, a similar challenge in coordinating approaches towards North Korea exists as the two allies work to align how each nation balances deterrence with diplomacy in their respective overarching strategies. The Moon government's strategic objective is to transform relations with North Korea and establish an enduring peace that no longer requires the alliance for deterrence purposes against the Kim regime. Simply, while deterrence remains an operational objective 'end' in ROK military strategy, it is not the currently preferred means to realise the higher-order national security aim of peace for this administration. Rather, many progressives in Seoul perceive the pathway to peace as consisting more of actions aimed directly at 'building' peace than at preparing for war.

Ultimately, the absence of a coherent encompassing security strategy is limiting ROK–US alliance planning. That is, the allies lack a shared understanding of escalation dynamics and of the role of deterrence in the

19 Anna Fifield and Mehdi Hasan, 'Why Does Sen. Lindsey Graham Think Killing Millions of Koreans Would Be "Worth It"?', *The Intercept*, 6 March 2018, theintercept.com/2018/03/06/why-do-u-s-politicians-think-killing-millions-of-koreans-would-be-worth-it/.

transformed strategic environment. Such strategic dissonance previously existed but has become more prominent in recent ROK–US alliance management regarding China and North Korea. Thus, despite respective military preparations to address these security challenges, political divergence is constraining combined alliance preparations.

Refitting Alliance Political-Military Mechanisms

The ROK–US alliance has a rich architecture of government-to-government political-military consultation mechanisms to address the above challenges. This includes the ROK–US Combined Forces Command and USFK Headquarters, ROK Deterrence Strategy Committee (DSC), Korea Integrated Defence Dialogue, Extended Deterrence Strategy & Consultative Group (EDSCG), Military Committee Meeting, Security Consultative Meeting, Foreign and Defence Ministerial (2+2)—all of which support ad hoc coordination and cooperation between the two respective national security offices/councils and heads of state. The mechanisms, however, must be refitted to be effective. In many ways, the alliance's success and strengths are now its greatest challenges. While it perfects operational coordination and defence preparations for the traditional conventional fight against North Korea, legacy practices and processes are inhibiting necessary alliance adaptations.

The US four-star-general–led ROK–US Combined Forces Command (CFC), USFK and UN Command are examples of this. The presence of this most senior military grade officer and 28,500 permanently stationed troops on the Korean Peninsula send a strong message of US commitment to the deterrence and defence of the Korean Peninsula. Further, their presence allows for daily integrated efforts to coordinate operations and plan for common defence. This includes support for the US Office of the Secretary of Defense and interagency understanding of the 'on-the-ground' perspectives to inform US policy development.

CFC, as a warfighting command, and USFK, with its train and equip mission, are generally focused on readiness to execute wartime OPLANs. Meanwhile, UN Command, as the 'home for international commitments', works predominently to maintain the armistice. Although they do support deterrence through presence and preparations for conflict with

North Korea, given the transformative shifts in the strategic environment, political-level strategic guidance may now be needed to update the parameters of the conflict for which they train to ensure they are preparing for the 'fight today' and not just a 'fight tonight'. Relatedly, although the ROK–US alliance established a combined counter-provocation plan and crisis action standard operating procedures to address challenges below the threshold of war, even these two mechanisms are operated with questionable consideration to the influence of North Korea's advancing asymmetric capabilities.

Policy coordination mechanisms—such as the DSC, EDSCG and 2+2—appropriately consist of representatives from both diplomatic and defence ministries/departments. Nevertheless, these fora are sometimes criticised as 'a lot of process, but no progress'. While their establishment alone once represented progress in facilitating alliance cohesion, transformed deterrence challenges now require their agendas be updated to tackle the implications of China's rise and a changing North Korean nuclear posture.

***

As China and North Korea cast shadows over and beyond the traditional scope of ROK–US security cooperation, the alliance needs to widen its aperture and raise the level of its discussions to address these shifts in the security environment. This includes strengthening strategic alignment on how to strengthen deterrence in peacetime through war. In particular, the allies must address the transforming challenges that for past and present reasons pose political tensions in the alliance. Ultimately, South Korea and the US must adapt the ways in which they cooperate and wage deterrence. Failure to do so will have the alliance operationally ready only for a conflict of the past and at risk of strategic defeat in the transformed campaign in which it must now actively engage.

8

Japan: The Political Costs of Deterrence

Tomohiko Satake[1]

This chapter analyses the US–Japan alliance and the continuing limits to Japan's contribution to the operational underpinnings of deterrence. While Japan's security environment has deteriorated in recent years, and although increased interoperability between the Japan Self-Defense Forces (SDF) and the US military has been achieved, there remain significant normative and constitutional constraints on Tokyo's ability to play an active military role in North-East Asia and beyond. Unless the Japanese Government undertakes significant reform of its security policy, it is likely that the US–Japan alliance will continue to be characterised by asymmetry in the foreseeable future.

From an Asymmetric to a Symmetric Alliance?

The US–Japan alliance, based on the US–Japan Security Treaty concluded in 1951 and renewed in 1960, is typified by its asymmetric defence obligations. Article 5 of the treaty states that Japan and the US would respond to armed attacks only 'in the territories under the administration

---

1   The views expressed in this chapter are those of the author and do not reflect the official views of NIDS or Ministry of Defence, Japan.

of Japan'. This means that the SDF has no legal obligation to protect the US homeland or the US military outside Japanese territory, while the US military is required to protect the Japanese homeland.

To offset these unilateral defence obligations, Article 6 of the treaty grants the US 'the use of land, air and naval forces of facilities and areas in Japan'. These facilities are not only for the defence of Japan, but also for international peace and security in the 'Far East'. As a result, the alliance came to consist of what is called 'asymmetric mutuality'—often described as the 'exchange between *mono* (materials, meaning US military bases) and *hito* (people, meaning US soldiers)'.[2]

However, Japan has gradually but surely expanded its security roles within the framework of the US–Japan alliance, especially since the end of the Cold War. After the 1991 Gulf War, Japan dispatched its Maritime SDF (MSDF) minesweepers to the Gulf of Aden in the Middle East for the first time. And, after the 1993–94 nuclear crisis on the Korean Peninsula, it enabled the SDF to provide logistical support to the US military in case of 'situations in areas surrounding Japan' (*Syuhen-Jitai*) that would have 'an important influence on Japanese peace and security'.[3] Further, after the 11 September 2001 terrorist attacks in the US, Japan dispatched MSDF refuelling ships to the Indian Ocean to contribute to the US-led multilateral military operation known as Enduring Freedom. Japan also dispatched Ground SDF units for reconstruction efforts in Iraq from 2003 to 2009.

Japan's security roles under the US–Japan alliance further expanded under Prime Minister Shinzo Abe's leadership. After being re-elected as Japanese prime minister in December 2012, Abe forcefully promoted Japan's defence reforms, including the build-up of defence capabilities. Those capabilities included the acquisition of 105 F-35 jet fighters, construction of the largest-ever *Izumo*-class multipurpose destroyers, establishment of the amphibious rapid deployment force, introduction of long-range stand-off missiles and development of a hypersonic anti-ship missile.

The Abe government also revised Japan's National Defense Program Guidelines (NDPG) twice, in 2013 and in 2018. The 2018 NDPG introduced the Multi-Domain Defence Force concept to enhance the SDF's joint operational capabilities across ground, maritime, air, cyber

---

2   Sakamoto Kazuya, *Nichibei Domei no Kizuna: Anpo Joyaku to Sougosei no Mosaku* [The Bond of the US–Japan Alliance: The Security Treaty and Search for Mutuality] (Tokyo: Yuhikaku, 2001), 63.
3   Ministry of Foreign Affairs of Japan, 'The Guidelines for Japan–US Defense Cooperation', 23 September 1997, www.mofa.go.jp/region/n-america/us/security/defense.html.

and space domains.[4] Under this initiative, Japan invested heavily in new domains such as cyber, space and electromagnetic. In May 2020, the SDF launched a Space Domain Mission Unit specialising in space security. To financially support such initiatives, Japan boosted its defence budget for nine consecutive years after 2012.

The Abe government introduced new security legislation that allowed Japan to exercise the right of collective self-defence for the first time in its history. Japan is now able to mobilise the SDF in case of an 'armed attack against a country other than Japan', as stipulated by the US–Japan defence guidelines updated in April 2015.[5] The new guidelines, as well as the new security legislation, enable the SDF to protect the military assets of the US and its partners during peacetime and in 'grey-zone' situations (which occur in neither peace nor wartime). In fact, the SDF has already conducted a number of 'asset protection' missions for vessels and aircraft of the US military.[6]

The new guidelines also realised more 'seamless' coordination between the SDF and the US military from peacetime to wartime by establishing the Alliance Coordination Mechanism (ACM). The ACM comprises policy, operational and military coordination groups. Unlike the previous Bilateral Coordination Mechanism, which could only function during emergencies, the ACM operates from peacetime and covers a wide range of incidents, including grey-zone situations. Indeed, the ACM was utilised for policy coordination after the North Korean nuclear test in January 2016. Japan and the US also agreed to establish a bilateral planning mechanism to prepare for various contingencies.[7]

As such, Japan has enhanced its roles, missions and capabilities under the US–Japan alliance, while continuously relying on US extended deterrence. With Japan's greater defence and security roles, and with enhanced coordination and integration between the SDF and the US

4   Ministry of Defense of Japan, 'National Defense Program Guidelines', 18 December 2019, www.mod.go.jp/en/d_act/d_policy/national.html.
5   Ministry of Foreign Affairs of Japan, 'The Guidelines for Japan–US Defense Cooperation', 27 April 2015, www.mofa.go.jp/files/000078188.pdf.
6   Elizabeth Shim, 'Report: Japan Increased Protection of US Military Assets after 2016', *UPI*, 29 March 2019, www.upi.com/Top_News/World-News/2019/03/29/Report-Japan-increased-protection-of-US-military-assets-after-2016/3861553864841/.
7   Ministry of Foreign Affairs of Japan, 'The Guidelines for Japan–US Defense Cooperation', 4.

military, some argue that the US–Japan alliance is no longer 'asymmetric', but has moved towards a 'more balanced, integrated, and coordinated security' partnership.[8]

Japan's Pacifism Remains Strong

Despite significant developments in alliance cooperation, some continuities exist in the US–Japan security relationship. Most notably, Japan's strong pacifism and anti-militarism, which originated from the devastating defeat of World War II, still constrain Japan's security policies.[9] Japan's pacifism and anti-militarism can be understood as the Japanese public's tendency to believe that the:

> Military is a dangerous institution that must be constantly restrained and monitored lest it threaten Japan's postwar democratic order and undermine the peace and prosperity that the nation has enjoyed since 1945.[10]

As will be discussed below, this belief has gradually changed over the past decades. Nevertheless, it still limits the utility of the US–Japan alliance by increasing the political (and sometimes financial) costs of Japan's deterrence to an unacceptable level for the Japanese Government.

Since the end of the Cold War, and in the face of an increasingly assertive China and North Korea, the Japanese public has gradually become supportive of a more realistic security policy for Japan. The Japanese public's impression of, and attitude towards, the SDF greatly improved in the wake of the SDF's massive rescue mission during the Great East Japan Earthquake in March 2011 and has continued to improve. Yet, during debates over the new security legislation, the Japanese Government faced a concerted anti-legislation campaign by members of the Japanese

---

8   Congressional Research Service, 'The US–Japan Alliance', updated 13 June 2019, fas.org/sgp/crs/row/RL33740.pdf.

9   For Japan's pacifism and anti-militarism, see Thomas Berger, 'From Sword to Chrysanthemum: Japan's Culture of Anti-Militarism', *International Security* 17(4), 1993, 119–50, doi.org/10.2307/2539024; Peter Katzenstein, *Cultural Norms and National Security: Police and Military in Postwar Japan* (Ithaca: Cornell University Press, 1998); Peter Katzenstein and Nobuo Okawara, *Japan's National Security: Structures, Norms and Policy Responses in a Changing World* (Ithaca: Cornell University Press, 2010).

10   Berger, 'From Sword to Chrysanthemum', 120.

public, intellectuals and politicians.[11] This caused considerable political turbulence when the new security legislation was passed in the Diet in September 2015.[12] According to one survey, the Cabinet's support rate dropped 6 percentage points while its disapproval rate increased 7 points after the passage of the legislation.[13]

After five years, the Japanese public seem to have accepted the legislation. A survey conducted in December 2020 revealed that 46 per cent of respondents approved of the 2015 security legislation, while 33 per cent disapproved of it.[14] Nevertheless, the 2015 incident revealed that, despite an increasingly severe security environment, Japanese policymakers should expect opposition if they want to change Japanese security policies that conflict with Japan's pacifism, which stems from Article 9 of the *Constitution of Japan*.

Recent examples of such normative constraints include the cancellation of plans to acquire the land-based Aegis Ashore Ballistic Missile Defence system in June 2020. According to the government's explanation, the major reason for the cancellation was the extra expense and time needed to ensure that rocket boosters used to launch the interceptor missiles would not fall on residential areas.[15] While the government must endeavour to safeguard lives in the local community, assuring 'zero-risk', especially in an emergency situation in which ballistic missiles have already flown to Japan, is hard to achieve, as intercepted missiles could also cause debris that may fall on residential areas. Although logical, such an argument is unlikely to become mainstream in Japanese society. One survey showed that 51 per cent of respondents supported the government's decision to withdraw the plan,

---

11 'Massive Protest Against Japanese Military Legislation', *VOA News*, 30 August 2015, www.voanews.com/a/massive-protest-against-japanese-military-legislation/2938322.html. For the opposition from scholars, see 'Association of Scholars Opposed to the Security-Related Bills', 15 June 2015, anti-security-related-bill.jp/index_en.html.

12 Yuki Oda and Anna Fifield, 'Protests Erupt in Japan as Committee in Parliament Approves Security Bills', *The Washington Post*, 15 July 2015, www.washingtonpost.com/world/asia_pacific/protests-erupt-in-japan-as-committee-in-parliament-approves-security-bills/2015/07/15/7267d88e-2afd-11e5-960f-22c4ba982ed4_story.html.

13 'Support for Japan's Abe Sags after Security Bills Passed', *Reuters*, 21 September 2015, www.reuters.com/article/us-japan-security-idUSKCN0RL08Z20150921.

14 See the result of a public opinion survey by *Asahi* conducted in November 2020, digital.asahi.com/articles/DA3S14736112.html [in Japanese].

15 'Kono Suspends Deployment of Aegis Ashore Defense System', *Asahi Shimbun*, 16 June 2020, www.asahi.com/ajw/articles/13462150 (site discontinued).

while only 29 per cent opposed the decision.[16] Consequently, the Japanese Government has been forced to consider an alternative plan, which is said to be even more costly than the original Aegis Ashore plan.

Another example is discussion over the introduction of 'enemy-bases strike capabilities' or *teki-kichi kogeki noryoku*. This debate has been ongoing for more than a decade, with some Liberal Democratic Party (LDP) politicians pushing for an increase in Japan's strategic options in an era of uncertainty. The SDF's strike capabilities, however limited, are expected to transform a traditional division of labour in the US–Japan alliance, which delegated the 'spear' role of offensive capability to the US and the 'shield' role of self-defence to Japan.[17] By building offensive capabilities, Japan could enhance its own deterrence capabilities while, at the same time, strengthening the alliance beyond a previous paradigm of role-sharing. Having offensive (or 'counter-striking') weapons could also save deterrence costs, which have been heavily dependent upon a costly missile defence system.

However, the introduction of enemy-bases strike capabilities met strong opposition inside and outside the Japanese Government. The LDP's coalition partner, the New Komei Party, stressed Japan's diplomatic efforts to forge a peaceful environment over acquiring its own deterrence capabilities. Some Japanese media outlets, including the *Asahi* newspaper, also opposed the plan, arguing that it would destabilise the region by promoting an arms race.[18] The Japanese public seemed to have had mixed feelings about the plan. One survey showed that 55 per cent of respondents were against initiating enemy-bases strike capabilities, while 37 per cent were in favour.[19] Another survey found that 50 per cent of respondents agreed that Japan should have 'capabilities to prevent enemy's attacks on its soil'.[20]

Given the controversial nature of the proposal, the Suga administration decided to postpone the decision to introduce strike capabilities, originally scheduled for the end of 2020. While the Japanese Government

---

16 The survey by the Japanese TV station can be seen at news.tbs.co.jp/newsi_sp/yoron/backnumber/20200704/q4-1.html [in Japanese].

17 James L. Schoff and David Song, 'Should the US Share the "Spear" With Japan?', *Japan Times*, 9 May 2017, www.japantimes.co.jp/opinion/2017/05/09/commentary/japan-commentary/u-s-share-spear-japan/.

18 'Allowing SDF to Strike Enemy Bases Would Alter Security Policy', *Asahi Shimbun*, 21 July 2020, www.asahi.com/ajw/articles/13564486 (site discontinued).

19 Survey by *Nikkei* newspaper, 20 July 2020, www.nikkei.com/article/DGXMZO61703540 Z10C20A7PE8000 [in Japanese].

20 The result can be seen at www.nhk.or.jp/senkyo/shijiritsu/archive/2020_08.html [in Japanese].

did decide to introduce long-range, stand-off missiles, it explained that they were designed 'to deal with ships and landing forces attempting to invade Japan, including remote islands, from the outside of their threat envelopes'.[21] Defence Minister Nobuo Kishi made it clear that Japan's stand-off missiles were not aimed at 'so-called enemy-bases strikes'.[22]

In the late 1960s and early 1970s, Japan undertook high-level studies to ascertain the costs and benefits of manufacturing a threshold nuclear capability, and national elites determined that such assessments did not justify a departure from Japan's non-nuclear stance.[23] In June 1976, Japan ratified the Treaty on the Non-Proliferation of Nuclear Weapons. Before the ratification, the Japanese Diet confirmed the implementation of 'Three Non-Nuclear Principles' that had originally been adopted in 1968, and pledged not to manufacture, possess or permit the introduction of nuclear weapons on Japanese soil. These principles have been widely supported by the Japanese public as they symbolise Japan's non-nuclear policy.

Today, Japan's so-called nuclear allergy remains strong, and has even increased since the disruption of the Fukushima Nuclear Reactor by the earthquake and tsunami in March 2011. According to a joint survey conducted by Japanese and American research institutes in 2017, given North Korea's nuclear development, 40 per cent of American respondents supported Japan's nuclear armament and 33 per cent were against it. By contrast, 69 per cent of Japanese respondents were against Japan's nuclear armament and only 12 per cent supported it.[24] A more recent survey found that nearly 60 per cent of Japanese respondents supported Japan signing the Treaty on the Prohibition of Nuclear Weapons, which entered into force in January 2021.[25]

Japan's anti-militarism and nuclear allergy limit Japanese and American strategic options. Following the end of the Intermediate-Range Nuclear Forces Treaty, the US reportedly considered deploying ground-based, intermediate-range missiles among its Asian allies, including Japan.

---

21 Ministry of Defense of Japan, *Defense of Japan 2019*, 221.
22 Ministry of Defense of Japan, 'Boei Daijin Kisya Kaiken' [Press Conference of Defense Minister], 11 December 2020, www.mod.go.jp/j/press/kisha/2020/1211a.html [in Japanese].
23 Akira Kurosaki, 'Nuclear Energy and Nuclear Weapons Potential: A Historical Analysis of Japan in the 1960s', *The Nonproliferation Review* 24(1/2), 2017, 52–54, doi.org/10.1080/10736700.2017.1367536.
24 The Genron NPO and Critical Issues Poll, 'US–Japan Opinion Survey 2017', 8 January 2018, www.genron-npo.net/en/US-Japan_2017.pdf (site discontinued).
25 'Survey: 51% Oppose Extension of "Go to Travel" Campaign', *Asahi Shimbun*, 17 November 2020, www.asahi.com/ajw/articles/13938137 (site discontinued).

The point would be to offset the 'strike gap' between China's ground-based strike power and America's air and sea-launched strike power.[26] It would also fill the strategic gap between the US, whose military bases in Asia are quite vulnerable to missile attacks by enemies, and China, which has vast strategic depth in its homeland.[27] Yet, the introduction of US offensive weapons on Japanese soil—even without nuclear warheads— could provoke a domestic counter-movement or at least vocal resistance by local communities.[28] While Japan has decided to develop its own long-range missiles, it is not clear to what extent those missiles can fulfil the abovementioned strategic gaps.

Legal Constraints

In addition to the Japanese public's anti-militaristic sentiment, legal constraints on Japan's defence policies remain strong, even after the introduction of the new security legislation. These legal impediments could limit the SDF's ability to escalate in a timely manner from peacetime to wartime, including in grey-zone situations.

As already stated, the new security legislation enables the SDF to protect military assets of foreign countries, including Australia, during peacetime or grey-zone operations. However, such operations are limited to the protection of foreign countries that engage in 'activities that contribute to the defence of Japan'. They are also limited to 'activities in the scene where the combat activities are actually being conducted'. Further, the legislation stipulates that operations should be immediately terminated once a conflict breaks out between foreign defence forces and enemy countries.[29]

The SDF is allowed to use force once foreign countries conduct an 'organised and planned' armed attack against Japan. However, the question

---

26 Sugio Takahashi and Eric Sayers, 'America and Japan in a Post-INF World', *War on the Rocks*, 8 March 2019, warontherocks.com/2019/03/america-and-japan-in-a-post-inf-world/.

27 Ken Jimbo, 'Post-INF Zenpai Joyaku: Saihaibi de Kinko Mosaku Ka' [Post-INF Treaty: Seeking a Balance by the Redeployment?], The Canon Institute for Global Studies, 2 April 2019, cigs.canon/ article/20190402_5711.html [in Japanese].

28 Koji Sonoda and Taketsugu Sato, 'Bei, Taichu Misairmou Keikaku Haibisaki, Nihonwa "Saiyuryokukouho"' [The United States' Missile Network Planning against China: Japan is the 'Most Likely Candidate'], *Asahi Shimbun Digital*, 8 July 2020, digital.asahi.com/articles/ASP7776F4P5 0UHBI03L.html [in Japanese].

29 Ministry of Defense of Japan, *Defense of Japan 2016*, 214, www.mod.go.jp/e/publ/w_paper/pdf/ 2016/DOJ2016_2-3-2_web.pdf (site discontinued).

of what counts as an armed attack is highly controversial, especially in grey-zone situations. For example, if a Chinese military vessel attacked or interfered with a Japanese coastguard vessel that was protecting the Senkakus, would this count as an 'organised and planned' attack against Japan? If a missile launched by North Korea hit a Japanese vessel in Japan's territorial waters or exclusive economic zone, would it be recognised as an armed attack against Japan?

Such ambiguities also exist in the joint planning of the US–Japan alliance. According to a former MSDF chief of staff, there are at least three uncertainties that may create the perception of a gap between the SDF and the US military, especially in grey-zone situations: 1) whether the actions of another country constitute an armed attack, 2) when to begin and end operations by the SDF, and 3) when an armed attack occurs.[30] Without common understandings of these highly subjective issues between Japanese and American policymakers, significant delays could occur in both countries' responses, creating a gap in the level of deterrence provided by the US–Japan alliance.

Problems also exist regarding the use of force by the SDF. If the Japanese Government recognises 'situations that will have an important influence on Japan's Peace and Security' (or 'important influence situations'), the SDF can provide logistical support, including weapons and ammunition, to the US and its allies. Yet the SDF's logistical support should also be conducted in a 'non-combatant area' and terminated once the area turns into a conflict zone. In principle, these activities need prior approval of the Diet. However, debating whether a situation meets the legal test of having 'an important influence on Japan's peace and security' would necessarily delay deployment of the SDF.

Conversely, if a situation is recognised as 'survival-threatening', the SDF could fully engage with a conflict alongside foreign militaries by exercising collective self-defence. However, such a situation is limited to occasions when:

> An armed attack against a foreign country that is in a close relationship with Japan occurs and as a result threatens Japan's survival and poses a clear danger to fundamentally overturn people's right to life, liberty and pursuit of happiness.[31]

---

30 Tomohisa Takei, 'Gray Zones and Vulnerability in the US–Japan Alliance: Operational and Legal Dimensions', *Asia Policy* 15(3), July 2020, 25–27, doi.org/10.1353/asp.2020.0041.
31 Ministry of Defense of Japan, *Defense of Japan 2016*, 219.

The use of force should be at the 'minimum necessary' level.[32] Again, whether a conflict in the South China Sea or the Taiwan Strait counted as a 'survival-threatening situation' would likely be a matter of considerable debate.

Of course, military commitment to a war or a conflict is controversial for any country. Such a commitment is based on highly subjective judgements of domestic or international law, as demonstrated by Australia's and NATO's exercise of the right of collective self-defence following the terrorist attacks on 11 September 2001 in the US. Unlike other countries, however, Japan has specified a range of possible SDF responses to various 'situations' (*jitai*) by taking a 'positive list' approach, rather than a 'negative list' approach.[33] As already discussed, such an approach could limit the SDF's ability to respond flexibly to actual contingencies that may happen beyond the 'situations' described by the Japanese Government. Indeed, this was one reason the Japanese Government had to draft a new 'special measures law' to dispatch the SDF to the Indian Ocean after the September 11 attacks, for although the government had established the *Syuhen-Jitai* concept in 1995, it was not applicable to that situation.

These legal impediments could also make it difficult for Japan and the US to conduct the flexible deterrent options (FDO) included in the 2015 defence guidelines. According to the US Joint Chiefs of Staff, FDO aims to avoid a crisis by correctly conveying one's intentions and decisions to the enemy through diplomatic, informational, military and economic channels. If a crisis occurs, FDO seeks to quickly reduce tension and resolve the crisis by strengthening deterrence towards further incursions.[34] However, because of the legal constraints mentioned above, the SDF could fail to upgrade its responses in line with the US military and in accordance with the escalation of a crisis. In this case, the US–Japan alliance would be seriously damaged at both political and operational levels.

---

32 Ibid.
33 For the difference between 'positive list' and 'negative list' approaches, see Michael Macarthur Bosack, 'Understanding Japan's "Positive List" Approach to Security', *Japan Times*, 29 May 2021, www.japantimes.co.jp/opinion/2021/05/29/commentary/japan-commentary/japan-security-laws/.
34 Joint Publication 5-0, *Joint Operation Planning*, US Joint Chiefs of Staff, 11 August 2011, Appendix E, Flexible Deterrent Options, E-1.

Japan's Response and its Limits

Since the end of World War II, Japan has struggled to adjust its defence and security policies to meet changing international realities on the one hand, and ongoing domestic pacifism on the other.[35] Despite changing strategic circumstances, Japanese policymakers have not touched Article 9 of the constitution, which has been the fundamental element of normative and legal constraints on Japanese security policies. Instead, Japan has taken incremental steps to expand the SDF's activities overseas by introducing 'special measures laws' or by reinterpreting the constitution. Dispatching the SDF to the Indian Ocean for refuelling missions between 2001 and 2010 was a case of the former while allowing the exercise of collective self-defence was a result of the latter.

This incremental approach—which Richard Samuels describes as a 'salami-slicing' strategy—has many limitations, some of which have already been experienced.[36] As the Diet debate over the constitutionality of collective self-defence demonstrates, enormous amounts of time and energy have already been expended by Japanese policymakers. Although debate is natural and positive under a rule of law, it has deprived the public and policymakers of important opportunities to discuss other essential strategic matters. Moreover, the complexity of the Japanese legal situation could create the perception of a gap between US and Japanese officials' ability to respond to a crisis.

Meanwhile, Japan continues to face growing security threats in its region. In January 2021, China adopted a new coastguard law that authorised the use of weapons by Chinese coastguard ships against foreign vessels on waters claimed by Beijing. It also allowed the Chinese coastguard to seize foreign ships entering those waters. Chinese coastguard ships have apparently been stepping up their 'law enforcement' activities, such as chasing Japanese fishing boats or intercepting Japanese coastguard ships, in waters near the Senkaku Islands, since mid-2020.[37]

---

35   Soeya Yoshihide, 'Japan: Normative Constraints Versus Structural Imperatives', in *Asian Security Practice: Material and Ideational Influences*, ed. Muthiah Alagappa (Stanford: Stanford University Press, 1998), 198–233.
36   Richard Samuels, 'Japan's Whack-a-Mole Foreign Policy', *The Boston Globe*, 30 September 2019.
37   Alessio Patarano, 'What is China's Strategy in the Senkaku Islands?', *War on the Rocks*, 10 September 2020.

In response, ruling LDP politicians called for the Japanese Government to strengthen measures to protect Japanese islands, including the use of weapons by Japanese coastguard ships against foreign vessels that do not comply with deportation orders.[38] While such measures may help to deter China's grey-zone activities, they could also escalate matters beyond grey-zone situations. As already discussed, Japan's legal constraints could inhibit the SDF's ability to respond in a timely and seamless manner to any escalation from grey zone to a more intensified conflict. This could incentivise China to thrust further into Japanese territorial waters, while tactically and carefully avoiding any US military intervention.

Nuclear-armed North Korea also remains an existential threat to Japan. Since his inauguration in 2012, North Korean leader Kim Jong-un has conducted at least 88 missile launches and four nuclear tests.[39] Meanwhile, North Korea has rapidly advanced its missile and nuclear technologies, including submarine-launched ballistic missiles and an intercontinental ballistic missile that can reach the US homeland. While the Kim government refrained from missile launches after March 2020, it would not be surprising if Pyongyang returned to provocations to extract concessions from the new US administration. Indeed, North Korea launched a seemingly new type of short-range missile for the first time in March 2021.[40]

***

In sum, Japan's security environment has rapidly deteriorated, while its domestic security reform continues to take a slow and 'incremental' approach. This inevitably makes Japan even more dependent on US protection. Unless Japan takes a significant step towards security reform, enabling it to provide greater flexibility with SDF operations under strict civilian control, the asymmetric nature of the US–Japan alliance will likely continue for the foreseeable future.

38 Reito Kaneko, 'Confirmation of Law on Coast Guard Action Will Help Japan Deter China, Officials Say', *Japan Times*, 17 March 2021.
39 As of October 2020. See Ministry of Defense of Japan, 'Recent Missile & Nuclear Development of North Korea', October 2020, www.mod.go.jp/en/d_act/sec_env/pdf/dprk_d-act_e_201111.pdf.
40 'North Korea Claims "New Tactical Guided" Missiles Launched', *BBC News*, 26 March 2021, www.bbc.com/news/world-asia-56533260.

9

Australia: Maximising Discretion in an Untested Alliance

Brendan Sargeant

A central feature of Australia's participation in the Australia–US alliance has been Australia's support for US strategic capabilities. Australia provides support for US capabilities through joint facilities at Pine Gap and elsewhere and through arms control monitoring and treaty verification.[1] Within this framework, Australia comes within the US policy of extended deterrence. This aspect of the Australia–US alliance has not featured prominently in the recent official discourse concerning the alliance, but this is changing due to the return of great power competition in the Indo-Pacific as the major strategic challenge facing Australia. Great power competition brings with it the risk of conflict. Understanding how crises might escalate, including escalation to a potential nuclear conflict, is a central concern for alliance management. This chapter gives a brief overview of Australia's alliance management in recent decades, including the role of deterrence in Australia's defence policy. It suggests some areas where traditional approaches to alliance management may not be fit for the emerging Indo-Pacific strategic environment.

---

1   Christopher Pyne, 'Ministerial Statements—Joint Facilities: Enhancing Australia's Security and Prosperity—Statement by the Minister for Defence', Parliament of Australia, 20 February 2019, parlinfo.aph.gov.au/parlInfo/search/display/display.w3p;query=Id%3A%22chamber%2Fhansardr%2Fe0e7b3e2-2c86-47b4-8de2-de9e8f0f224b%2F0026%22;src1=sm1.

Deterrence and the Alliance in Australian Strategic Policy

Deterrence as an element of strategic policy is embodied in Australia's policy of self-reliance—the ability to defend Australia and its interests and be a security provider in the near region. This rests on an understanding of Australia's strategic geography, validated by historical experience. In this respect, self-reliance recognises that Australia will need to operate alone or with minimal assistance from its alliance partner against threats from within its own neighbourhood, especially Indonesia.[2] The need for conventional deterrence capabilities has been a primary driver of the development of the Australian Defence Force structure, particularly through the acquisition of submarine and air strike capabilities.

Notwithstanding the different emphasis of defence white papers and other policy documents over many years, the idea of self-reliance and the capacity to defend Australia with minimal assistance remains an enduring feature of Australia's strategic policy. The *1987 Defence White Paper* expressed strategic and defence policy as one of self-reliance within a framework of alliances and agreements.[3] This latter qualification (of alliances and agreements) speaks to the reality that Australia has always sought to engage with larger global strategic systems and to participate in the development and maintenance of regional and global strategic architectures and institutions.

The Australia–US alliance sits at the centre of Australian strategic policy and contributes to Australian deterrence because it ties Australia in close relationship to the US. Like all alliances, it brings obligations, the most important being the obligation to consult in the event of a crisis. The 1951 Australia, New Zealand, United States Security Treaty states:

> Each party recognises that an armed attack in the Pacific area on any of the parties would be dangerous to its own peace and safety and declares that it would act to meet the common danger in accordance with its constitutional processes.[4]

---

2   Stephan Frühling, 'Australian Defence Policy and the Concept of Self-Reliance', *Australian Journal of International Affairs* 68(5), 2014, 531–47, doi.org/10.1080/10357718.2014.899310.
3   Department of Defence, *1987 Defence White Paper* (Canberra: Australian Government Publishing Service, 1987).
4   Department of External Affairs, *The ANZUS Treaty 1951* (Canberra: Australian Government Publishing Service, 1952).

Within the broad alliance framework underpinned by the treaty, Australia and the US have developed a robust culture of collaboration across the full spectrum of defence activities. For Australia, participation in the alliance brings incommensurable benefits, and the cost of non-participation is potentially great. This applies particularly to capability, where interdependency has increased substantially in recent decades.[5] By providing access to capabilities and intelligence otherwise not available, the alliance contributes to Australia's capacity for self-reliant conventional deterrence.

Extended Deterrence in Australian Strategic Policy

The salience of extended deterrence in Australian strategic policy has varied in response to strategic circumstances. During the Cold War, Australia's strategic contribution was to participate in US systems designed to advance Western strategic interests in South-East Asia, including the Southeast Asia Treaty Organization, and its commitment to the Vietnam War. Extended deterrence was one element of the broader alliance policy architecture, but Australia was more a partner in extending it to regional partners in South-East Asia than a recipient. As Stephan Frühling has discussed, 'extended deterrence was never truly effected in Australia's case and as a result, Australia was spared most of the difficult political and military dilemmas inherent in receiving extended deterrence'.[6] In this respect, its policy significance has been political rather than practical.

In the 2000s, the East Timor crisis and the 9/11 attack by Al-Qaeda focused Australian Defence Force activity on a series of operational commitments. This included the stabilisation of East Timor and involvement in the response to other regional challenges, including to crises in Bougainville and Solomon Islands. More important in terms of the alliance was participation as a coalition partner with the US in Afghanistan and Iraq as part of the response to 9/11 and the challenge of global terrorism. This shifted the emphasis of the alliance towards

---

5   James Goldrick, 'Interoperability', in *Australia's American Alliance*, ed. Peter Dean, Stephan Frühling and Brendan Taylor (Melbourne: Melbourne University Press, 2016), 163–78.

6   Stephan Frühling, 'The Fuzzy Limits of Self-Reliance: US Extended Deterrence and Australian Strategic Policy', *Australian Journal of International Affairs* 67(1), 2013, 18–34, doi.org/10.1080/103 57718.2013.748273.

activity where Australia's primary role was directed to providing political and operational support for the US. The strategic environment did not highlight potential confrontation between great powers that could escalate to a nuclear confrontation as a first-order issue.

In 2017, however, during one of the periodic crises that characterise North Korea's relations with its neighbours, the US and other countries in the Indo-Pacific, North Korea raised the prospect of using nuclear weapons. It issued direct nuclear threats against Australia in April and October 2017.[7] These threats were dealt with in the context of crisis management at the time.[8] However, there were longer-term implications for the US–Australia alliance. The first was that there was little that Australia could do unilaterally. Policy responses, of which there were limited options, could only be undertaken in the context of crisis management by the US. In this respect, Australia was unprepared.[9] Second, the policy of extended deterrence returned to the public discourse. During that period, there was a lively discussion among commentators about extended deterrence and its continuing relevance. The foreign minister at the time, Julie Bishop, in several interviews, referred to extended deterrence as one element of Australia's strategic response.[10] Third, the crisis signalled that the Indo-Pacific was an arena where a nuclear crisis could emerge quickly, potentially escalate and Australian strategic interests were engaged.

The question that arises from this concerns how extended deterrence might operate in an environment that continues to have features created during the Cold War along with those that have emerged more recently. Specifically, how relevant is it to contingencies that might involve China?

---

7   'North Korea Threatens Australia with Disaster if it Continues to Support US Stance on Pyongyang', *ABC News*, 15 October 2017, www.abc.net.au/news/2017-10-15/north-korea-warns-australia-face-disaster-continues-support-us/9051156; 'North Korea Threatens Australia with Nuclear Strike over US Allegiance', *news.com.au*, 24 April 2017, www.news.com.au/world/north-korea-threatens-australia-with-nuclear-strike-over-us-allegiance/news-story/2cf2f736bf4e530e59f99e8d04d913b3.

8   Stephen Dziedzic, 'North Korea Threatens Australia with "Disaster", Julie Bishop Says Nation Is Not a Primary Target', *ABC News*, 15 October 2017, www.abc.net.au/news/2017-10-15/julie-bishop-speaks-on-north-korea/9051912.

9   Andrew O'Neil, Brendan Taylor and William T. Tow, 'Australia and the Korean Crisis: Confronting the Limits of Influence?', *Centre of Gravity* 40, 2018.

10   'ABC 7.30 Report, Interview with Leigh Sales', Minister for Foreign Affairs The Hon Julie Bishop MP, 29 August 2017, www.foreignminister.gov.au/minister/julie-bishop/transcript-eoe/abc-730-report-interview-leigh-sales; 'ABC AM, Interview with Sabra Lane', Minister for Foreign Affairs The Hon Julie Bishop MP, 30 August 2017, www.foreignminister.gov.au/minister/julie-bishop/transcript-eoe/abc-am-interview-sabra-lane-2.

In this respect, the effect of the North Korean crisis was to highlight the complexity of the nuclear dimension of the Indo-Pacific strategic environment and the immaturity of existing strategic architectures.

Managing the Alliance

Contemporary Australian strategic policy thus faces two entirely different challenges. The first challenge is how Australia might *participate effectively* in a global alliance system managed by the US and underpinned by US nuclear capability. This challenge is made more complex by changes occurring across the Indo-Pacific combined with the acquisition of nuclear capabilities (or the potential to acquire them quickly) by Indo-Pacific countries. The second challenge is developing effective conventional deterrence in the context of major power threats that might emerge in Australia's near region.

The *2020 Defence Strategic Update* recognises that deterrence capabilities are needed to provide Australia with the capacity to resist challenges by major powers in Australia's neighbourhood.[11] The *Strategic Update* also emphasises developing infrastructure and levels of interoperability with the US that strengthen Australia's capacity to operate with the US in the broader Indo-Pacific.[12] This is not necessarily a contradiction, but it is a challenge to policy and operational cultures because crisis preparation needs to develop the capacity to manage across the potential spectrum of future possibilities. A crisis in the near region may require a very different response and capability to one that might occur in North Asia.

Australia's management of the alliance since the Vietnam War through to the beginning of the Trump era responded to a strategic environment that was relatively stable and, in terms of potential crises, relatively low risk. The superpowers had protocols and modes of communication to ensure effective crisis management. There were many local crises, but the larger pattern of forces that structured the global order was remarkably stable, providing a secure strategic environment for Australia. Strategic assessments at the time were confident that there would be at least a decade-long warning before a major military threat to Australian security would

---

11 Department of Defence, *2020 Defence Strategic Update*, www1.defence.gov.au/sites/default/files/2020-11/2020_Defence_Strategic_Update.pdf, 33.
12 Ibid., 26.

emerge.[13] This was built on the assumption that the struggle between the US and the Soviet Union, though existential and all-encompassing in its range and intensity, was a force for stability. Australia's strategic security was underpinned by US extended deterrence across the region, which was explicit in the case of US alliances in North-East Asia and more implicit in the case of Australia itself.

In this context, Australia has managed its alliance relationship by establishing processes that enable it to maximise its discretionary decision-making capacity.[14] Australia has developed a set of arrangements and protocols that enable it to condition participation, particularly in relation to decisions that might involve Australia in US strategic or operational activities. Perhaps the most prominent example is the 'full knowledge and concurrence' arrangements at Pine Gap and other joint facilities.[15] What this means in practice is that they are established as *joint* facilities, not US bases, with integrated workforce and management arrangements, and where activities that occur or go through those facilities do so with the full knowledge and concurrence of the Australian Government. Other examples include the management of US aircraft and ship visits and the framework governing the rotational deployments of the US Marines to Darwin initiated under the Gillard government.[16]

Australian policy, in its practical application, has been operationally focused, concerned with managing participation in the context of a domestic environment where elements of the alliance are contested, and in an international environment that was relatively stable and where major crises were managed at the superpower level. This has enabled Australia to gain the deterrence benefits of the alliance while minimising the cost in terms of commitments that might intrude on Australia's capacity to exercise independent decision-making in its national interest.

---

13 Department of Defence, *1976 Defence White Paper* (Canberra: Defence Publishing Service, 1976); Department of Defence, *1987 Defence White Paper*; Department of Defence, *1991 Force Structure Review* (Canberra: Defence Publishing Services, 1991).

14 Kim Beazley, 'Sovereignty and the US Alliance', in *Australia's American Alliance*, ed. Peter Dean, Stephan Frühling and Brendan Taylor (Melbourne: Melbourne University Press, 2016), 203–23.

15 Stephen Smith, 'Full Knowledge and Concurrence', Parliament of Australia, 26 June 2013, parlinfo.aph.gov.au/parlInfo/search/display/display.w3p;query=Id%3A%22chamber%2Fhansardr% 2F4d60a662-a538-4e48-b2d8-9a97b8276c77%2F0016%22.

16 Department of Foreign Affairs and Trade, *The Force Posture Agreement between the Government of Australia and the Government of the United States of America* (Canberra: Department of Foreign Affairs and Trade, 2014).

Understanding Mutual Expectations within the Alliance

The *2020 Defence Strategic Update* signalled that Australian policy could no longer rely on past assumptions about the extent of the warning time decision-makers might have before and during a crisis.[17] This has many consequences and profound implications for defence planning. It also has implications for alliance management.

The increasingly adversarial relationship between the US and China means that the possibility of an incident occurring between American and Chinese military forces has increased. This is overlaid on the Indo-Pacific strategic environment, which has several potential flashpoints. Each of these flashpoints, through either intention or accident, has the potential to escalate to a major confrontation. In some circumstances, particularly with Taiwan, the potential for escalation to a nuclear confrontation exists. Putting to one side the political context, the practical reality for Australia is that very high levels of interdependence with US strategic and operational systems mean that, in some contingencies, Australian participation would reduce the burden on US capabilities. A decision not to participate would have major implications for the alliance.

A major crisis, such as a Taiwan contingency, will therefore confront Australia with real dilemmas. First, due to the degree of integration with US forces across the Indo-Pacific, and given the infrastructure that Australia would be contributing to the capacity of those forces to operate, Australia will have a degree of involvement regardless of decisions that it may wish to make. While it is likely to have some discretion over the degree of involvement, that very much depends on circumstances at the time. Second, Australia will not be in control of the process of escalation. This means that policy will be directed not only at managing participation in response to the crisis but also at Australia's relationship with its alliance partner. Third, given the interdependent economic, trading and cultural linkages that Australia has across the Indo-Pacific, including with potentially adversarial countries, a major crisis in which Australia does not control escalation is likely to be a major disruptor to existing and future patterns of activity, and what emerges may not necessarily be in Australia's interests.

---

17   Department of Defence, *2020 Defence Strategic Update*, 14.

In the current environment, particularly in the context of the potential crises that could occur, the central alliance question concerns each party's expectations in a crisis and how these expectations would be expressed in operational arrangements. In this respect, Australian policy, at least as declared publicly, is ambiguous. Intelligence arrangements continue broadly within frameworks established decades ago. Operational activity in the form of exercises, training and participation in US fleet activities continues. Infrastructure is being developed in Australia that will strengthen the capacity of the US to operate from Australia. However, agreements and arrangements governing US activities in Australia are carefully designed to place limits on the ability of the US to act without close consultation and the implied consent of the Australian Government.[18] This adds up to strategic imperatives that seem to be suggesting greater degrees of integration but policy frameworks that also seek to maximise discretion in Australian Government decision-making. The question is whether this ambiguity would withstand the pressure of a major strategic crisis such as a Taiwan contingency.

Understanding Time as a Diminishing Strategic Resource

The most important resource in crisis management is time. One of the features of the contemporary strategic environment is that time is an increasingly diminishing resource, as a result of both technology (and particularly of cyber technologies) and the increased proximity of countries in contested domains. In this respect, Australian alliance management processes, including the deterrent posture they imply and the capabilities that it might develop, need to create more time for positioning and decision-making, both strategically and operationally.

Effective deterrence creates time and secure spaces. The *2020 Defence Strategic Update* has signalled a focus on deterrence both as policy and in prospective capability development. However, in the context of the alliance, a different type of discussion also needs to occur. This involves

---

18   For example: Department of Foreign Affairs and Trade, *The Force Posture Agreement between the Government of Australia and the Government of the United States of America* (Canberra: Department of Foreign Affairs and Trade, 2014); 'Agreement with the Government of the United States of America Relating to the Establishment of a Joint Defence Space Research Facility [Pine Gap NT]', Australian Treaties, 9 December 1966, www.austlii.edu.au/au/other/dfat/treaties/1966/17.html.

coming to an understanding and negotiation of mutual expectations in relation to future crisis management and response. The results of this need to be approved by government and translated into operational protocols. What is Australia prepared to do and what are its limits? There is no absolute answer to this question, but it needs to be discussed and some understandings reached. This is particularly important from an Australian perspective because crisis management may largely be the management of alliance partner expectations. This suggests that the alliance planning infrastructure needs to be formalised to a greater degree than it is at the moment. This has both an operational and a political dimension.

Finally, in a crisis, ministers through the National Security Committee of Cabinet chaired by the prime minister will be the ones responsible for the overall management of the response and the key decision-making. As part of the development of a stronger alliance planning infrastructure, the role of ministers must be central. One implication of this is that ministers will also need to take a much stronger interest and involvement in planning and managing the operational environment, particularly in terms of potential contingencies and to understand their role in shaping operational responses within a broader national interest and alliance framework.

***

The *2020 Defence Strategic Update* signals a policy shift in response to change in Australia's strategic environment. The rise of China and its increasingly adversarial stance in the region, including in relation to the US, are driving other large forces for change. The Indo-Pacific has become more crowded, more contested, and regional decision-making institutions have become less capable of establishing agreement on how the strategic order should be managed in the future.[19]

In a crisis (and in crisis preparation), the US—being in control of escalation management—will want certainty and the capacity to plan and act on agreed assumptions. The imperative for the smaller partner is to create space that enables them to act in their own interests, even when it may be against the interests of the major partner. As noted above, Australian alliance management has sought to maximise discretionary space while at the same time implying commitment in a future crisis. In

---

19 Department of Defence, *2020 Defence Strategic Update*, 6.

recent decades, particularly in relation to participation in Afghanistan and Iraq, Australian policy has been to maximise the value of participation both in the context of the particular operations and more broadly in the context of the alliance, while minimising operational and strategic risk. The question now is whether traditional approaches to alliance management are sufficient in the context of a potential nuclear crisis in the Indo-Pacific.

We can consider, as an example, a crisis that has the potential to escalate to a nuclear confrontation. Such a crisis would be managed by the US. Australia will have equities, but the interests of the US could constrain the capacity to pursue them as it manages the crisis. Extended deterrence functions as a kind of guarantee of security from nuclear attack, yet in a major crisis, it is not certain how such a guarantee would be understood and implemented in practice. In this respect, crisis management should not rest on the assumption that Australia's strategic interests are so intertwined with those of the US that the US would, in its response, recognise and act in Australia's interests. This assumption has not been tested and assumes a convergence of strategic interests that in some circumstances may not exist.

Part III:
Nuclear Weapons and Non-Nuclear Capabilities

10

New Capabilities and Nuclear Deterrence in Europe

Łukasz Kulesa

By and large, Europeans treat the nexus between new technologies and nuclear deterrence with suspicion rather than optimism. European countries and the European Union (EU) are more than happy to aspire to leadership in the civilian part of the ongoing technological revolution. European militaries and the armament industry are busy looking for next-generation capabilities for future conventional weapon systems.[1] Yet, to the extent that the evolution of the relationship between nuclear weapons and new military technologies is discussed beyond military experts, it is primarily seen as a risk factor.[2]

Further complicating the picture are the differences regarding views on deterrence inside Europe. A 2018 study by the European Council on Foreign Affairs divided the European NATO members into four categories: True Believers in nuclear deterrence (e.g. France and the United Kingdom but also Poland and Romania), the Conflicted (e.g. Germany), the Pragmatists (who accept without enthusiasm its necessity) and the

---

1   This includes sixth-generation combat air systems, FCAS and Tempest, or an array of projects developed in the framework of the European Defence Fund and the EU's Permanent Structural Cooperation. See 'About Pesco', Pesco, accessed 14 September 2021, pesco.europa.eu/.

2   See Katarzyna Kubiak, Sylvia Mishra and Graham Stacey, 'Nuclear Decision-Making under Technological Complexity', European Leadership Network, March 2021, www.europeanleadership network.org/wp-content/uploads/2021/03/ELN-Pilot-Workshop-Report-1.pdf.

Conformists (the largest and most passive group).[3] The 'deterrence IQ' within the alliance is therefore not evenly distributed, and 'emerging technologies IQ' even less so. In some countries there is considerable hesitation to discuss not only the nuclear dimension, but also broader requirements for deterrence and escalation management.

Conventional Deterrence Nexus and the Role of New Technologies

European ambivalence about the impact of new technologies on deterrence stems from several sources. Generally speaking, there is widespread scepticism within the political classes about the ability of new military technology to assist in resolving major contemporary strategic dilemmas, such as the West's relationship with Russia and China. Political, economic, technological and societal factors are seen as far more important aspects bearing on the future of these relationships than military power. This may be best demonstrated in Europe's lack of interest in territorial ballistic missile defence.

A substantial segment of government and expert communities share the view that the emergence and deployment of new capabilities would become a source of heightened instability both at the global level and in the European context. This includes concerns about the security and safety of existing nuclear weapons systems and command and control infrastructure (especially their vulnerability to cyber interference), the perils of the development of fully autonomous or artificial intelligence–enabled strategic systems, the destabilising effects of the misuse of social media and escalation in deepfakes, and an inadvertent escalation from conventional to nuclear conflict due to the entanglement of nuclear and non-nuclear systems.[4]

There also is a doctrinal 'firewall' between nuclear weapons and other means of deterrence in the strategies of two European nuclear possessors: the UK and France. This thinking seems to be also influencing the

---

3   Manuel Lafont Rapnouil, Tara Varma and Nick Witney, 'Eyes Tight Shut: European Attitudes towards Nuclear Deterrence', European Council on Foreign Relations, Flash Scorecard, December 2018, www.ecfr.eu/page/-/ECFR_275_NUCLEAR_WEAPONS_FLASH_SCORECARD_update.pdf.
4   See, for example, research cited in: Andrew Futter and Benjamin Zala, 'Strategic Non-Nuclear Weapons and the Onset of a Third Nuclear Age', *European Journal of International Security* 6(3), 2021, 8–10, doi.org/10.1017/eis.2021.2.

conceptual approach of NATO. From the political viewpoint, maintaining firm control over decisions on the employment of nuclear weapons and separating these from conventional elements of deterrence posture remain of paramount importance for most members of NATO.

The Russian Challenge for NATO

Europeans' scepticism regarding the strategic value of new capabilities does not make them impervious to specific challenges in this area stemming from Russia. European states have already been subjected to a number of Russia-originated cyber attacks and remain in range of Russian short and intermediate-range, precision-guided missiles. In 2017, Russia reportedly used one of its satellites to intercept transmissions from the French–Italian satellite, demonstrating the potential to conduct assertive space operations.[5]

Russia has shown determination in integrating a broad set of approaches, tactics and capabilities to reach the desired strategic effect. Some past pronouncements of the Russian military leadership pointed to the aspiration of gradually reducing the reliance on nuclear weapons through development of 'non-nuclear deterrence' forces—understood primarily as long-range, conventional, precision-guided ballistic cruise and hypersonic systems. However, subsequent developments suggested instead a drive to advance in parallel in a range of domains, including conventional, nuclear, cyber and electronic warfare, space capabilities, and air and missile defence, as well as military implementation of emerging technologies such as artificial intelligence.[6] New technologies are also utilised—alongside other means—for grey-zone activities and for probing NATO and national responses.

In any crisis or conflict with NATO, Russia would not only aim to maximise the effects of its possession of nuclear weapons (which should not be reduced to early use of non-strategic weapons options), but also pursue confrontation in multiple domains simultaneously, aiming to capture the strategic initiative and bring a quick end to the conflict on favourable

---

5   'Russia "Tried to Spy on France in Space"—French Minister', *BBC News*, 7 September 2018, www.bbc.com/news/world-europe-45448261.

6   The evolution is described in: Kristin Ven Bruusgaard, 'Russian Nuclear Strategy and Conventional Inferiority', *Journal of Strategic Studies* 44(1), October 2020, 3–35, doi.org/10.1080/01402390. 2020.1818070.

terms.[7] Such a posture is partly grounded in a sense of vulnerability; Russia remains convinced that US technological breakthroughs give it an advantage in conflict, including the ability to attack Russia's command and control system and/or its nuclear assets and thus prevent nuclear retaliation, and that some US non-nuclear strategic systems have been developed with this decapitation goal in mind.

European Responses

Against such an opponent, the survivability of nuclear forces, and maintaining the ability to resort to their use and successfully execute a nuclear strike, becomes paramount. France and the UK are therefore looking into safeguarding their nuclear systems against the use of new technologies by Russia and any other actors. This includes increasing the resilience of their command and control system and aspects of cybersecurity, and avoiding detection of their ballistic missile–carrying submarines. France is exercising the air component of its nuclear forces to be able to overcome a modern air defence system utilising a whole range of countermeasures and new technologies. Both countries are also planning to incorporate new technologies into their future nuclear systems, including new designs for submarines (e.g. the UK's Dreadnought class and France's SNLE 3G program). In the case of France, its next-generation nuclear cruise missile (the ASN4G) is to utilise hypersonic technologies. The UK's new nuclear warheads, to be developed jointly with the US, are to include an improved set of penetration aids allowing them to overcome existing and prospective missile defence systems.

France and the UK are investing heavily in new non-nuclear capabilities, and multi-domain integration is seen by both as essential for the modern battlefield. At the same time, both countries treat nuclear deterrence as the only credible response to major threats to vital national interests, and the nuclear dimension is seen as being complemented, but not replaced by non-nuclear capabilities. As highlighted by French President Emmanuel Macron in a 2020 speech, 'conventional military manoeuvre[s]' can be used for deterrence purposes, but nuclear deterrence remains the key to France's security and freedom of action, as it 'prevents adversaries from

---

7 On the role of nuclear versus non-nuclear forces in escalation, see M. Kofman, A. Fink and J. Edmonds, 'Russian Strategy for Escalation Management', *CNA*, April 2020, 18–29.

betting on escalation, intimidation and blackmailing to achieve their ends'.[8] This is further elaborated in France's security doctrine, which describes the objective of French nuclear forces as preventing conventional forces from being circumvented 'from above' through escalation.

The UK, in its March 2021 Integrated Review, announced an increase in the salience of nuclear weapons. The document envisages raising the cap on UK nuclear warheads from 180 to 260 and limiting transparency on warhead and missile deployment numbers. This was justified by 'recognition of the evolving security environment, including the developing range of technological and doctrinal threats'.[9] While the document focuses on the development of nuclear doctrine and the capabilities of potential adversaries as the reason for the shift, the change may also be related to concerns about the long-term effect of non-nuclear systems on the credibility of British deterrence. UK Secretary of State for Defence Ben Wallace subsequently mentioned advances in Russian ballistic missile systems as having influenced the UK's decision to raise its warhead numbers—a likely reference to Moscow's defence system, which incorporates both nuclear and non-nuclear elements. The document includes the caveat that the UK can review its negative security assurances (i.e. its pledge not to use nuclear weapons) if 'emerging technologies that could have a comparable impact [to nuclear weapons use]' make it necessary.

NATO is in the process of adapting to the challenges and opportunities brought by the growing pace of developments in the emerging and disruptive technologies (EDT) area. The alliance has been slow to address the challenges and consequences of its deterrence posture and relationship with Russia. It was preoccupied in the 2010s, first and foremost with establishing a forward deployment posture along its eastern flank, increasing the availability of conventional forces and their level of readiness and mobility. This was accompanied by an increased focus on countering 'hybrid warfare' activities below the threshold of war, including

---

8   'Speech of the President of the Republic Emmanuel Macron on the Defense and Deterrence Strategy', France Diplomacy, 7 February 2020, www.diplomatie.gouv.fr/en/french-foreign-policy/security-disarmament-and-non-proliferation/news/2020/article/speech-of-the-president-of-the-republic-emmanuel-macron-on-the-defense-and.
9   Global Britain in a Competitive Age. The Integrated Review of Security, Defence, Development and Foreign Policy, March 2021, 76, assets.publishing.service.gov.uk/government/uploads/system/uploads/attachment_data/file/969402/The_Integrated_Review_of_Security__Defence__Development_and_Foreign_Policy.pdf.

the malign use of cyberspace (recognised only in 2016 by NATO as an operational domain) and disinformation. Towards the end of the 2010s, high-level political interest in EDT surged, fuelled internally by the US's promotion of the effects of its third offset strategy and externally by a growing realisation of the technological advances made by potential adversaries. In 2019, NATO's EDT roadmap was adopted. A major report by the NATO Science and Technology Organization, published in March 2020, built on the roadmap, identifying eight EDTs considered to be 'major strategic disruptors' for the period 2020–40: data, artificial intelligence, autonomy, space, hypersonics, quantum, biotechnology and materials.[10] The report drew attention to the need to look at these technologies comprehensively, as their effects will be augmented through the integration and interactions between them. Still, as noted by the NATO 2030 Reflection Group, the alliance needs a 'strategic surge' in this area, more cooperation with the private sector and to firmly anchor EDT in its strategic thinking, planning and operations.[11]

The impact of specific EDT and/or their cumulative weight on NATO's nuclear deterrence have been noted. Examples include the ability to use improved sensors and big data analysis to locate allies' nuclear delivery systems, and the capacity of hypersonic systems to deliver successful strikes against high-value NATO targets without crossing the nuclear threshold, which would have 'potentially profoundly destabilising' effects.[12] These considerations had probably already had an impact on the operational side of NATO's nuclear mission in terms of updating nuclear, command, control and communication systems against cyber and other forms of interference;[13] identifying ways to increase the survivability of nuclear assets assigned to NATO during a potential conflict; and conducting nuclear-related exercises. However, so far they have not altered NATO's strategy regarding the role of nuclear weapons or the function of

---

10 *Science and Technology Trends 2020–2040. Exploring the S&T Edge*, NATO, Science and Technology Organization, March 2020, www.nato.int/nato_static_fl2014/assets/pdf/2020/4/pdf/190422-ST_Tech_Trends_Report_2020-2040.pdf.

11 *NATO 2030: United for a New Era, Analysis and Recommendations of the Reflection Group Appointed by the NATO Secretary General*, November 2020, www.nato.int/nato_static_fl2014/assets/pdf/2020/12/pdf/201201-Reflection-Group-Final-Report-Uni.pdf.

12 *Science and Technology Trends*, 91.

13 See Y. Afina, C. Inverarity and B. Unal, *Ensuring Cyber Resilience in NATO's Command, Control and Communications Systems*, Chatham House Research Paper, July 2020, www.chathamhouse.org/sites/default/files/2020-07-17-cyber-resilience-nato-command-control-communication-afina-inverarity-unal_0.pdf.

new capabilities in deterrence and in managing escalation. The preparation of NATO's new strategic concept, scheduled to be finished in 2022, could provide an opportunity to address these issues.

Consequences for NATO and the Relations of European Allies with the US

The impact of new technologies and emerging military capabilities on nuclear deterrence is the subject of intense debate among experts, with multiple and often contradictory hypotheses.[14] Some assert that the nature of nuclear deterrence will be radically transformed and that the increased vulnerability of nuclear systems and improved defences will lead to the role of nuclear weapons becoming marginalised, an increase in the number of nuclear weapons or the adoption of more dangerous nuclear postures by some possessors (e.g. pre-delegation, launch-on-warning, pre-emption). But there are also more conservative predictions—namely that new technologies may not fully deliver on their disruptive promises and/or that their offensive advantages would be balanced by defensive countermeasures, leaving the role of nuclear deterrence more or less intact.

The analysis conducted so far in this chapter seems to indicate that the European True Believers (in nuclear deterrence) remain unconvinced that any radical changes are approaching. The UK and France are taking steps to safeguard the functioning of their nuclear deterrence in a more challenging environment, utilising the assistance of new technologies. But they continue to see the role of nuclear weapons as 'ultima ratio' in escalation management and retaliation, to which no comparable alternative is likely to emerge. This is likely to remain the default position.

The future trajectory of development and deployment of new non-nuclear capabilities by the US will have an impact on the alliance's nuclear deterrence posture, especially regarding the rationale for maintaining US forward-deployed nuclear forces in Europe and continuing NATO's nuclear sharing. If US non-nuclear capabilities are seen as providing the same or perhaps a higher level of deterrence as nuclear weapons deployed in Europe, this may strengthen the case for their withdrawal to the US

---

14   Brad Roberts, 'Emerging and Disruptive Technologies, Multi-Domain Complexity, and Strategic Stability: A Review and Assessment of the Literature', Center for Global Security Research, Lawrence Livermore National Laboratory, February 2021, 19–20.

or complete elimination. One can envisage, for example, deployment of intermediate-range conventional hypersonic systems in Europe as substitutes for B61 nuclear bombs. In that case, the main axis of frictions may be between the US and those states that are particularly attracted to the forward deployment of nuclear weapons (even if they are not stationed on their territories), such as Poland and other eastern flank countries. These would most likely point out that Russia would treat the replacement of nuclear assets with non-nuclear ones as an invitation to escalate any crisis to the nuclear level, and that a nuclear-sharing model that includes direct involvement of a number of European allies cannot easily be replicated with regard to most of the new capabilities.

A number of other political-military challenges may arise. First, we may face the emergence of a gap in thinking about escalation management and the employment of new capabilities between the US and its allies, with consequences for the nuclear sphere. The US is likely to maintain its pre-eminence in terms of the development and deployment of new technologies, and of formulating conceptual approaches as regards their use. Since individual NATO countries, most importantly the UK and France, aim to actively contribute their own ideas and approaches to discussions on issues such as artificial intelligence development, space and cyber policy, common NATO positions can be formulated. However, the US is likely to be far ahead of the majority of NATO allies. Further, the US and other technologically advanced allies may not be willing to share the full details of some of the more sensitive technologies they possess at NATO fora. The September 2021 announcement of the creation of the trilateral security partnership between the US, Australia and the UK (AUKUS) can be seen as potentially contributing to this trend. While the initial attention was focused on the nuclear-powered submarines, the participants also pledged closer cooperation on cyber capabilities, artificial intelligence, quantum technologies and other undersea capabilities. This may lead to strengthening the links and interoperability between the three countries, but would not engage NATO (which has a broad partnership relationship with Australia) as a whole.

Consequently, in a crisis, allies may be surprised by certain US actions and their escalatory effects. This may not necessarily be caused by any lack of consultation or advanced warning but may happen because of their lack of understanding of the doctrinal, technological and military aspects of the US's approach to operations.[15] The reverse may also be true. The US may be forced to react to developments arising from the employment of new technologies by some of its NATO allies, including a situation in which such an action escalates conflict to the nuclear threshold (e.g. cyber attack on the adversary's nuclear command and control). The alliance's response to this challenge will need to take the form of in-depth consultations, developing joint doctrinal documents and investment in simulations and wargaming.

Second, integration of new capabilities and new domains into the deterrence and defence toolbox seems inevitable. Some changes will have important consequences at the tactical and operational levels (e.g. ubiquity of low-cost unmanned systems and their increased level of autonomy and effectiveness) and some may reach the strategic level. Any sudden devaluation of nuclear deterrence due to a technological breakthrough—for example, the end of ballistic missile submarines' 'near-invulnerability'—would have major ramifications and force the three NATO nuclear possessors to re-evaluate their posture, with major consequences for the alliance. But less revolutionary changes may be significant, as they would impact on traditional NATO approaches to burden and risk-sharing, deterrence and assurance.

In the foreseeable future, a scenario of US military disengagement from NATO and Europe remains far-fetched, which means that Europe can rely on the full range of US capabilities when facing Russia. However, if the US or other allies were able to provide advanced strategic non-nuclear assets for common defence and deterrence, they may be inclined to reduce the 'traditional' contributions of their armed forces. The UK's recent Integrated Review may pave the way, as it highlights the contribution of UK offensive cyber and precision strike capabilities (as well as nuclear forces) to NATO, while simultaneously reducing the size of its land forces. Other allies may follow the same logic. For example, some of the European states currently hosting US nuclear weapons may be interested in exploring the option of providing specific new capabilities to the alliance instead of continuing with their nuclear mission. However, the question would arise as to whether such a rebalancing and new division of labour would increase the credibility of deterrence or be seen as weakening NATO's ability to provide the necessary levels of 'boots on the ground'.

---

15   See, for example: Justin Anderson and James R. McCue, 'Deterring, Countering, and Defeating Conventional-Nuclear Integration', *Strategic Studies Quarterly* 15(1), 2021, 28–60.

Third, there is a danger of increased polarisation between the allies interested in making full use of the opportunities created by EDT and those advocating more restraint and engagement with potential adversaries as the best way to reduce the destabilising effects of new technologies.[16] In the NATO context, one can expect future discussions about the deployment of specific weapon systems, which may resemble Cold War–era debates between the proponents of strengthening deterrence and pursuing arms control. For example, should NATO countries move forward with, or rather aim to limit, the deployment of certain categories of autonomous or hypersonic systems, looking for similar restraint from Russia?

Finally, NATO's adversaries will have a vote in deciding the future role of nuclear weapons and new capabilities in the alliance's deterrence mix. The further pursuit of new military technologies by Russia, and increased lethality of its own mix of offensive and defensive non-nuclear capabilities, will necessitate a periodical review and adaptation of NATO's approach. The issue will become particularly pressing if Russia manages to achieve dominance on some non-nuclear 'rungs' of escalation—for example, hypersonic precision strike systems or counterspace capabilities. The alliance may then be forced to broaden the role of nuclear weapons to maintain the credibility of its deterrence strategy, including potentially an explicit threat of nuclear retaliation to non-nuclear strategic attacks, or prepare its own non-nuclear response, using a range of new technologies.

---

16 For examination of the employment of EDT for bolstering deterrence, see D. Jankowski, 'NATO and the Emerging and Disruptive Technologies Challenge', in *NATO in the Era of Unpeace: Defending against Known Unknowns*, ed. D. Jankowski and T. Stępniewski (Lublin: Institute of Central Europe, 2021), 96–99; A. Lanoszka, 'How Emerging Technologies Might Affect Baltic Security', in *The Return of Deterrence: Credibility and Capabilities in a New Era*, ed. William G. Braun III, Stéfanie von Hlatky and Kim Richard Nossal (Carlisle: US Army War College Press, 2019), publications.armywarcollege.edu/pubs/3703.pdf.

11

Nuclear Sharing and NATO as a 'Nuclear Alliance'

Alexander Mattelaer

The North Atlantic Treaty Organization's (NATO's) capstone document, its 2010 Strategic Concept, explicitly stated that 'as long as nuclear weapons exist, NATO will remain a nuclear alliance'.[1] This wording put new emphasis on a reality that has been part of the alliance since its very foundation—namely, that the nuclear arsenal of the United States, later supplemented by those of the United Kingdom and France, constitutes the supreme guarantee of the security of the allies.[2] Yet the mere existence of these nuclear arsenals and extended deterrence commitments does not make NATO a nuclear alliance. Politically, NATO's nuclear posture is shaped by the Nuclear Planning Group (NPG)—that is, it is developed in a multilateral process of consultation and coordination. Militarily, different allies participate to varying degrees in the nuclear deterrence enterprise. This ranges from providing support to nuclear operations to taking part in nuclear sharing by hosting US nuclear weapons and fielding dual-capable aircraft (DCA). While the

---

1   NATO, *Active Engagement, Modern Defence: Strategic Concept for the Defence and Security of the Members of the North Atlantic Treaty Organization* (Lisbon: NATO Summit, 2010), www.nato.int/cps/en/natohq/official_texts_68580.htm.
2   For a critical discussion, see Kjølv Egeland, 'Spreading the Burden: How NATO Became a "Nuclear" Alliance', *Diplomacy & Statecraft* 31(1), 2020, 143–67, doi.org/10.1080/09592296.2020.1721086.

nuclear debate in NATO features some longstanding dilemmas, the close involvement of allies makes the deterrence posture materially tangible and thus more credible.[3]

This chapter explores the interplay between nuclear-sharing arrangements and NATO's organisational identity as a nuclear alliance. It does so with the aim of reviewing the contemporary relevance of nuclear sharing and the dynamics of extended deterrence in the European and Indo-Pacific theatres. The argument proceeds in three parts. The first section focuses on the threefold logic that underlies NATO's nuclear-sharing arrangements. Why have allies come to consider nuclear sharing in the first place? A combination of concerns over nuclear proliferation, the political cohesion of the alliance and the military credibility of extended deterrence provides for a multifaceted response. Yet all three dimensions face considerable challenges today. The second section discusses the institutionalisation of nuclear policy in the NATO alliance. How do NATO nuclear policy and posture come into being? The role of the NPG, the function of DCA and bilateral security relations all account for part of the answer. The third section compares the extended deterrence dynamics at play in the European and Indo-Pacific theatres. While the institutional features of US extended deterrence commitments in both regions may vary, their political dynamic is similar. Ongoing nuclear modernisation efforts suggest that the challenge of managing deterrence in alliance relationships is an enduring one. The renewed emphasis on nuclear communication in NATO summit declarations indicates that political debates on the future of alliance relationships cannot help but confront deterrence and arms control questions head-on.

The Threefold Logic of Nuclear Sharing — and its Challenges

NATO's nuclear deterrence relies in part on US nuclear weapons being forward deployed in Europe and on capabilities and infrastructure provided by allies. In particular, this concerns the fielding of DCA fleets in the air forces of Belgium, Germany, Italy and the Netherlands that are

---

3   Cf. Josef Joffe, 'NATO and the Dilemmas of a Nuclear Alliance', *Journal of International Affairs* 43(1), 1989, 29–45.

able to jointly deliver US nuclear weapons.[4] More than anything else, these nuclear-sharing arrangements constitute a symbol of the indivisible security of the alliance. Precisely because nuclear weapons are unique, the collective management thereof underscores the nuclear nature of the alliance. Before turning to the institutional specifics—allowing for comparison between different extended deterrence commitments—it is well warranted to recall the threefold logic that underlies the concept of nuclear sharing itself. First, nuclear sharing helps restrain proliferation pressures; second, nuclear sharing helps cement the political cohesion of the NATO alliance; third, nuclear sharing strengthens the military credibility of NATO's deterrence by providing a wider array of graduated force options. While all three dimensions face contemporary challenges, the overall logic remains compelling.

When conceptualising the rationale for nuclear sharing, the historical link with non-proliferation comes first. After the UK had acquired nuclear weapons in 1952 and France had started its nuclear program, the sharing of nuclear weapons by the US was conceived as a way to limit the proliferation of additional nuclear arsenals. A key element of the 'nuclear stockpile' arrangement agreed in 1957, nuclear sharing sought to obviate the need for more European allies to provide for their own existential security independently. During several years of negotiations on procedural and technical details in the late 1950s and early 1960s, the deployment of US nuclear weapons in Europe and the close involvement of allied forces came into being.[5] NATO's nuclear-sharing arrangements were concluded before the Treaty on the Non-Proliferation of Nuclear Weapons (NPT) came into effect, hence ensuring the conformity of the former with the obligations of the latter.[6] This entailed that NATO nuclear sharing was accepted under the NPT regime as long as the US maintained full peacetime custody of its forward-deployed nuclear weapons in Europe.

---

4   The status of Turkey in NATO's nuclear sharing is currently in doubt: while Turkey has long hosted US nuclear weapons on its territory, the participation of the Turkish Air Force in the nuclear strike mission has been discontinued. See, for example: Dustin Hinkley, 'US–Turkey Nuclear Energy Sharing', Turkish Heritage Organization, 2020, www.turkheritage.org/Uploads/US---turkey--nuclear-energy-sharing.pdf.

5   Marc Trachtenberg, *A Constructed Peace: The Making of the European Settlement 1945–1963* (Princeton: Princeton University Press, 1999).

6   William Alberque, *The NPT and the Origins of NATO's Nuclear Sharing Arrangements*, Proliferation Papers No. 57, 2017, www.ifri.org/sites/default/files/atoms/files/alberque_npt_origins_nato_nuclear_2017.pdf.

While the recent Treaty on the Prohibition of Nuclear Weapons (TPNW) has put the spotlight on the lack of progress on nuclear disarmament efforts under the NPT regime, the fact that all NATO allies have abstained from the TPNW indicates their ongoing concern about their fundamental security needs.[7] In particular, the history of nuclear sharing raises a question about whether the abandonment of NATO's nuclear guarantee would further the cause of disarmament or have the opposite effect.

The second function of nuclear sharing—arguably the principal one today—is to cement the political cohesion of the alliance. After all, nuclear sharing ties different allies together in a way that is altogether unique, in the sense that it ensures that their security is indivisible. Both through political consultation process and the military readiness that the nuclear mission entails for the allies concerned, the nuclear-sharing arrangements make the deterrence posture of the alliance more legitimate and more robust than any conceivable alternative.

It is of course true that the political cohesion of the alliance has been put to the test in recent years by sharp transatlantic discussions on burden sharing and the lack of consultation among allies, especially in the eastern Mediterranean. This challenge has been clearly recognised and, to some extent, explicitly addressed by the NATO 2030 Reflection Group.[8] As far as the nuclear dimension of alliance cohesion is concerned, broad recognition thereof is increasing: both those allies who are already participating in nuclear sharing and those interested in becoming more closely involved are stating so on the record.[9]

The third and least understood function of nuclear sharing concerns its military-strategic utility. While critics often argue that such 'tactical' nuclear weapons delivered by fighter aircraft and gravity serve no military function—hence reducing these to their political symbolism—this claim is

---

7   'North Atlantic Council Statement as the Treaty on the Prohibition of Nuclear Weapons Enters into Force', NATO Press Release, 20 December 2020, www.nato.int/cps/en/natohq/news_180087.htm.

8   *NATO 2030: United for a New Era, Analysis and Recommendations of the Reflection Group Appointed by the NATO Secretary General*, November 2020, www.nato.int/nato_static_fl2014/assets/pdf/2020/12/pdf/201201-Reflection-Group-Final-Report-Uni.pdf.

9   In Belgium, for instance, a parliamentary resolution to join the TPNW (doc 55K0372001) failed to gather a majority in a plenary vote. Meanwhile, allies like Poland and Estonia occasionally flag an interest in becoming more involved in the nuclear deterrence mission. See, for example: Jonatan Vseviov, *Constructing Deterrence in the Baltic States* (Tallinn: International Centre for Defence and Security, 2021), icds.ee/wp-content/uploads/2021/02/ICDS_Analysis_Constructing_Deterrence_in_the_Baltic_States_Jonatan_Vseviov_February_2021-1.pdf.

incorrect.[10] Nuclear deterrence rests on a combination of communication, capability and resolve. Given that these sharing arrangements provide NATO with nuclear capability, they provide (and are intentionally used as) the prime vehicle for communicating deterrence messages on behalf of the alliance as a whole. The visibility of DCA that can jointly train, be deployed or recalled is not just a military vulnerability, but a strategic function that is hard to replicate with other delivery systems. The regime of annual Steadfast Noon exercises they engage in helps in turning this capability into a key instrument for deterrence signalling, especially in times of crisis.

In addition, limited nuclear response options have a specific function on the escalation ladder—namely, to deter a limited Russian strike against which strategic retaliation would be disproportionate.[11] Finally, but perhaps most fundamentally, nuclear sharing provides allies with a degree of nuclear expertise and capability, allowing them to transform into nuclear weapon states at the turning of a US key at a time of crisis.[12] While these arguments would have struck many observers as outlandish in the security environment of the 1990s and 2000s, the gradual erosion of the arms control architecture and the abandonment of the Intermediate-Range Nuclear Forces Treaty in particular have upended widespread assumptions about the fading relevance of nuclear deterrence in the European theatre.

The Institutional Specifics of NATO as a Nuclear Alliance

Bearing in mind these varied arguments for nuclear sharing, it becomes possible to make sense of the way in which the NATO alliance articulates its nuclear deterrence policy. This concerns the role of the NPG, the different supporting capabilities provided by non-nuclear allies and the bilateral agreements that enable nuclear sharing to work on the basis of a dual-key arrangement. Individually, these institutional specifics highlight different

---

10 For a critical view, see Tom Sauer, 'US Tactical Nuclear Weapons: A European Perspective', *Bulletin of the Atomic Scientists* 66(5), 2010, 65–75, doi.org/10.1177/0096340210381338.

11 For discussion, see Hans Binnendijk and David Gompert, 'Decisive Response: A New Nuclear Strategy for NATO', *Survival* 61(5), 2019, 1–16, doi.org/10.1080/00396338.2019.1662119.

12 Cf. Barry Posen, 'In Reply: To Repeat, Europe Can Defend Itself', *Survival* 63(1), 2021, 41–49, doi.org/10.1080/00396338.2021.1881252.

dimensions of NATO's nuclear identity. Collectively, they underscore the fact that NATO is not just an alliance that includes nuclear weapon states but is indeed a nuclear alliance itself.

The NPG constitutes NATO's senior body on nuclear matters. With the exception of France, which prides itself on its fully autonomous (national) deterrent capabilities, all NATO allies participate in the consultative process on the nuclear arrangements of the alliance. Established at the end of 1966, and in sync with the drafting of the Harmel Report balancing deterrence and dialogue, the NPG provides a forum for consensual decision-making relating to deterrence communication, nuclear planning and force posture, consultation about nuclear use, nuclear weapons safety and arms control issues. While generally meeting at the level of defence ministers, the activities of the NPG are supported by the (ambassador-level) NPG Staff Group and the High-Level Group involving national policymakers (at policy director level). As such, all allies but France acquire a diplomatic voice in a multilateral consultation process. Individual capitals can choose to amplify their own voice by means of nuclear burden and risk-sharing: by assuming ownership over part of the deterrence posture, they acquire more control over the nuclear policy of the alliance. As decisions are taken by consensus, the NPG articulates the common positions of the alliance members and thus embodies alliance solidarity and commitment to indivisible security and burden sharing.[13]

The strategic nuclear forces of the US, the UK and France constitute the backbone of NATO's nuclear capabilities. This particularly concerns the continuous at-sea deterrents that all three allies maintain—hence ensuring second-strike capability tied to three separate centres of decision—and the unique 'missile sink' function of the US arsenal of intercontinental ballistic missiles. The latter makes it virtually impossible for any adversary to overwhelm the alliance in a surprise attack. Yet the supporting capabilities and infrastructure provided by non-nuclear allies do help to strengthen NATO's posture. This goes beyond simply supporting nuclear operations with conventional air tactics (e.g. by escorting bombers with fighters), which is a mission in which many allies participate. It can also involve the hosting of US weapons that are forward deployed and making personnel and infrastructure available for NATO

13 Cf. Rose Gottemoeller, 'NATO Nuclear Policy in a Post-INF World', Speech by NATO Deputy Secretary at the University of Oslo, 9 September 2019, www.nato.int/cps/en/natohq/opinions_168602.htm.

nuclear deterrence, and can include fielding DCA. For the latter, US weapons are married to a delivery system that is owned and operated by individual allies, turning it into a multinational extension of the nuclear posture of the US and latent nuclear powers. While the US maintains full custody over the weapons, the DCA allies obtain some degree of control over their hypothetical use. In effect, this shared capability can only be employed with the consent of both the US and the ally concerned—the so-called dual key.

Political control over NATO is exercised via the NPG and command authority is exercised from the top political level to military commanders. Nuclear decision authority rests ultimately with the political leadership of the nuclear powers (i.e. without delegation to commanders in the field).[14] However, the technical operationalisation of nuclear sharing builds on NATO's military command structure, led by the supreme allied commander Europe, as well as a broad array of bilateral agreements with individual allies involved in the nuclear mission. This system of bilateral consultations within an alliance framework facilitates the technical and legal support that are required for the mission. It also allows for minor technical variation across different allies and avoids the scenario in which the technical implementation of the alliance's posture is complicated by the unanimity requirement governing the political work of the NPG. While NATO functions as an integrated, multilateral alliance, its structure also builds on strong bilateral ties with individual allies.[15]

Interplay between Extended Deterrence in Europe and the Indo-Pacific

By keeping the nuclear-sharing model in mind, the differences and similarities between extended deterrence in the European and Indo-Pacific theatres are accentuated. Ultimately, the US nuclear arsenal provides the fundamental security guarantee for allies as diverse as Japan, the Republic of Korea, Australia and the different NATO countries. For this reason, the fate of extended deterrence in both theatres is deeply intertwined:

14 Simon Lunn, 'NATO Nuclear Sharing', in *Building a Safe, Secure, and Credible NATO Nuclear Posture*, 2018, www.jstor.org/stable/pdf/resrep17630.12.pdf.
15 Jeffrey A. Larsen, 'NATO Nuclear Adaptation since 2014: The Return of Deterrence and Renewed Alliance Discomfort', *Journal of Transatlantic Studies* 17, 2019, 180, doi.org/10.1057/s42738-019-00016-y.

the communication and credibility of the US strategic deterrent in one theatre cannot help but affect the other. Yet these security guarantees are operationalised in different ways—politically and militarily. Understanding NATO's identity as a nuclear alliance thus also benefits from such a comparative approach.

The institutionalisation of nuclear sharing in NATO engages allies in a multilateral process that binds their security more closely together. This in turn makes the promise of extended deterrence materially tangible. After all, the armed forces of different allies take part in nuclear exercises and deterrence messaging. Taken together, this makes NATO's nuclear deterrence posture more credible and more reliable precisely because it involves different actors and therefore greater redundancy. Being implicated in the formulation and signalling of nuclear deterrence also implies embracing responsibility and helping to share the burden of risk. Such nuclear co-ownership comes at a cost: it requires political capital in justifying deterrence. Yet the level of public support for deterrence is often underestimated. Worries about accidental nuclear use tend to be more prevalent than principled opposition to nuclear deterrence, thereby putting a premium on institutional excellence in terms of security protocols. Finally, while it is generally accepted that the credibility of NATO's deterrence posture influences elite perceptions among US allies in Asia, this relationship also works in the other direction. Especially as US–China competition is downgrading Europe to being a secondary theatre, NATO's role in setting the gold standard of extended deterrence would benefit from taking this Indo-Pacific dimension on board.[16]

For US allies such as South Korea, Japan and Australia, the prospect of taking part in a similar endeavour of nuclear sharing in the Indo-Pacific would arguably mitigate the fear of abandonment. It would also involve them more closely in the formulation of nuclear strategy and posture discussions. This would substantially expand the model of extended deterrence dialogues that have featured in the framework of the Japan–US alliance since 2010, for instance. It would also entail accepting the mutual interdependence that such multilateralisation would entail. In order to be credible, this would require their political leadership to contemplate, however remotely, the possibility of nuclear use. Quite apart from financial

16 Luis Simon, Linde Desmaele and Jordan Becker, 'Europe as a Secondary Theater? Competition with China and the Future of America's European Strategy', *Strategic Studies Quarterly*, Spring 2021, 90–115.

or budgetary discussions, the fundamental willingness to engage in nuclear deterrence is perhaps the hardest question of all. Yet without such political willingness on the part of US allies, it is equally fair to ask whether the US extended deterrence commitment can be fully relied upon. Simply put, can one ask one's ally to do what one is not, as a matter of principle, willing to do for oneself? In turn, the multifaceted and technologically advanced nature of the China challenge with which South Korea, Japan and Australia are most familiar are reshaping the character of deterrence in ways that impact the discussion of NATO's future security as well. The attention paid to emerging and disruptive technologies in the report by the NATO 2030 Reflection Group constitutes clear evidence of this.[17]

* * *

Deteriorating trends in the security environments of both Europe and the Indo-Pacific have put renewed emphasis on the importance of extended deterrence relationships and the nuclear guarantee underpinning these. The evolution of the nuclear language contained in NATO summit declarations from 2014 onwards constitutes a clear indication of this. This implies that the nuclear identity of the NATO alliance is far from mere symbolism. Instead, ongoing political debate on the future of the alliance suggests that questions pertaining to deterrence commitments, burden sharing and arms control need to be addressed, taking the changed security environment and the evolving military balance into account. As the military balance in the Indo-Pacific and the European theatres cannot avoid impacting on one another, a detailed comparison between the two regions offers an enhanced understanding of the extended deterrence provided by the US in both theatres. The latter is, of course, not new. Just as the Korean War was instrumental in endowing NATO with a standing command structure, the origins and contemporary relevance of NATO's nuclear-sharing arrangements may offer inspiration to defence planners in the Indo-Pacific as well.

---

17 'North Atlantic Council Statement as the Treaty on the Prohibition of Nuclear Weapons Enters into Force'.

12

US Nuclear Weapons and US Alliances in North-East Asia

Michito Tsuruoka

In North-East Asia, the United States maintains alliances with Japan and South Korea and extends nuclear deterrence to them. Yet it no longer maintains forward-deployed nuclear weapons in the region. The lack of any US nuclear presence is one of the most notable characteristics of the deterrence and defence posture of the US alliances in the region, and contrasts strongly with the fact that all the other regional players—namely, China, North Korea and Russia—possess nuclear weapons.[1]

Two more major factors need to be taken into account. First, China, North Korea and Russia are all modernising and expanding their nuclear arsenals in one way or another, raising questions as to whether the current deterrence and defence posture of the US–Japan and US–Korea alliances remains adequate. Second, the balance of military power in North-East Asia and the wider Western Pacific region between the US and its allies on the one hand, and China on the other, is rapidly changing in favour of the latter, which raises questions about the credibility and sustainability of the US commitment to the region.

---

1   Whereas China and Russia are nuclear weapon states recognised by the Treaty on the Non-Proliferation of Nuclear Weapons (NPT), North Korea is only a de facto nuclear state, and is not allowed to have nuclear weapons under the NPT. Yet the fact remains that North Korea possesses nuclear weapons.

Against this background, it is no surprise that the level of interest in the region on issues related to extended deterrence by the US and the role of nuclear weapons is on the rise. This chapter examines how the US and its allies have sought to maintain the credibility of extended deterrence, particularly in the context of the US–Japan and US–South Korea alliances, looking at the history and the characteristics of their postures and approaches to consultation and cooperation in the nuclear domain. Possible prospects of post-INF Treaty challenges and US nuclear modernisation will also be explored at the end of the chapter.

The Myth of the Asia Model

It is commonplace to argue that, unlike the North Atlantic Treaty Organization (NATO) model of nuclear deterrence that in part relies on the forward deployment of US tactical nuclear weapons on allied territories, the Asian model lacks such a physical element. This is currently correct, although the degree to which NATO's deterrence posture relies on its unique system of nuclear sharing beyond symbolism is debatable; the alliance's security is ultimately guaranteed by US strategic weapons. The US, however, did maintain nuclear weapons in North-East Asia for a substantial period during the Cold War. A nuclear weapons deployment in South Korea began in 1958 and lasted until as late as 1991.[2] The US also deployed a number of nuclear weapons in Okinawa until the island's reversion to Japan in 1972. Indeed, Okinawa saw one of the earliest deployments of nuclear weapons outside the US mainland, in December 1954.[3] Since Okinawa at that time was under US control, it was not considered a deployment to Japan. Yet the deterrence posture of the Japan–US alliance was underpinned by the presence of nuclear weapons in Okinawa as well as the deployment of non-nuclear components on mainland Japan, such as aircraft that were supposed to deliver nuclear warheads in wartime. That was the 'Cold War East Asian model'.[4] Without a reliable intercontinental ballistic missile capability, the role of forward-deployed tactical and theatre nuclear weapons was more prominent in the 1950s and 1960s.

---

2   Hans Kristensen and Robert Norris, 'A History of US Nuclear Weapons in South Korea', *Bulletin of the Atomic Scientists* 73(6), 2017: 349–57, doi.org/10.1080/00963402.2017.1388656.
3   Robert Norris, William Arkin and William Burr, 'Where They Were', *Bulletin of the Atomic Scientists* 55(6), 1999, 30–31, doi.org/10.1080/00963402.1999.11460389.
4   Brad Roberts, *The Case for US Nuclear Weapons in the 21st Century* (Stanford: Stanford University Press, 2015), 207, doi.org/10.1515/9780804797153.

Further, US surface vessels as well as submarines were believed to be routinely carrying nuclear weapons during the Cold War. Due to the US policy of neither confirming nor denying the location of its nuclear weapons, it was not clear which vessels were carrying what number of nuclear weapons at any given moment. However, that US vessels and submarines *did* carry nuclear weapons constituted an important element of allied deterrence posture in the region. These vessels visited allied ports including those in Japan on a regular basis.

Unlike NATO, the US did not introduce a nuclear-sharing arrangement in Asia. Yet the alliance deterrence posture in the US alliances with Japan and South Korea used to be dependent, at least partly, on forward-deployed nuclear weapons. Therefore, the dichotomy between the NATO and Asian models is not as clear-cut as it first appears.[5]

The Consultative Approach

Nonetheless, one of the biggest differences between the European and East Asian models of extended deterrence was the degree of institutionalisation of nuclear consultation. While NATO has a highly institutionalised mechanism for nuclear consultation, called the Nuclear Planning Group (NPG), both US–Japan and US–Korea alliances had long lacked a similar mechanism. The Obama administration, together with Tokyo and Seoul, agreed to institute bilateral dialogue on nuclear issues as part of the 2010 Nuclear Posture Review (NPR). One of the aims of such dialogue was to discuss the retirement of the Tomahawk Land Attack Missile – Nuclear (TLAM-N) and the issues of modernising dual-capable aircraft before decisions are made.[6] Such efforts were pertinent in light of the fact that 'some US allies in Asia' were expressing concerns about the retirement of the TLAM-N.[7]

---

5   Michito Tsuruoka, 'The NATO vs. East Asian Models of Extended Nuclear Deterrence? Seeking a Synergy beyond Dichotomy', *The ASAN Forum*, 30 June 2016.
6   Roberts, *The Case for US Nuclear Weapons*, 202.
7   William Perry et al., *America's Strategic Posture: The Final Report of the Congressional Commission on the Strategic Posture of the United States* (Washington: United States Institute of Peace Press, 2009), 26. On Japan's concerns, see also Nobuyasu Abe and Hirofumi Tosaki, 'Understanding Japan's Nuclear Dilemma: Deterrence before Disarmament', in *Disarming Doubt: The Future of Extended Nuclear Deterrence in East Asia*, ed. Rory Medcalf and Fiona Cunningham (Woollahra: Lowy Institute for International Policy, 2012), 25–28.

From an American perspective, it was largely a misunderstanding that the credibility of US extended nuclear deterrence was heavily dependent on the TLAM-N, which was believed to be more or less redundant.[8] It was, therefore, in America's own interest to 'educate' the allies, by sharing more information about the workings of US nuclear deterrence. One could argue that the logic that brought about the establishment of the NPG in NATO in the 1960s worked again vis-a-vis Japan and South Korea, in the sense that Americans 'were convinced that they could change their allies' positions by changing their minds, and this change could come through a nuclear education'.[9] Crucially, the Japanese and Koreans were also eager to understand the thinking and mechanisms underpinning US nuclear deterrence strategy.

It was thus natural that the nuclear dialogue that had started in the run-up to the 2010 NPR continued and became institutionalised as an Extended Deterrence Dialogue with Japan and Extended Deterrence Policy Committee with South Korea, the latter renamed the Extended Deterrence Strategy and Consultation Group. These dialogue sessions have included not just normal policy dialogues, but also tabletop exercises and visits to US bases where the country's strategic assets are housed.[10] While not much has been revealed to the public about the nature and result of those dialogues, judging from the fact that the dialogue frameworks have continued, it seems reasonable to assume that both the US and its allies have found them a useful, if still modest and largely invisible, pillar of the alliances.

Towards a New Nuclear(-Related) Cooperation

However, talks are just talks. One could argue that what gives credibility to the alliance deterrence posture are the physical elements. Also, it is undeniable that there is an element of 'the grass is always greener on the

---

8   Jeffrey Lewis, 'Japan Loves TLAM/N', Arms Control Wonk (blog), 8 May 2009, www.arms controlwonk.com/archive/202284/japan-tlamn/; Roberts, *The Case for US Nuclear Weapons*, 202.
9   Timothy Andrews Sayle, 'A Nuclear Education: The Origins of NATO's Nuclear Planning Group', *Journal of Strategic Studies* 43(6–7), 2020, 954, doi.org/10.1080/01402390.2020.1818560.
10   Michito Tsuruoka, 'Nuclear Proliferation, Deterrence and Strategic Stability in East Asia: The United States, China and Japan in a Changing Strategic Landscape', in *Routledge Handbook of Nuclear Proliferation and Policy*, ed. Joseph Pilat and Nathan Busch (London: Routledge, 2015), 59–61.

other side'—meaning that some Asians, including Japanese and Koreans, regard the nuclear-sharing arrangement in NATO with a measure of envy (which is somewhat ironic given that an increasing number of Europeans regard NATO's nuclear sharing as obsolete).[11] Calls to introduce an Asian NPG are also popular in some quarters in Asia.[12] In addition, there are calls for a (re)deployment of US tactical nuclear weapons on their soils in view of a NATO-like arrangement of nuclear sharing in South Korea and, to a lesser extent, Japan. At least for the foreseeable future, it is highly unlikely for such an arrangement to be established between the US and Japan or South Korea, since the US would not see it as having any strategic rationale or imperative. When calling for the deployment of US tactical nuclear weapons or nuclear sharing, the concrete objectives to be achieved through such measures need to be defined in a realistic way. Those arrangements cannot be a panacea for the threats and challenges from China or North Korea. Still, given the delicate and psychological nature of deterrence, simply saying that strategic weapons based in the US would do the entire job may not be always sufficient. Some 'visibility' may be needed in maintaining the credibility of deterrence.[13]

Short of nuclear sharing, various other possibilities of allied involvement in US nuclear operations can be envisaged, some of which have already been taking place in the US–Japan and US–South Korea contexts. The most visible of those in recent years is joint training involving US strategic bombers, including the B-1B, B-2 and B-52. US bombers have been flying in the region for decades, but recently they have been used as a tool of strategic messaging to North Korea, evidenced by the fact that the US has been flying such aircraft mainly following North Korea's nuclear and ballistic missile tests. Japanese and South Korean fighters have escorted US bombers more frequently in recent years. Based on what has already been done, the countries involved could think of more substantial involvement in possible nuclear missions beyond escorting.

The challenge of making joint training with US bombers more substantial is also related to the fact that the US seems to be using its strategic bombers more widely, meaning that the US now conducts joint training with an

11   Michito Tsuruoka, 'Why the NATO Nuclear Debate is Relevant to Asia and Vice Versa', *Policy Brief*, German Marshall Fund of the United States, October 2010.
12   Chuck Hagel et al., *Preventing Nuclear Proliferation and Reassuring America's Allies*, Task Force Report, Chicago Council on Global Affairs, February 2021.
13   Elaine Bunn, 'The Future of US Extended Deterrence', in *Perspectives on Extended Deterrence*, Recherches & Documents, No. 03/2010 (Paris: Fondation pour la Recherche Stratégique, 2010), 41.

increasing number of countries, including non-allies. In the context of its new concept of Dynamic Force Employment, strategic bomber operations are more active across the globe, involving not just formal allies, but also partners like India and Ukraine. A B-1B bomber landed in India for the first time in February 2021, escorted by Indian Air Force *Tejas* fighters.[14] Tokyo certainly does not have any objection to the US cooperating with those countries, but some cannot help wondering whether the meaning of joint training with US bombers is being diluted: is it no longer special? Extended 'nuclear' deterrence has long been thought of as the 'premium content' of US extended deterrence, not (explicitly) extended to all the allies.[15] While the B-1B is currently not nuclear capable, strategic bomber fleets as a whole (operated by Strategic Command) represent the very core of US strategic deterrent capability, which is why bombers have been used to deliver strategic messages to US adversaries.

In addition to participation in bomber training/operations, allies' other areas of involvement in US nuclear deterrence include ballistic missile defence (BMD) and anti-submarine warfare (ASW). Japan has invested heavily in BMD over the past two decades or so, and ASW is one of the strongest capabilities of its Maritime Self-Defense Force. Given that China's *Jin*-class nuclear-powered ballistic missile submarines are now operational, constituting the country's first credible sea-based nuclear deterrent, Japan–US cooperation in ASW has become even more important.[16]

A Return of Nuclear Weapons to the Region?

The Trump administration's 2018 NPR stated that the US would 'in the longer term, pursue' a modern Sea-Launched Cruise Missile – Nuclear (SLCM–N).[17] This could have a significant impact on extended

---

14 'B-1B Makes First US Bomber Visit to India Since 1945', *Air Force Magazine*, 8 February 2021.
15 Andrew O'Neil, *Asia, the US and Extended Nuclear Deterrence: Atomic Umbrellas in the Twenty-First Century* (Abingdon: Routledge, 2013), 121.
16 On the US assessment of China's ballistic submarine missile capability, see Department of Defense, *Military and Security Developments Involving the People's Republic of China 2020: Annual Report to Congress*, September 2020, 45, 86, media.defense.gov/2020/Sep/01/2002488689/-1/-1/1/2020-DOD-CHINA-MILITARY-POWER-REPORT-FINAL.PDF.
17 Department of Defense, *Nuclear Posture Review*, February 2018, 54, media.defense.gov/2018/Feb/02/2001872886/-1/-1/1/2018-NUCLEAR-POSTURE-REVIEW-FINAL-REPORT.PDF.

deterrence in North-East Asia. The 2018 NPR argued that SLCM as well as low-yield submarine-launched ballistic missiles (SLBM) would 'enhance the flexibility and responsiveness of US nuclear forces' and emphasised the fact that SLCM will 'not require or rely on host nation support to provide deterrent effect'.[18] Despite some Democrats in the US being fiercely opposed to the further development of SLCM–N,[19] the Biden administration took an early decision to begin research and development of a nuclear-armed SLCM.[20]

The SLCM–N issue raises a number of fundamental and politically sensitive questions about the future of extended nuclear deterrence in East Asia. For example, it highlights the issue of whether forward-deployed (and less-destructive) nuclear weapons make the US commitment more credible in the eyes of allies. Given the fact that the 2010 NPR argued that the role of the TLAM-N could be substituted by dual-capable aircraft (DCA) and strategic bombers, the US will need to explain why a new SLCM–N is needed. If China's increasing capability is cited as a reason, what specific aspect will need to be addressed by the SLCM–N?[21]

Unlike DCA, SLCM–Ns will 'not require or rely on host nation support'; however, as US Navy Virginia-class and Los Angeles-class attack submarines often visit foreign bases, including Yokosuka and Sasebo, this will inevitably cause domestic political controversies in Japan if and when those submarines are nuclear-armed. During the Cold War, Japan tacitly allowed nuclear visiting and transiting through a series of secret agreements and understandings between the two governments. All such arrangements were revealed in 2010. Subsequently, the Japanese Government's position has been that, as there are no US vessels carrying nuclear weapons on a regular basis (with the exception of ballistic missile submarines), there is no need to worry about nuclear visiting.[22] The development and deployment of the SLCM–N will present a new challenge for Tokyo.

---

18 Ibid., 52–55.
19 'Lawmakers Aim to Prevent Sea-Based Nuclear Cruise Missile', *Defense News*, 4 March 2021.
20 Kingston Reif, 'Biden Continues Trump Nuclear Funding', *Arms Control Today* 56(6), 2021.
21 For an authoritative assessment of the merits of SLCM-N, see 'Strengthening Deterrence and Reducing Nuclear Risks, Part II: The Sea-Launched Cruise Missile–Nuclear (SLCM-N)', *Arms Control and International Security Papers* (Department of State) 1(11), 23 July 2020.
22 Katsuya Okada, *Gaikou wo hiraku: kaku gunshuku, mitsuyaku mondai no genba-de* [Opening Diplomacy: From the Frontline of Nuclear Disarmament and Secret Agreements Problems] (Tokyo: Iwanami Shoten, 2014), 92–93.

Finally, the role of the SLCM–N will have to be put in the context of a broader debate on the ways in which the US could address the 'strike gap' with China in a post–INF Treaty strategic environment. The low-yield SLBM that the 2018 NPR decided to pursue and is already being deployed should also be considered in this context.[23] It needs to be remembered that only conventional missiles are envisaged regarding a possible deployment of intermediate-range missiles in Asia (and Europe for that matter). Nevertheless, given that many missiles in China's arsenal are dual-capable and that both conventional and nuclear missiles constitute the deterrence posture of the US and its allies, dealing with conventional and nuclear missiles as if they were from different planets will become untenable. Further, even for conventional missiles, both Japan and South Korea will struggle to build a domestic consensus on accepting the deployment of US ground-based missiles on their territories, which could become one of the most difficult challenges in their respective alliances with the US.

* * *

Japan and South Korea face threats and challenges from both China and North Korea, and the reality is that the balance of military power is changing in Beijing's favour, making extended deterrence, including nuclear deterrence, even more important. Both allies have strengthened and institutionalised their respective nuclear consultations with the US and increased their involvement, particularly in bomber operations, in the region. Nonetheless, it remains to be seen whether such measures will prove to be sufficient in view of China's rapid build-up of its military, including its nuclear arsenal. A more fundamental rethinking of the allied deterrence posture in East Asia could turn out to be necessary.

---

23 Jacob Cohn, Timothy Walton, Adam Lemon and Toshi Yoshihara, *Leveling the Playing Field: Reintroducing US Theater-Range Missiles in a Post-INF World* (Washington: Center for Strategic and Budgetary Assessments, May 2019).

13

The Impact of New Capabilities on the Regional Deterrence Architecture in North-East Asia

Masashi Murano

The development of technology and the new capabilities that make use of it have had a major impact on the security environment and strategy. The 'nuclear revolution' is a major example, which has been supported by the combination of two deterrence concepts: punishment and denial. A strategy that emphasises deterrence by punishment is based on the view that nuclear weapons are 'absolute weapons'—weapons that are too destructive to ever be used for military purposes—and that their role is limited to deterrence by retaliation.[1] Based on this view, the minimum second-strike (i.e. assured destruction) capability required to destroy critical infrastructure such as an adversary's capital would be enough to deter the adversary, which has the advantage of keeping the cost of deterrent force structure relatively low.

However, there is a fundamental problem with a deterrence strategy focused on retaliation. This is because retaliation occurs only after deterrence has failed—that is, after an adversary has launched a nuclear or non-nuclear attack and changed the status quo—and it does nothing

---

1   Bernard Brodie, ed., *The Absolute Weapon: Atomic Power and World Order* (New York: Harcourt, Brace, 1946).

to prevent the adversary from taking action or limiting damage. From the perspective of escalation control, denial capability at any level of conflict is thus ideal for a deterrent posture. However, developing a denial-based deterrence posture that was fully capable of damage limitation through nuclear and conventional counterforce capabilities and missile defences was impossible during the Cold War.

New technological developments and the current security environment are forcing the United States and its allies to take the development of denial and damage limitation capabilities more seriously than ever before.[2] Technologically, the advantage of taking an offensive rather than a defensive position is becoming more apparent; however, this also provides a wider range of active denial and damage limitation options than before. This chapter discusses these developments and their implications for alliances in relation to three main areas: deterrence in space, the role of conventional prompt-strike (CPS) capabilities in North-East Asia and the role of low-yield nuclear warheads introduced in the 2018 Nuclear Posture Review (NPR).

Space Systems in Regional Deterrence Architecture

Since the 1991 Gulf War, ensuring space control has become an essential element of joint operations for US and modern allied forces. Challengers such as China are attempting to take advantage of this vulnerability. In 2007, China destroyed a satellite as part of a test of a kinetic anti-satellite (ASAT) missile modified from the DF-21 medium-range ballistic missile (MRBM), generating a large quantity of uncontrollable debris. As China expands its own use of space, including operation of the *Beidou* positioning satellite (its version of a global positioning system) and manned space missions, such as its space station, 'hit-to-kill' kinetic counterspace systems such as ASAT missiles and co-orbital killer satellites will present risks to China's own space activities. Therefore, while it continues to develop kinetic ASAT, China is also simultaneously developing a variety of non-kinetic ASAT systems. These include laser

---

2   The following is an early argument for the importance of damage limitation: Keith B. Payne, *Deterrence in the Second Nuclear Age* (Lexington: University Press of Kentucky, 1996).

dazzling against optical sensors of reconnaissance satellites, uplink and downlink jamming and spoofing of satellite signals, as well as cyber attacks against space control systems.[3]

Non-kinetic counterspace capabilities increase the complexity of escalation control. In general, non-kinetic countermeasures are difficult to recognise. This is because it is difficult to determine in real time whether the damage is accidental or intentional, attacks are difficult to attribute and the function of systems may be restored with no lasting damage when the attack stops. Such capabilities can thus easily enable the creation of a grey zone, making the threshold that justifies proportional response ambiguous and deterrence by punishment difficult. Reversible disruptions could also have a lower threshold of use than irreversible damaging attacks. Therefore, to deter such interference, it is necessary not only to strengthen the resiliency of space systems, but also to possess and operate similar counterspace capabilities and conduct dynamic escalation control. In this regard, Japan's decision to acquire countermeasures in the space domain in its 2018 National Defense Program Guidelines is notable and a step in the right direction.[4]

Since ambiguity in Space Situational Awareness (SSA) can lead to delays in decision-making and disruptions to command and control, it is essential to improve SSA, first and foremost through international cooperation, to address these problems. At the same time, it is necessary to strengthen the technological resilience, as well as the political resilience, of space systems to deter interference and disruption to space assets. Technological resilience means dispersing vulnerabilities through enhanced interoperability, miniaturisation and constellation of satellites to maintain mission capabilities and speed up recovery even in the event of an attack. One of these efforts is the Blackjack program led by the US Defense Advanced Projects Agency, which aims to demonstrate how an autonomous small satellite constellation deployed in low Earth orbit can replace the same functions traditionally performed by larger, more expensive satellites deployed in geostationary orbit.[5] In both areas—SSA and space resilience—allies have the ability to make real contributions through their own efforts.

---

3   Todd Harrison, Kaitlyn Johnson and Thomas G. Roberts, *Space Threat Assessment 2019*, CSIS, April 2019, www.csis.org/analysis/space-threat-assessment-2019.
4   Ministry of Defense of Japan, 'National Defense Program Guidelines', 18 December 2018, www.mod.go.jp/en/d_act/d_policy/national.html.
5   Stephen Forbes, 'Blackjack', DARPA, accessed 14 September 2021, www.darpa.mil/program/blackjack.

Conversely, political resilience is an effort to raise the bar for attack by complicating the adversary's strategic calculations. One way to do this is through hosted payloads in which mission equipment is carried as an extra load on board a different country's satellite. For example, the Japanese and US governments exchanged letters under the Mutual Defense Assistance Agreement in December 2020 to carry US SSA sensors on Japan's Quasi-Zenith Satellite System, units 6 and 7, which are scheduled to be operational by the 2023 fiscal year, and to cooperate in improving SSA capabilities.[6]

From the point of view of a potential aggressor, the risk of horizontal escalation arises when attacking a satellite carrying the payload of multiple countries rather than a satellite operated by a single country. Further, if hosted payloads are possible not only between the US and Japan but also between partners that do not necessarily share a common geographic theatre, such as Japan–Australia, Japan–Europe, US–Europe and US–Australia, it could have a cross-regional deterrent effect that is not limited to specific scenarios. For example, if China attempts to disrupt a satellite in the case of a Taiwan contingency, and the target US or Japanese satellite is shared by a European country or Australia, this would complicate China's calculations and may dissuade an attack on the satellite. But similar considerations would also extend to Russian attacks on the same system.

Conventional Prompt-Strike and Deterrence by Denial

One of the features of today's security environment and military-related technologies is the increase of operational tempo. While the development of command, control, communications, computers, intelligence, surveillance and reconnaissance (C4ISR)—including space systems—and other factors are responsible for this increase in operational tempo, it is also due to the growing impact of long-range, prompt-strike weapons in the region.

---

6   Ministry of Foreign Affairs of Japan, 'Exchange of Letters on Hosted Payload Cooperation under the Mutual Defense Assistance Agreement between Japan and the United States of America', 15 December 2020, www.mofa.go.jp/mofaj/press/release/press3_000392.html [in Japanese]; 'Japan's Office of National Space Policy Signs Historic MOU with the US Space Force', *Space Force Public Affairs*, 18 December 2020, www.spaceforce.mil/News/Article/2451728/japans-office-of-national-space-policy-signs-historic-mou-with-the-us-space-for/.

Conventional prompt global strike (CPGS) weapons, as conceived by G. W. Bush's administration in the 2000s, were originally intended to address two related problems: first, to give the US the ability to hit targets across the globe in a short period; second, to provide a strike option that was non-nuclear. This was because, until the introduction of low-yield W76-2 warheads in the 2018 NPR, the only US prompt global strike options were intercontinental ballistic missiles (ICBMs) or submarine-launched ballistic missiles (SLBMs) with high-yield nuclear warheads. However, this challenge has not been fully resolved to date. US CPS programs that are under way have an intermediate range, and do not yet include truly global strike options.[7] This means that, even if these weapons are deployed in the near future, forward deployment will be essential to their operation. Therefore, the role of allies is critical.

The nature of intermediate-range or theatre-range CPS differs from both CPGS and the low-yield nuclear SLBM. What the low-yield SLBM and previous plans for CPGS have in common is that they are deployed in very small numbers.[8] Limited numbers of these warheads are intended to help with escalation control, especially against limited nuclear use by Russia, rather than in a counterforce strike disarming campaign against peer competitors such as Russia or China. However, unlike strategic hypersonic weapons, theatre-range hypersonic weapons will be battlefield weapons used for actual warfighting purposes.

These weapons have the potential to significantly change the strategic stability of the region. However, it should not be overlooked that China and North Korea deployed many prompt conventional strike weapons (basically, most ballistic missiles reach hypersonic speeds) before the US. This is important in considering the appropriate combination of strike and defence capabilities that the US and its allies should develop now that the Intermediate-Range Nuclear Forces Treaty is no longer in place.

---

7   In this program, the US Navy and Army will develop a shared 34.5-inch, two-stage solid rocket motor with a common hypersonic glide body, or C-HGB, but its range is expected to be around 1,400 miles (2,250 km). The US Air Force's hypersonic glide weapon program, Air-Launched Rapid Response Weapon (ARRW), also has a range of less than 575 miles (925 km). See Kelley M. Sayler, *Hypersonic Weapons: Background and Issues for Congress*, Congressional Research Service, 26 April 2021.

8   Department of Defense, *Nuclear Posture Review*, February 2018, 54, media.defense.gov/2018/Feb/02/2001872886/-1/-1/1/2018-NUCLEAR-POSTURE-REVIEW-FINAL-REPORT.PDF.

China has already deployed nearly 1,250 short and medium-range missiles and more than 500 mobile launchers as counter-power projection capabilities, and it would be impossible for the US and its allies to quickly neutralise them if a crisis happened.[9] On the other hand, China would need more than missile strikes to secure air and maritime superiority over the first island chain in a crisis. Ultimately, that would require continuous deployment of air and naval power. Therefore, to defeat the Chinese theory of victory, forward-deployed CPS weapons should be used to target Chinese air and naval bases and forces, not mobile missile launchers. Ballistic missiles (or hypersonic glide vehicles) are effective for achieving mission-kill against hard targets, even with conventional warheads. For example, if the Chinese Air Force's 3,000-metre class runways are attacked with ballistic missiles at equal intervals, they will be rendered inoperable, weakening China's offensive counter-air capabilities.[10] If the US and its allies are able to deploy deep-strike capable CPS weapons against mainland China, China would need to invest more in modernising its air defence systems to mitigate the risk. Hence, even short of use, the deployment of these systems would be an effective cost imposition strategy for the US and its allies.

However, the reaction of North Korea to such a deployment will be different from that of China. North Korea is currently estimated to have around 250 mobile missile launchers for short-range ballistic missiles and MRBMs.[11] Their production rates are uncertain, but it is almost certain that they will be able to produce medium-sized transporter erector launchers domestically, and there is no doubt that their volumes will increase until the 2030s. Also, solid-fuel missiles are comprising an increasing share of the theatre-range missile force, and the time window for identifying, targeting and destroying these systems is becoming very limited. Unlike in the Chinese case, this missile force would be the central target of allied CPS.

---

9   Department of Defense, *Military and Security Developments Involving the People's Republic of China 2020: Annual Report to Congress*, September 2020, china.usc.edu/department-defense-military-and-security-developments-involving-peoples-republic-china-2020.

10   See also the discussion below on post-INF strike options: Masashi Murano, 'The Japan–US Alliance in a Post-INF World: Building an Effective Deterrent in the Western Pacific', nippon.com, 18 December 2019; Masashi Murano, 'The Modality of Japan's Long-Range Strike Options', *Texas National Security Review*, 1 October 2020.

11   National Air and Space Intelligence Center and Defense Intelligence Ballistic Missile Analysis Committee, *Ballistic and Cruise Missile Threat*, July 2020, media.defense.gov/2021/Jan/11/2002563190/-1/-1/1/2020%20BALLISTIC%20AND%20CRUISE%20MISSILE%20THREAT_FINAL_2OCT_REDUCEDFILE.PDF.

However, it is highly unlikely that North Korea could or would develop and deploy an advanced missile defence system like the one deployed by the US and its allies, or which could be deployed by China, to counter CPS. As the US and its allies are acutely aware, the cost of acquiring and operating mid-course missile defence systems is enormous. Therefore, Pyongyang's strategic portfolio will remain focused on mobile missiles and nuclear weapons.

In short, the deployment of CPS by the US and its allies will not structurally change North Korea's strategic portfolio. Instead, its increasing number of mobile missiles will make it more costly for the US and its allies to continue investing in missile defence. In other words, the CPS needs to be positioned as a genuine denial and damage limitation option rather than as leverage to change the nature of the confrontation.

Since the 1991 Gulf War, US air-strike campaigns have been conducted primarily with fighter-based strike packages and subsonic cruise missiles, such as Tomahawk. However, it would take around an hour for a subsonic fighter or cruise missile sortie from Japan to reach North Korea. This does not lend itself to strikes that could immediately suppress mobile missiles that are at high launch readiness. Therefore, to suppress North Korea's mobile missiles, the use of ground-launched, medium-range CPS combined with advanced space-based and airborne intelligence, surveillance and reconnaissance assets should be considered. A precision-guided MRBM or hypersonic glide vehicle that could hit North Korea within minutes from Japan might solve the current problems associated with the use of aircraft or subsonic cruise missiles. Nevertheless, given the growing number of North Korea's mobile launchers, such damage limitation strikes might need to be combined with low-yield nuclear options.

Low-Yield Nuclear Weapons in North-East Asia

The 2018 NPR decided to strengthen the flexibility of US nuclear force structure, especially with the low-yield W76-2 warhead on Trident D5 SLBM. In addition, it foreshadowed the development of a new low-yield and sea-based nuclear cruise missile. The NPR described them as serving a deterrent role against Russia's 'escalate to de-escalate' strategy by non-strategic nuclear forces.[12] Yet these sea-based systems also have a global impact.

Certainly, the visibility of the airborne leg of the nuclear triad (i.e. the strategic bombers) with air-launched cruise missiles is effective as a deterrent signal. In addition, forward-deployable, dual-capable aircraft (DCA) can deliver B61 gravity bombs with low yields, which can provide the essential flexibility for tailored deterrent architecture in North-East Asia. However, as mentioned earlier, given the increase in theatre-range missile threats from North Korea and China, the US and its allies will need to re-evaluate the risks of deployment of these aerial assets to nearby forward bases in Japan, South Korea and even in Guam when military tensions rise. Since US dual-capable stealth assets are hard to detect and intercept in the air, adversaries have an incentive to use their theatre-range strike capabilities against them early in a confrontation. This is because detection and neutralisation have a much higher probability of success while such assets are on the ground.

A sea-based, survivable low-yield nuclear option has different roles and characteristics than air assets. According to the 2018 NPR, these low-yield options are not intended for nuclear warfighting, but to deter adversaries, especially Russian limited nuclear use in a conflict. However, the 2018 NPR emphasises substantial US counterforce capabilities and describes the specific tailored deterrence strategies for each country. As the nuclear forces of China and North Korea are composed mainly of road-mobile systems, it makes sense to include targets such as mobile missiles and their hardened shelters in consideration of the new capabilities, as well as Chinese air and naval forces.

In the current environment, the targets that might need immediate suppression are North Korean nuclear-tipped mobile ballistic missiles. This includes MRBMs such as the *Nodong*, *Scud*-ER (able to attack Japan), intermediate-range *Hwasong*-12 (which puts Guam within range), *Hwasong*-14/15/16 and North Korea's ICBM. In addition, North Korea has already finished developing several solid-fuel missiles, such as the *Pukguksong*-2 MRBM. A conflict on the Korean Peninsula would be a very

---

12   Department of Defense, *Nuclear Posture Review*.

challenging situation for Japan, and it is necessary to at least consider all various countermeasures, including a nuclear first-use option to suppress the North Korean mobile missile bases or the missiles themselves.

Even when considering a confrontation with China, low-yield SLBMs have an essential role. According to Indo-Pacific Command (INDOPACOM) estimates, China has already gained a significant temporal advantage over the US in terms of the forces that can be deployed into the Western Pacific in a short time.[13] Until the US and its allies can deploy sufficient CPS in the region to offset this temporal disadvantage, the prompt-strike capability of low-yield SLBM will also play a supplementary role on the escalation ladder as part of the regional deterrence architecture. Further, despite the growing precision-strike capability of its missile forces, the People's Liberation Army's continued and improved capability to 'hot-swap' conventional and nuclear warheads on the DF-26 suggests they have an 'escalate to de-escalate' strategy with nuclear weapons at the theatre level. Survivable, forward-deployable and prompt low-yield nuclear options are needed to negate China's dangerous confidence in such a strategy.

Three Recommendations for Managing Escalation in North-East Asia

As discussed in this chapter, new capabilities are essential for appropriate and flexible escalation control in a security environment in which offensive advantage is becoming more prominent. However, effective deterrence using these capabilities also requires close coordination among allies.

First, to build the denial capability needed for deterrence and prevent escalation of the conflict, it is critical that allies work together to accurately gauge the threat, assess their joint capability (with respect to targets, weapon systems, deployment sites, logistical support and so forth), identify any capability gaps that need to be filled and optimise the allocation of roles, missions and capabilities.

---

13 Mallory Shelbourne, 'US Indo-Pacific Command Wants $4.68B for New Pacific Deterrence Initiative', *USNI News*, 2 March 2021, news.usni.org/2021/03/02/u-s-indo-pacific-command-wants-4-68b-for-new-pacific-deterrence-initiative; Chris Dougherty, 'Moving Beyond A2/AD', CNAS, 3 December 2020, www.cnas.org/publications/commentary/moving-beyond-a2-ad.

Second, allies need to establish a common operational picture and a joint targeting coordination board. To manage the risk of escalation, Japan should be an active and responsible partner in the drafting and implementation of an operational plan detailing when, how and for what targets CPS and counterspace systems would be used. The Japanese Self-Defense Force's active involvement in US operational planning should also reduce the political risks of deploying US CPS systems to Japan.

Third, allies need to improve conventional-nuclear integration in the context of extended deterrence. Unlike during the Cold War, nuclear operations are no longer the responsibility of US regional combatant commands, but of Strategic Command (STRATCOM). Therefore, linking the agenda of the Extended Deterrence Dialogue with the joint operational planning process through the US–Japan Bilateral Planning Committee would seamlessly construct an escalation ladder from the grey zone to the conventional and nuclear domains, leading to more specific nuclear options for the defence of Japan. Based on these plans, it is desirable to conduct regular US–Japan joint exercises that include not only US Forces Korea and INDOPACOM, but also STRATCOM, to test assumptions and improve cooperation. In particular, the risk to forward-deployed DCA and strategic bombers at a time of crisis, the frequency of deployment of ballistic missile submarines in Guam and the use of low-yield SLBMs against time-sensitive targets, based on the necessity of their use as a prompt means of suppression of hostile missiles, should be a focus of these activities.

14

Australia's Shrinking Advantages: How Technology Might Defeat Geography

Andrew Davies

For many decades Australia's defence strategy has rested on three comparative advantages, sometimes explicitly stated and sometimes implicit.[1] First, that its strategic geography provides Australia with a significant buffer against hostile power projection. Second, that Australia's alliance with the United States provides a high level of conventional and nuclear deterrence to would-be adversaries. And third, that Australia's armed forces enjoy a significant technological advantage over those of regional nations. But economic, geopolitical and technological evolutions have diminished those comparative advantages, especially in the past decade, and the next generation of theatre and global-range weapons will only continue the trend. Australia's current strategic settings and force structure are likely to require some significant rethinking.

Australian defence planning, at least in terms of the resources allocated, has long focused on the maintenance of a 'balanced force', centred on sophisticated but traditional land, sea and air platforms. In fact, the Australian Defence Force (ADF) of today bears a striking resemblance to the force developed by the Menzies government in the 1960s.

---

1   This chapter updates and expands upon previous work the author produced for the Australian Strategic Policy Institute, including some collaborative work with Benjamin Schreer.

For much of the intervening period, that has been adequate, but, as recent Australian Government white paper assessments have noted, the strategic environment is changing for the worse. New military technologies are available to regional nations and the military power of the People's Republic of China is steadily growing. Cyberspace is already a highly contested area and allows remote attacks on Australia's military and national systems. The emergence of hypersonic strike weapons, some of which are likely to enter service this decade, will greatly reduce the safety bestowed by distance from North Asian power competitions for Australian and allied forces. It is also possible that we will see the weaponising of orbital space.

Australia's comfortable defence assumptions of the past few decades will not pertain in the future. This paper explores some of the possible impacts of new technologies on Australian defence planning and implications for the US alliance.

Geography and Australia's Links to the US

In defence planning, Australia has both benefited and suffered from its geography. Scale is a disadvantage for a nation with only the resources of a small population that has to defend across continental distances and police its jurisdiction over 10 per cent of the Earth's oceans. For example, a routine transit between fleet bases at Sydney and Fremantle represents a lengthy voyage for many European navies. Because of that, the ADF has to be structured as an expeditionary force even if the operational focus is limited to local operations.

But the huge distances of the Pacific theatre have also worked heavily in Australia's favour in the past, in two different but complementary ways: its long approaches complicate adversary logistic planning, and its location is a useful secure base for operations further afield. During World War II, imperial Japan was unable to muster the capability to project power across a hemisphere to overwhelm Australia, despite having swept through South-East Asia with few difficulties. In those days of industrial warfare, when massed forces were required to deliver a strategic effect, Australia was distant enough from Japan's centres of power to mean that an invasion was never seriously considered. The air attacks that did take place, from land bases in the archipelago supplemented by the occasional foray from naval aircraft, amounted to little more than nuisance value, being much less intense than air attacks in the European theatre or in those parts of Asia where forces could be concentrated at ranges suited to the platforms of the day.

Precisely because of the strategic sanctuary provided by its geographical separation from the centres of power in North Asia, Australia has long been seen by strategists in the US as an important staging point for its own strategic projection capability. In 1911, naval strategist Alfred Thayer Mahan wrote that the sea lines of communication between a rapidly developing west coast of North America and Australia would give the US a foothold even when Asian powers (particularly Japan after its defeat of Russia in 1905) held sway further north:

> *The Western Pacific will remain Asiatic, as it should* ... The question awaiting and approaching solution is the line of demarcation between the Asiatic and European elements in the Pacific. The considerations advanced appear to indicate that it will be that joining Puget Sound and Vancouver with Australia.[2]

Mahan's assessment was vindicated in the first year of the Pacific War. When planning for the war against Japan after the initial setbacks at Pearl Harbor and the Philippines, the US Joint Chiefs of Staff came to the conclusion that the:

> Entire Allied strategy in the Pacific depended on two cardinal points: Hawaii must not fall, and Australia must not fall ... the new Pacific Fleet chief, Admiral Nimitz, [was ordered] to secure the seaways between Midway, Hawaii and the North American mainland. That was to be his first priority. The second, in only a 'small degree less important' was to protect the lifeline between North America and Australia ... By those means the allied war machine would be built up in Australasia.[3]

Australia's geography again offered advantages to the US during the Cold War, though this time the attraction was more to do with the ability to extend the US and Five Eyes' global command, control, communications, computers, intelligence, surveillance and reconnaissance (C4ISR) capability, manifested in joint facilities located on Australian soil.

---

2   A.T. Mahan, 'The Panama Canal and Sea Power in the Pacific', *Century Magazine*, June 1911. Reprinted in *Armaments and Arbitration* (New York: Garland Publishing, 1972).

3   Ian W. Toll, *Pacific Crucible: War at Sea in the Pacific 1941–42* (New York: W. W. Norton & Co., 2012), 182.

In the absence of a credible regional peer adversary, the US Navy had virtually free rein in the Western Pacific after the Vietnam War. In that environment, Australia's defence outlook was benign. With the possible exception of Singapore, Australia fielded the most sophisticated military forces in the region and faced no potential adversaries with effective power projection capabilities.

But that was a somewhat artificial situation in the immediate aftermath of World War II and the post-colonial upheavals that followed. Because Asian economies enjoyed a period of high average economic growth and much greater internal stability (with a few exceptions) from the 1990s on, the region could afford militaries with modern platforms and capabilities, including air and maritime forces providing power projection beyond borders, rather than predominantly inwardly focused land forces.

Pre-eminent among Asia's resurgent military capability is China. The People's Liberation Army (PLA) has developed a formidable-looking—though untested in practice—anti-access/area denial (A2/AD) posture, and is now starting in earnest to develop a blue water power projection capability centred on aircraft carrier task groups and nuclear-powered submarines. China's A2/AD posture is designed to keep foreign powers, especially the US, at a distance. As a result, today's power relativities resemble the Asia that Mahan saw when looking west a century ago. Though not yet the case, it is now conceivable that Washington will, in the future, come to judge that the Western Pacific will again be 'Asiatic' rather than its own sphere of influence.

A corollary is that the more contested space of North Asia has once again raised the value of Australia's geographical position in the eyes of its major ally. A 2015 joint study by The Australian National University's Strategic and Defence Studies Centre and the Center for Strategic and International Studies (CSIS) observed that:

> Australia's geographic location is more important to the United States today than it has been at any time since the Second World War. Australia serves both as a link between the Indian and Pacific Oceans and as a sanctuary from China's anti-access/area denial capabilities.[4]

---

4   Michael J. Green, Peter J. Dean, Brendan Taylor and Zack Cooper, *The ANZUS Alliance in an Ascending Asia*, SDSC Centre of Gravity series, July 2015, sdsc.bellschool.anu.edu.au/sites/default/files/publications/attachments/2015-12/COG_%2323_Web_4.pdf.

That conclusion is supported by an analysis of China's missile capabilities by the Missile Defense Project at CSIS. The number, type and range of Chinese missiles based along its coastline, including ballistic and cruise missile systems, provide effective coverage of its maritime approaches as far as the east coast of Japan. Beyond that, hundreds of medium-range ballistic missiles cover much of the South China Sea and Indonesia as far south as Jakarta.[5] Submarine-launched weapons or launchers forward deployed on features in the South China Sea effectively extend that range to cover Australia's northern approaches.

The enduring presence of one or more Western powers in its strategic approaches is an affront to the Chinese Government—the 'century of humiliation' at the hands of Western powers looms large in Chinese strategic thinking. Consequently, Beijing is serious about its intentions to be able to deny its extended approaches to what it termed in its 2008 defence white paper 'strategic manoeuvres and containment from the outside' (a phrase echoed many times since).[6] In fact, the Chinese military first articulated 'active off-shore defense' as PLA Navy doctrine in 1985.[7] Decades of consistent double-digit GDP growth have allowed it to manifest that concept as a force in being.

The US has a few possible responses. It can double down on its posture and harden its forward-deployed forces within range of Chinese weapons, it can pull back at least some of those forces to safer locations or it can cede strategic ground to China. In practice, it has done a little of all those, while developing new concepts for operations in an A2/AD environment, such as the 'Air-Sea Battle Concept' and its subsequent evolutions.[8] Not surprisingly, an increased presence in Australia—though only modest so far—has featured in some recent US force posture initiatives. A greater footprint in Australia is a rational response to the growth in China's power projection and strike capabilities over the past 20 years. If nothing else, keeping beyond the range of the many short to medium-range weapons greatly reduces the chance of a debilitating strike in the early stages of a conflict.

---

5   Missile Defense Project, 'Missiles of China', *Missile Threat*, Center for Strategic and International Studies, 14 June 2018, missilethreat.csis.org/country/china/.

6   *China's National Defense in 2008*, Information Office of the State Council of the People's Republic of China, 20 January 2009, www.china.org.cn/government/whitepaper/node_7060059.htm.

7   Alexander Chieh-cheng Huang, 'The Chinese Navy's Offshore Active Defense Strategy: Conceptualization and Implications', *Naval War College Review* 47(3), 1994, 7–32.

8   Jan van Tol, Mark Gunzinger, Andrew F. Krepinevich and Jim Thomas, 'AirSea Battle: A Point-of-Departure Operational Concept', Center for Strategic and Budgetary Assessments, 18 May 2010, csbaonline.org/research/publications/airsea-battle-concept.

From an Australian perspective, providing a safe harbour for US forces also bolsters our own position, as any hostility projected towards Australia would necessarily engage the US as well. As it has done in the past, the strategic geography of the region has pushed Australian and US interests together. However, it is not clear that the current advantages are sustainable. For reasons explained below, today's alliance posture may be at best meta-stable, and the refuge provided by geography might not be as enduring as we hope. Developments in technology continue to effectively shrink the world, while national interests and vulnerabilities in cyberspace and space transcend terrestrial geography.

The Future—Australia's Defence in a Shrinking World

The above discussion is very much couched in terms of traditional military platforms such as ships, submarines and aircraft. If the only defence problems were the protection of territory and sea lines of communication, as was the case during industrial-age warfare, that might be an adequate view. But today's world also places a high value on information, making cyberspace an important arena of competition between nations.

There is no doubt that attacks in cyberspace can be extremely damaging, as Estonia's experience in 2007 showed. But defence against cyber attack is also possible, and arguably the window of early opportunities to exploit and attack underprepared national-level cyber architecture has largely closed (though the wider economy is likely still vulnerable). While some once talked up the possibility of a hugely damaging cyber strike—a 'cyber Pearl Harbor' in the language of former US Secretary of Defense Leon Panetta[9]—others argued against such a dramatic take, suggesting that cyber activities are a new manifestation of the age-old practices of espionage, subversion and sabotage.[10] The latter view is consistent with the observations of constant background cyber activity, including espionage, the probing of systems and the conduct of information operations (such as Russia's manipulation of a section of the US public during the 2016 presidential election). That said, the lack of an example

---

9   Leon E. Panetta, 'Remarks by Secretary Panetta on Cybersecurity to the Business Executives for National Security', New York City, 11 October 2012, www.hsdl.org/?view&did=724128.
10   Thomas Rid, 'Cyber War Will Not Take Place', *Journal of Strategic Studies* 35(1), 2012, 5–32, doi.org/10.1080/01402390.2011.608939.

of a massive and dramatically damaging cyber strike is not necessarily comforting; the successful erosion of democratic norms is potentially as damaging to Western states in the longer term. While Australia and the US have similar interests in minimising the harm done by hostile actors in cyberspace, geography does nothing to help against such attacks.

More pertinently for questions of hard defence, it seems increasingly possible that there will be a significant weaponisation of space in the next couple of decades. Space has been an arena for communications, intelligence gathering and surveillance activities since the 1960s. The advantages of hosting ground stations in Australia have been a net positive for Australia in providing value to the US. To date, space has not been a potential source of conventional kinetic strikes. But that could change; though the deployment of nuclear weapons in orbit has long been outlawed by treaty, several nations are developing a new generation of conventionally armed, global-range hypersonic strike weapons, some of which could be pre-deployed in orbit.[11]

There are two broad classes of hypersonic weapon systems of relevance to the discussion here: vehicles that re-enter from orbit and air-breathing cruise missiles.[12] As an example of the former, the Pentagon's research and development program includes a 'common glide vehicle'—a hypersonic re-entry vehicle—at the centre of its conventional prompt global strike program.[13] The aim of the program, as the name suggests, is to provide the US with the capability of rapidly delivering conventional weapons anywhere on Earth—within tens of minutes. Hypersonic glide vehicles could be either first boosted into orbit from terrestrial launchers before re-entry or pre-deployed in orbit to provide a shorter response time. They are intended to augment existing conventional strike capabilities that require launch platforms to first manoeuvre within firing range, and thus potentially be exposed to A2/AD systems. As well, ephemeral mobile

---

11 *Treaty on Principles Governing the Activities of States in the Exploration and Use of Outer Space, including the Moon and Other Celestial Bodies*, United Nations Res. 2222 (XXI), 1966, www.unoosa. org/oosa/en/ourwork/spacelaw/treaties/outerspacetreaty.html.

12 For an overview of hypersonic systems and some of the strategic issues they raise, see Andrew Davies, 'Coming Ready or Not: Hypersonic Weapons', Australian Strategic Policy Institute, 23 March 2021, www.aspi.org.au/report/coming-ready-or-not-hypersonic-weapons.

13 *Conventional Prompt Global Strike and Long-Range Ballistic Missiles: Background and Issues* (Washington: Congressional Research Service, 14 February 2020), crsreports.congress.gov/product/pdf/R/R41464.

targets such as road-mobile launchers have proven extremely difficult to effectively target in the past. Prompt-strike capabilities that shrink the time between detection and a weapon on target offer a possible remedy.

The US has no monopoly on such systems and, in fact, may lag behind others in some respects. Russian leader Vladimir Putin has boasted of Russian systems with global capabilities—though it is not clear how seriously to take some of his wilder claims, such as a global-range nuclear-powered weapon. China has also been active in developing hypersonic glide vehicles, including integrating them on to its existing ballistic missile launchers.[14] Chinese weapons are perhaps of more immediate concern for Australia's defence planning, although truly global strike capabilities mean that vital US C4ISR facilities located in Australia could be targeted early in a European conflict, for example.

In a different category, hypersonic cruise weapons offer fast strike capabilities over similar ranges to short and intermediate-range ballistic missiles—between 500 and 5,000 kilometres. According to a study by the Center for Strategic Budgetary Assessment in Washington, intermediate-range hypersonic glide or cruise weapons are competitive with intermediate-range ballistic missiles in both range and expected development cost. They also potentially offer better capability, being harder to detect and more manoeuvrable, so they travel on less predictable trajectories in the terminal phase and can approach targets from multiple directions.[15] Again, the US is only one of several active players in the area, and many observers expect operational hypersonic cruise weapons to be fielded by China, Russia and the US before the decade is out. There are considerable strategic destabilisation risks that come with those developments; they raise (and sometimes exacerbate) the same issues that led to the negotiation of the Intermediate-Range Nuclear Forces Treaty during the latter stages of the Cold War. The US Congressional Research Service has suggested that treaty arrangements

---

14 Mike Yeo et al., 'Hypersonic and Directed-Energy Weapons: Who Has Them, and Who's Winning the Race in the Asia-Pacific?', *Defense News*, 15 March 2021, www.defensenews.com/global/asia-pacific/2021/03/15/hypersonic-and-directed-energy-weapons-who-has-them-and-whos-winning-the-race-in-the-asia-pacific/.

15 Jacob Cohn et al., 'Leveling the Playing Field: Reintroducing US Theatre-Range Missiles in a Post-INF World', Center for Strategic and Budgetary Assessments, 19 May 2019, csbaonline.org/research/publications/leveling-the-playing-field-reintroducing-us-theater-range-missiles-in-a-post-INF-world.

to deal with hypersonic weapons might be desirable to help manage the escalatory issues that could arise, but there seems to be little enthusiasm for such discussions.

Weapons with ranges of 2,000 kilometres or more deployed as part of China's A2/AD force posture would effectively negate the buffer of distance for bases and facilities in the north of Australia. Prompt global strike weapons would almost negate the advantages of geography entirely. For the ADF there would be one upside to the availability of such weapons, given that it has lacked the ability to strike targets at distances much beyond 500 kilometres since the retirement of the F-111 bomber. Intermediate-range hypersonic cruise weapons might prove attractive as a way to reinstate that capability. But even that would need careful consideration. The strategic need that drove the 1960s decision to acquire the F-111 was the risk of aggression from Indonesia, to be countered by the ability to strike targets as far away as Jakarta, with no Indonesian capability of responding in kind. Today's environment is quite different, and the logic of a technological imbalance between Australia and Indonesia simply does not apply to China. If Australia (either with or without US cooperation) was to pursue an intermediate-range strike capability as part of a deterrence posture, China could respond in kind and forward deploy its own systems—perhaps to the South China Sea—to be able to rapidly strike Australian targets. A widespread proliferation of hypersonic weapons (or even intermediate-range ballistic weapons) would go a long way to eroding Australia's geographical advantage.

***

For much of the second half of the twentieth century, the prevailing military paradigm was that territorial integrity was by far the most vital interest to be protected through military force. Australia's defence planners have long been able to take comfort in the fact that force projection against the nation is formidably difficult due to the distances involved. And that calculus improves when augmented by a major power alliance that raises the stakes even higher for a would-be adversary. Not that there was much power projection capability—or even much in the way of sophisticated forces of any kind—to worry about in Australia's part of the world until recently. The net result is an ADF that has long been centred on a small number of high-performance (and expensive) platforms. It is a force designed to deal with any likely threat from South-East Asia, run independent operations in its local neighbourhood and have enough expeditionary capability to make real contributions to coalition operations with its major ally, the US.

The days in which that was enough, and the right type of, capability are rapidly coming to an end. US hegemony has been good for Australia, but it is now coming under challenge. Technological advantages are being rapidly eroded—and may not exist at all in some strategically important emerging technologies. We are currently in a transition period between US dominance and the US having to contemplate operating against a near-peer adversary in the Pacific theatre—a situation it has not experienced for 80 years. Australia's value to the Australia, New Zealand, United States Security Treaty (ANZUS) alliance depends in part on geography, and Australia's location and geographical separation from North Asia still provide some natural advantages. But, like the technological gap, those advantages are diminishing. In the absence of international conventions that limit the proliferation of new weapon technologies, the ability for an adversary to strike at Australia's core military capabilities and national infrastructure will increase markedly. It is possible that Australia will be able to establish a sort of détente, possibly by deploying similar systems itself, and probably in cooperation with the US. But, at best, it will certainly require some different thinking about the way in which Australia approaches its defence planning. At worst, it may also significantly diminish the geographic value that Australia has had for its main ally.

Part IV: Bringing the Public Along: Talking about Nuclear Weapons and Deterrence

15

Non-Nuclear Allies and Declaratory Policy: The NATO Experience

Michael Rühle

Extended nuclear deterrence, being the willingness of the United States to commit nuclear weapons to the defence of its allies, has become a central pillar of the international order. Today, over 30 countries in Europe and the Asia-Pacific region are considered to be under the US 'nuclear umbrella'. Critics of this concept often assert that the US would never risk its own destruction in order to protect its allies. Yet, despite this inherent credibility dilemma, the US and its allies consider this arrangement to be of existential importance. As Lawrence Freedman observes, nuclear weapons 'can have a deterrent effect well beyond their logical limits'.[1] By explicitly extending its nuclear (and conventional) deterrence to other countries, Washington sends a powerful signal that it regards their security as a fundamental national security interest.[2]

---

1   Lawrence Freedman, 'Disarmament and Other Nuclear Norms', *Washington Quarterly* 36(2), 2013, 102, doi.org/10.1080/0163660X.2013.791085.
2   Moreover, the 'nuclear umbrella' also relieves allies from the need to develop nuclear weapons of their own. While the causality between extended deterrence and non-proliferation is sometimes questioned, some cases demonstrate that US allies who felt abandoned by Washington had started nuclear programs, only to halt them once relations with the US had recovered. See Rebecca K.C. Hersman and Robert Peters, 'Nuclear U-Turns: Learning from South Korean and Taiwanese Rollback', *Nonproliferation Review* 13(3), November 2006, 539–53, doi.org/10.1080/10736700601071629.

The specific implementation of US extended nuclear deterrence commitments varies considerably. In the Asia-Pacific region, Washington maintains bilateral relationships with like-minded but diverse democracies such as Australia and Japan. In Europe, by contrast, Washington's nuclear relationships are largely managed through the North Atlantic Treaty Organization (NATO), an alliance of currently 30 countries with a longstanding shared 'culture' of nuclear cooperation and planning. These different regional approaches are also reflected in nuclear declaratory policy. Whereas NATO statements are negotiated among 30 allies, pronouncements on nuclear matters in the Indo-Pacific region reflect the individual nature of each bilateral relationship. However, despite these differences, the basic challenges surrounding nuclear declaratory policy are quite similar. Based on NATO's experience, which dates back over seven decades, this chapter seeks to identify the most pertinent challenges.

The Multi-Directional Character of Declaratory Policy

Political declarations on security matters, whether issued by individual governments or by coalitions of states, usually have several recipients: one's own political elites; one's broader population; one's (real and potential) opponents; and—in the case of the US—one's allies benefiting from extended deterrence protection, including their political elites and publics.[3] Ideally, each of these addressees would understand the message exactly as its originators intended. The political elites would be reassured that 'radical departures in policy have been avoided and that no commitments have been made to anything that will cause upset at home or, even worse, require extra funds'.[4] The broader population, it may be hoped, would come away with the comforting feeling that their security was being taken care of. The allies would be reassured about the continued US commitment to their security. And the opponents would be impressed—and deterred—by a strong sign of national or collective resolve. In practice, however, these lines are often blurred.

---

3   On the complexity of US extended deterrence messaging, see Brad Roberts, *The Case for US Nuclear Weapons in the 21st Century* (Stanford: Stanford University Press, 2015), 214–34, doi.org/10.1515/9780804797153.

4   Lawrence Freedman, *The Primacy of Alliance: Deterrence and European Security*, Proliferation Papers No. 46, March–April 2013, www.ifri.org/sites/default/files/atoms/files/pp46freedman.pdf.

As far as alliances such as NATO are concerned, the major goal of such a communications exercise is not the exposition of military-strategic detail, but rather the mutual reaffirmation of the alliance's broader purpose and, above all, unity. The German term '*Selbstvergewisserung*' (slightly awkwardly translated as 'self-assurance') perhaps captures it best: for an alliance of 30 countries, with governments from across the entire political spectrum, unity is the most precious asset. More than any specific instruments of military power, it is the political power of a cohesive coalition of like-minded states that serves as the ultimate key to security. This is not to say that military questions are merely an afterthought; however, they must never be seen to dominate (and possibly derail) regular alliance business.

This primacy of alliance unity over military posture is particularly obvious when it comes to nuclear matters. After all, it is here that asymmetries among allies—in terms of military power but also in terms of status—are most obvious, and where even a small rhetorical misstep by one ally can cause massive damage to alliance cohesion. As the history of NATO has amply demonstrated, what may come across as a statement of resolve designed to impress an opponent and thus strengthen nuclear deterrence may also incite fear and antagonism among one's own population. For an alliance that features three nuclear powers (who are also permanent members of the United Nations Security Council) and 27 non-nuclear states, agreeing on proclamations on nuclear matters is sometimes akin to walking on eggshells.

The NATO allies' careful stance when it comes to public declarations on nuclear matters is not the result of an assumed blanket anti-nuclear bias among their own populations. While numerous opinion polls suggest that such a bias does indeed exist, the respondents' answers are highly dependent on the wording of the questions asked by the pollsters and are thus of little value in terms of guiding established policy.[5] Even in countries with strong anti-nuclear civil society groups that have made nuclear weapons a prominent election issue, nuclear weapons are not an issue that, in themselves, would be the determining factor in election outcomes.

---

5   See Thomas W. Graham, *American Public Opinion on NATO, Extended Deterrence, and Use of Nuclear Weapons: Future or Fission?* (Lanham: University Press of America, 1989). Graham notes that, when it comes to nuclear weapons, people often hold multiple contradictory beliefs. On the rise and fall of the US Freeze Movement in the 1980s, see J. Michael Hogan, *The Nuclear Freeze Campaign: Rhetoric and Foreign Policy in the Telepolitical Age* (East Lansing: Michigan State University Press, 1994). For an overview of the cultural context of nuclear weapons and nuclear energy, see Spencer R. Weart, *The Rise of Nuclear Fear* (Cambridge: Harvard University Press, 2012).

Other factors, such as the economy, matter much more.[6] However, as has been demonstrated many times, within NATO as well as within the Australia, New Zealand, United States Security Treaty (ANZUS), nuclear weapons can become an issue for domestic political skirmishes and party politics.[7] Hence, the major reason for the care exerted by allies in their public pronouncements is the desire to offer no cause for—inadvertent or deliberate—misunderstandings that could result in political disputes.[8]

The Nuclear Paradox

Nuclear weapons represent the ultimate paradox. Their enormous destructive power makes their use potentially suicidal, yet it is precisely these possible disastrous consequences that exercise restraint on the behaviour of states. Thus, while the nuclear age has seen many conventional wars, no nuclear powers have used nuclear weapons against each other. Nuclear deterrence cannot prevent every kind of war, but it is always present when existential issues are at stake. As former US defence secretary James Schlesinger observed, in this sense, nuclear weapons are being 'used' every day.[9] NATO, for its part, has repeatedly stated that as long as nuclear weapons exist, it will remain a nuclear alliance.[10]

---

6   This is not to say that nuclear weapons per se are not an important factor in elections. See, for example: Ian McAllister and Anthony Mughan, 'The Nuclear Weapons Issue in the 1983 British General Election', *European Journal of Political Research* 14, 1986, 651–67, doi.org/10.1111/j.1475-6765.1986.tb00854.x.

7   On the demise of ANZUS due to a change of government in one member state, see Gerald Hensley, *Friendly Fire: Nuclear Politics and the Collapse of ANZUS, 1984–1987* (Auckland: Auckland University Press, 2013).

8   In addition to communiqués, speeches and other statements, high-level NATO officials can also send political messages to specific audiences. For example, when a debate started to heat up in Germany over that country's continued participation in nuclear-sharing arrangements, the NATO secretary general published an article in a major German daily that underlined Germany's crucial role. See Jens Stoltenberg, 'Germany's Support for Nuclear Sharing is Vital to Protect Peace and Freedom', NATO, 11 May 2020, www.nato.int/cps/en/natohq/opinions_175663.htm?selectedLocale=en, originally published by *Frankfurter Allgemeine Zeitung*.

9   See Melanie Kirkpatrick, 'Why We Don't Want a Nuclear-Free World', *Wall Street Journal*, 13 July 2009, www.wsj.com/articles/SB124726489588925407.

10   The term 'nuclear alliance' was first used in NATO's 2010 Strategic Concept, see *Strategic Concept for the Defence and Security of the Members of the North Atlantic Treaty Organization, adopted by Heads of State and Government at the NATO Summit in Lisbon 19–20 November 2010*, NATO, www.nato.int/strategic-concept/pdf/Strat_Concept_web_en.pdf. However, a few months earlier, Hillary Clinton, then US secretary of state, said at a meeting of NATO foreign ministers in Tallinn:

We should recognize that as long as nuclear weapons exist, NATO will remain a nuclear alliance
… As a nuclear alliance, sharing nuclear risks and responsibilities widely is fundamental.

Quoted in Mark Landler, 'US Resists Push by Allies for Tactical Nuclear Cuts', *The New York Times*, 22 April 2010, www.nytimes.com/2010/04/23/world/europe/23diplo.html.

Orthodox Western security policy seeks to utilise the destructive potential of nuclear weapons to prevent war. This task is considered rather easy when it comes to protecting the homeland of a nuclear power, as nuclear retaliation in the face of an existential threat appears credible. By contrast, extending nuclear deterrence protection to non-nuclear allies is a much more complex matter, since their security is not necessarily essential for the survival of the protector. Extended nuclear deterrence is therefore burdened with perennial doubts as to its credibility. This dilemma was perhaps best captured by Denis Healey, the United Kingdom's minister for defence in 1964–70, in what he termed the 'Healey Theorem': 'It takes only five per cent credibility of American retaliation to deter the Russians, but ninety-five per cent credibility to reassure the Europeans'.[11]

To minimise the uncertainties associated with the concept of extended nuclear deterrence, the non-nuclear ally seeking nuclear protection will try to obtain an ironclad commitment by its nuclear guarantor that the latter will be willing and able to use nuclear weapons in defence of its ally. By contrast, the nuclear protector will seek to minimise any risk of becoming entrapped in any kind of escalatory automatism and will thus try to protect its autonomous decision-making. In the same vein, while the non-nuclear ally will seek commitments from its protector that a military response to an act of aggression will be swift and decisive, the protector will want to preserve a degree of flexibility to contemplate its actions and assess their potential consequences.

Despite sometimes long and controversial debates among allies, this inherent tension between the expectations of the non-nuclear allies and the hesitation of the US to satisfy them in full could never be completely resolved. However, in the late 1960s, a workable compromise was finally agreed upon: US nuclear weapons in Europe would reinforce the credibility of the US commitment, while European delivery means and a newly created Nuclear Planning Group would address the European desire to exert influence on US nuclear planning.[12] These nuclear-sharing arrangements would also ease European, notably West German, worries with regard to signing the Treaty on the Non-Proliferation of Nuclear Weapons (NPT): the very notion of 'sharing' would qualify the NPT's

---

11 Denis Healey, *The Time of My Life* (London: Michael Joseph, 1989), 243.
12 See Timothy Andrews Sayle, 'A Nuclear Education: The Origins of NATO's Nuclear Planning Group', *Journal of Strategic Studies* 43(6–7), 2020, 920–56, doi.org/10.1080/01402390.2020.18185 60. Also see the contribution of Alexander Mattelaer in this volume.

inherently discriminatory character by suggesting, at least in intent, a tendency towards equalising the status of allies. In conformity with the logic of the NPT, the US would retain control of its nuclear arsenal, yet European allies would participate in the nuclear mission, both materially and conceptually.[13]

Deterrence versus Reassurance

The intra-alliance debates that led to these compromises were sometimes fierce, but they never fully made it into the public discussions. This changed in the late 1970s, when certain procurement decisions by NATO and individual governments became the subject of intense public scrutiny—and opposition. US plans to deploy a new type of nuclear weapon in West Germany had to be cancelled due to political and party resistance in Bonn as well as public concerns. While the controversy about the 'neutron bomb' was largely a bilateral US–West German affair, the use of slogans and imagery to exploit perennial nuclear fears turned out to be a harbinger of a much more severe controversy that followed shortly thereafter and led to a major crisis in the Western alliance: NATO's so-called dual-track decision of December 1979.[14]

The NATO allies, worried about the deployment of a new category of Soviet 'Eurostrategic' nuclear missiles that might challenge the nuclear 'coupling' across the Atlantic, decided to deploy their own new nuclear missiles in this range category. Even though this decision was eventually combined with an arms control offer to Moscow, NATO's 'dual-track' decision led to a crisis that still shapes NATO's cautious approach to nuclear matters. For the first time in decades, issues of nuclear deterrence, including the consequences of the employment of nuclear weapons, were discussed by a broader public that appeared totally unprepared. Already worried by the breakdown of détente in general, and careless talk by members of the Reagan administration about a 'winnable' nuclear war in particular, many Europeans became outright afraid of an impending war that would engulf Europe while sparing the 'sanctuaries' of the Soviet

---

13   France is not—and has never been—a member of the Nuclear Planning Group.
14   Kristina Spohr Readman, 'Germany and the Politics of the Neutron Bomb, 1975–1979', *Diplomacy & Statecraft* 21(2), 2010, 259–85, doi.org/10.1080/09592296.2010.482473.

Union and the US.[15] This debate revealed, in the words of British military historian Michael Howard, that the focus of Western governments on acquiring new military capabilities to restore deterrence had led them to lose sight of the political imperative of reassuring their own publics.[16]

This discussion need not be reviewed in detail.[17] However, it generated several key lessons that still determine NATO's approach to the handling of the nuclear dossier. The first lesson was that an extensive public debate on nuclear deterrence should be avoided. A rational discussion on nuclear employment options may be possible among like-minded experts, but no Western government should expect that its broader constituency would be willing to buy into the logic of 'deliberate escalation', 'limited nuclear employment' or similar intellectual constructs. As NATO's dual-track crisis vividly demonstrated, while the basic logic of deterrence is not difficult to grasp, public agreement with established policies tends to wane the more detailed the policy rationale becomes. With this backdrop, the 'democratization of national security issues' is but a euphemism for acrimonious debates that could jeopardise allied cohesion.[18]

The second lesson was that a debate over nuclear security was not just a debate between NATO governments and their publics, but also included the Soviet Union as well as Western 'counter-experts' who challenged NATO nuclear orthodoxy and often reinforced Moscow's arguments.[19] Moreover, some citizens of Western nations were susceptible to Soviet threats, in particular to Moscow's claim that any newly deployed US ballistic missiles or cruise missiles, due to their alleged 'first strike

---

15 For an excellent overview, see David S. Yost, 'The Delegitimization of Nuclear Deterrence?', *Armed Forces and Society* 16(4), Summer 1990, 487–508. For a detailed discussion on the various protest movements and their beliefs, see Benjamin Ziemann, 'A Quantum of Solace? European Peace Movements during the Cold War and their Elective Affinities', *Archiv für Sozialgeschichte* 49, 2009, 351–89.

16 See Michael Howard, 'Reassurance and Deterrence: Western Defence in the 1980s', *Foreign Affairs* 61, 1982–83, 311.

17 For an overview, see Stephanie Freeman, 'The Making of an Accidental Crisis: The United States and the NATO Dual-Track Decision of 1979', *Diplomacy & Statecraft* 25, 2014, 331–55, doi.org/10.1080/09592296.2014.907071; Josef Joffe, 'Peace and Populism: Why the European Anti-Nuclear Movement Failed', *International Security* 11(4), Spring 1987, 3–40, doi.org/10.2307/2538836. On the Dutch 'Hollanditis', see Ruud van Dijk, 'A Mass Psychosis: The Netherlands and NATO's Dual-Track Decision, 1978–1979', *Cold War History* 12(3), 2012, 381–405, doi.org/10.1080/14682745.2011.621750.

18 Richard Flickinger, 'Public Opinion: The Peace Movement and NATO Missile Deployment', *Peace & Change* 9(1), 1983, 26.

19 See the exchange between Jeffrey Herf, Gert Krell, Harald Müller and Matthew Evangelista in: 'Correspondence', *International Security* 11(2), 1986, 193–215, doi.org/10.2307/2538966.

capabilities', would inevitably become the initial targets of a Soviet strike. NATO governments, parliamentarians and military experts were forced to engage in public debates on detailed nuclear scenarios, in which the political character of the East–West competition got lost. Soviet leaders had sensed correctly that raising the spectre of 'Euroshima' would divert attention away from systemic differences between open and closed societies. In short, with 'mutual survival' becoming the key concern, the East–West relationship became de-politicised.

The third, and in many ways most painful, lesson was that nuclear fears trumped alliance politics. The whole point of NATO's dual-track decision—namely, to prevent a 'de-coupling' of Europe from the US—almost disappeared in the heated debate. Instead, the US, the main provider of extended nuclear deterrence for NATO Europe, was criticised as 'trigger happy', while the Soviet Union, which had caused the entire predicament through its massive conventional and nuclear force modernisation program, was seen by many as a victim of US belligerence. Instead of appreciating NATO as a security blanket, citizens of alliance nations perceived NATO as a political-military straitjacket that held the European member states hostage to American omnipotent fantasies.[20] Even if the crisis ultimately had a happy ending—Moscow finally accepted Western proposals, resulting in the historic 1987 Intermediate-Range Nuclear Forces (INF) Treaty that banned this entire weapon category— allied governments had learned that a public discussion on the nuclear dossier risked becoming emotionally and politically counterproductive and, hence, had to be avoided. The price they had to pay for ending this episode—namely, to allow arms control to trump nuclear strategy considerations—was considerable, but seemed tolerable.[21]

These lessons remain valid and have been assimilated—consciously or subconsciously—by NATO allies. For example, in 2019, Russian violations of the INF Treaty by deploying a new missile type were met with a response that was measured both in tone and in substance. Rather than espousing a 'tit-for-tat' logic, which would have called for NATO's deployment of similar ground-based nuclear-capable missile systems, the allies declared that they would respond with a range of

---

20 See Andreas Lutsch, 'Merely "Docile Self-Deception"? German Experiences with Nuclear Consultation in NATO', *Journal of Strategic Studies* 39, 2016, 535–58, doi.org/10.1080/01402390. 2016.1168014.
21 See Andreas Lutsch, 'The Zero Option and NATO's Dual-Track Decision: Rethinking the Paradox', *Journal of Strategic Studies* 43(6–7), 2020, 27, doi.org/10.1080/01402390.2020.1814259.

non-nuclear measures.[22] While the Russian deployments were not yet on a numerical par with the SS-20 deployments in the late 1970s, NATO's response nipped any potential controversy in the bud.

Signalling

Some observers have argued that NATO's declaratory statements are too anodyne to allow for internal strategy development, let alone serious signalling towards potential opponents, pointing to 'a disconnect between agreed-upon, but ambiguous, policy statements, and precise and doctrinal direction necessary to guide action, a significant "gap"'.[23] Others point to what they believe to be inconsistencies in NATO's messaging—for example, by declaring that NATO's nuclear posture is adequate even while agreeing that the state of European security had changed for the worse.[24]

However, such criticism reveals a fundamental misunderstanding of intra-alliance dynamics. For example, to believe that NATO would publicly declare that Russia's illegal annexation of Crimea in spring 2014 had rendered NATO's nuclear policy and posture inadequate, requiring a fundamental overhaul of this delicate dossier, reflects a simplistic—if common—expectation that the allies would stand to benefit from making such pronouncements. NATO's experience suggests the exact opposite. If changes in the strategic environment occur, one may indeed need to start reviewing certain established policies; however, given the potential difficulties (and the prospective long time frame for enacting change), the first (and most important) response vis-a-vis the public must be to reassure, not to alarm.[25]

---

22 See Rose Gottemoeller, 'NATO Nuclear Policy in a Post-INF World', Speech by NATO Deputy Secretary General at the University of Oslo, 9 September 2019, www.nato.int/cps/en/natohq/opinions_168602.htm?selectedLocale=en.

23 Andrew Corbett and Annamarie Bindenagel Šehović, *Acculturation of the Core Concepts of European Security*, NATO Science and Technology Organization, SAS-141.

24 For example, Karl-Heinz Kamp notes that NATO's 2012 Deterrence and Defence Posture Review described NATO's nuclear posture as 'adequate', yet even a game-changing event such as Russia's illegal annexation of Crimea in 2014 had not changed NATO's evaluation. See Karl-Heinz Kamp, 'Nuclear Reorientation of NATO', *NATO Defense College Commentary*, 5 February 2018, www.ndc.nato.int/download/downloads.php?icode=537.

25 Military details are principally dealt with in classified follow-on documents. By the same token, changes in NATO's nuclear planning and posture—such as changing alert levels and exercise scenarios, providing non-nuclear support for nuclear missions or the procurement of new dual-capable aircraft—proceed without detailed references in public documents. However, many of them are known through certain think tanks and other non-governmental sources.

NATO nuclear declaratory policy may indeed be fairly general, with certain key phrases being repeated literally for decades. However, while the most cryptic parts of this esoteric communication among allies need to be 'decoded',[26] it is not too difficult to identify elements of change and gauge their political meaning. One example was the characterisation of nuclear weapons as 'weapons of last resort'[27] in the 1990 London Summit Declaration. This new terminology was seen by some as risky, as it could have been read as a substantial downgrading of nuclear weapons and nuclear deterrence.[28] Accordingly, the term 'last resort' did not appear in subsequent declarations. However, in retrospect, the choice of the term at this specific historical juncture appears prescient: to persuade Moscow not to try to arrest the political changes that were happening at home and in its Eastern European glacis, it had to be assured about NATO's benign intentions. The downgrading of the salience of nuclear weapons implicit in the phrase 'last resort' sent the desired signal.

A similar logic applied to the nuclear Deterrence and Defence Posture Review (DDPR)—a process initiated in 2010 and concluded in 2012. The main rationale for this process was the need to consolidate NATO's nuclear *'acquis'* in light of certain countervailing developments, such as US President Obama's 'Prague agenda' on nuclear disarmament. This US policy had led some European NATO governments to envisage the withdrawal of European-based US nuclear weapons from the continent. Contrary to some expectations, however, the DDPR process turned into a strong reaffirmation of NATO's nuclear basics, all the more so as the US itself rejected any hasty disarmament moves in the NATO context. By encouraging the 'broadest possible participation of allies'

---

26   Freedman, *The Primacy of Alliance*, 8.

27   With the total withdrawal of Soviet stationed forces and the implementation of a CFE agreement, the Allies concerned can reduce their reliance on nuclear weapons. These will continue to fulfill an essential role in the overall strategy of the Alliance to prevent war by ensuring that there are no circumstances in which nuclear retaliation in response to military action might be discounted. However, in the transformed Europe, they will be able to adopt a new NATO strategy making nuclear forces truly weapons of last resort.

'Declaration on a Transformed North Atlantic Alliance', Issued by the Heads of State and Government participating in the meeting of the North Atlantic Council ('The London Declaration'), 5–6 July 1990, www.nato.int/cps/en/natohq/official_texts_23693.htm.

28   Accordingly, British Prime Minister Thatcher explained that, in order to keep 'the full deterrent effect', the phrase 'last resort' should be construed in the context of 'the comprehensive concept phraseology' employed in the entire paragraph of the Summit Declaration. See Margaret Thatcher, 'Press Conference after London NATO Summit', 6 July 1990, www.margaretthatcher.org/document/108139. The author is indebted to David Yost for his research on this episode.

in nuclear sharing and related arrangements, allies provided a carefully worded, yet clear statement about the continued value of these unique nuclear arrangements.

The DDPR thus rebuffed those voices from politics and academia who had been arguing that nuclear-sharing arrangements were obsolescent and thus could safely be discarded. Moreover, rather than defining arms control and non-proliferation as NATO's overarching objectives, the DDPR embedded these concepts in the broader context of NATO's comprehensive deterrence and defence policies.[29] In sum, the carefully worded endorsement of NATO's existing nuclear policy and posture in the DDPR reined in the critical views and thus helped maintain alliance unity on the nuclear dossier.

A final example is the unusually strong emphasis on nuclear deterrence in the 2016 Warsaw Summit Declaration. While much of the language was known from previous communiqués, the sheer amount of language on nuclear matters, as well as the way in which certain statements were presented, was not lost on Western observers and, presumably, any potential adversaries.[30]

Defending Nuclear Core Principles

NATO nuclear policy statements may be general, yet when it comes to defending the basic principles of the alliance's nuclear character—as opposed to military-operational details—allies are willing to speak up. For example, NATO's collective response to the Treaty on the Prohibition of Nuclear Weapons (TPNW) was tougher and more categorical than some observers had expected. Having recognised that this treaty, despite its professed universal vocation, is largely intended as an assault on Western, notably NATO nuclear policies, allies resorted to rather unambiguous language. When the treaty entered into force, allies restated their collective

---

29 See Michael Rühle, *The Broader Context of NATO's Nuclear Policy and Posture*, NATO Defense College Research Report No. 89, January 2013, www.ndc.nato.int/download/downloads.php?icode=366.

30 See Stephan Frühling, 'NATO Summit: Collective Defence and Nuclear Deterrence', Australian Institute of International Affairs, 14 July 2016, www.internationalaffairs.org.au/australianoutlook/nato-summit-collective-defence-nuclear-deterrence/.

opposition, 'as it does not reflect the increasingly challenging international security environment and is at odds with the existing non-proliferation and disarmament architecture'.[31]

Critics were quick to point out that this 'tone-deaf' rejection of the TPNW would make it more difficult to strike a middle ground.[32] However, the genesis of the treaty, as well as the language employed by some of its supporters, suggests that the very idea of a middle ground is, to say the least, questionable. The treaty seeks to outlaw nuclear cooperation and thus appears to be directed, first and foremost, against the US and its allies.[33] Moreover, the fact that some long-time partner countries of NATO, who initially had lobbied for the de-legitimisation of nuclear weapons, have started to rethink their national approaches, suggests that NATO's unambiguous messaging will not undermine the success of its partnership policies.[34]

Finally, contrary to the impression that TPNW advocates are trying to convey, the treaty has no significant traction in allied public opinion. As previously mentioned, opinion polls that are deliberately conducted without context mean very little, all the more so as nuclear fears do not currently rank high among the Western populace.[35] Hence, like previous initiatives such as 'Global Zero', the TPNW movement, despite being awarded the Nobel Peace Prize in 2017, remains a narrow elite project without significant political momentum. Since no nuclear power or any

31 'North Atlantic Council Statement as the Treaty on the Prohibition of Nuclear Weapons Enters Into Force', Press Release (2020) 131, NATO, 15 December 2020, www.nato.int/cps/en/natohq/news_180087.htm?selectedLocale=en.

32 Tweet by George Perkovich (@perkovichG), 16 December 2020, 4.14 pm.

33 See Brad Roberts, 'Ban the Bomb? Or Bomb the Ban?', European Leadership Network Policy Brief, 22 March 2018, www.europeanleadershipnetwork.org/wp-content/uploads/2018/03/180322-Brad-Roberts-Ban-Treaty.pdf.

34 See, for example: 'Inquiry into the Consequences of a Swedish Accession to the Treaty on the Prohibition of Nuclear Weapons', Swedish Foreign Ministry, 2019, www.regeringen.se/48f047/contentassets/756164e2ca3b4d84a3070a486f123dbb/rapport_execsummary.pdf.

35 For a typical example of hyping an inconsequential poll, see International Campaign to Abolish Nuclear Weapons, 'NATO Public Opinion on Nuclear Weapons', January 2021, d3n8a8pro7vhmx.cloudfront.net/ican/pages/234/attachments/original/1611134933/ICAN_YouGov_Poll_2020.pdf?1611134933. A more nuanced analysis is provided by Manuel Lafont Rapnouil, Tara Varma and Nick Witney, 'Eyes Tight Shut: European Attitudes towards Nuclear Deterrence', European Council on Foreign Relations, 19 December 2018, ecfr.eu/special/eyes_tight_shut_european_attitudes_towards_nuclear_deterrence/. On the current public disinterest in nuclear matters in the US, see Ashley Lytle and Kristyn L. Karl, 'Understanding Americans' Perceptions of Nuclear Weapons, Risk and Subsequent Behavior', *International Journal of Communication* 14, 2020, 299–323. For a review of nuclear attitudes in the 1980s, see Yost, 'The Delegitimization of Nuclear Deterrence?'.

ally benefiting from extended nuclear deterrence has signed the treaty, it is likely to remain a symbolic and aspirational document rather than a true game-changer in global disarmament.[36]

The possibility that a future government in a NATO member state may change its mind and seek to sign the TPNW or effect major changes in NATO's nuclear policy can never be ruled out. However, in a strategic environment characterised by increasing great power competition, allied governments are likely to give preference to allied solidarity rather than undermine that very solidarity by opposing what is likely to remain an important element of NATO's political and military *acquis*.

***

The asymmetry between nuclear and non-nuclear allies in terms of military power and status may be profound, and occasionally has led to allied disagreements over nuclear strategy. However, even though the US is the linchpin of NATO's nuclear deterrent, and thus is *primus inter pares*, it cannot determine alliance strategy or declaratory policy on its own. Recognising that political unity is of key importance, the US has to take into account the sensitivities of its non-nuclear allies, in terms of both strategy development and declaratory policy. The latter remains influenced by the primacy of communicating allied unity and of reassuring allied publics. While this may come at the expense of terminological precision or tailored messaging vis-a-vis an opponent, the alternative—a highly emotional and politically counterproductive debate within allied countries—would seem a net loss. This is all the truer in an age in which the (dis-)information space is increasingly dominated by social media. In such an environment, reassuring one's allies must take precedence over impressing one's adversaries with tough public messages intended to show 'resolve'.

This need for reassurance should not be misunderstood as a licence for passivity, however. In an era in which nuclear deterrence is being questioned politically, morally, technologically and legally in Western societies, the political class of a country that intends to retain nuclear protection must be able to make a cogent case for nuclear deterrence, without appearing to trivialise its risks. This requires that political leaders

---

36 See Jean-Baptiste Jeangène Vilmer, 'The Forever Emerging Norm of Banning Nuclear Weapons', *Journal of Strategic Studies* 2020, 1–27, doi.org/10.1080/01402390.2020.1770732.

make a conscious effort to engage in public discussions about the nuclear dossier.[37] It also requires like-minded nations to reinforce their case for nuclear deterrence by stating it collectively. In the end, communicating the reality of cohesion between nuclear and non-nuclear allies—across the North Atlantic and the Asia-Pacific—may send the strongest message in terms of both deterrence and reassurance: a united West.

---

37   See the contribution of Brad Roberts in this volume.

16

Public Communication on Nuclear Deterrence and Disarmament: The Challenge for Australia

Tanya Ogilvie-White

'Foreign policy doesn't lend itself to clear storytelling. Much of its work is elusive and incremental and happens behind closed doors and over time. It's the work of persuasion.'[1] These are the words of Allan Gyngell, president of the Australian Institute of International Affairs and author of *Fear of Abandonment: Australia in the World Since 1942*. As someone who has spent most of his life behind the closed doors to which he refers, and who is now responsible for drawing the Australian public into debate on foreign and defence issues, he knows better than most the communication challenges that governments face. When it comes to engaging the public on the US alliance, and its nuclear dimension in particular, these challenges are complex and growing. This chapter explores these challenges, some of which are unique to Australia. It argues that Canberra's decision-makers have reached a critical juncture in their attempts to reconcile Australian approaches to nuclear deterrence and disarmament: policies that have been problematic for years are threatening to backfire, the result of declining legitimacy, domestic political missteps and events that are beyond Canberra's control.

---

1   Allan Gyngell, 'Australian Foreign Policy: Does the Public Matter? Should the Community Care?', *Australian Outlook*, 7 December 2017, www.internationalaffairs.org.au/australianoutlook/foreign-policy-should-community-care/.

It then sets out a proposal for Australian decision-makers to consider, which would help narrow the gaps between Australia's nuclear deterrence and disarmament policies and public opinion.

The Treaty on the Prohibition of Nuclear Weapons and Extended Deterrence

In Australia, as in other countries that rely on US extended deterrence for their security, government policies on nuclear deterrence and disarmament are facing a growing legitimacy problem. This is not new, but it has become more difficult to manage since the adoption and entry into force of the Treaty on the Prohibition of Nuclear Weapons (TPNW), which has significantly advanced a global norm against nuclear weapons possession and reliance. Conscious of the new treaty's challenge to the legitimacy of nuclear deterrence doctrines, including nuclear assurance, the Australian Government attempted to derail TPNW negotiations and, having failed to do so, strongly and consistently denounces the new treaty, despite widespread support for it among the Australian public.[2] This raises serious questions about the credibility and legitimacy of Canberra's longstanding approach to reconciling nuclear deterrence and disarmament—that is, quietly relying on extended deterrence while focusing domestic attention on nuclear disarmament as a long-term goal. Decades of intense secrecy and exceptionally narrow and restricted public engagement on nuclear issues could now backfire, as Australia's decision-making elite try to sell the strengths of its nuclear arrangements to a wary public.

---

2   Although none of Australia's leading think tanks has published polls on Australian attitudes to the TPNW, data are available from other sources. In September 2017, a ReachTel survey of 1,669 Australian residents found 73 per cent of Australians want the government to sign the TPNW and 11 per cent oppose it. It also found 77 per cent of respondents think nuclear weapons make the world less safe and more than half of those surveyed said they would be more likely to vote for a party that supports a ban on nuclear weapons. In 2018, an Ipsos public opinion poll found 78.9 per cent of Australian respondents supported Australia joining the TPNW and only 7.2 per cent opposed, with 10.1 per cent undecided. In 2019, the ICRC's 'Millennials on War' survey of 16,000 young adults in 16 countries, including Australia, found millennials overwhelmingly supported nuclear disarmament and opposed the use of nuclear weapons (80 per cent), but found most of the people they surveyed had not heard of the TPNW. See Greenpeace Australia Pacific, 'Poll on Australians' Attitudes to Nuclear Weapons', 19 September 2017, www.greenpeace.org.au/blog/poll-australians-attitudes-towards-nuclear-weapons/; Ipsos Public Opinion Poll, cited in International Human Rights Commission, 'Australia and the Treaty on the Prohibition of Nuclear Weapons', December 2018, hrp.law.harvard. edu/wp-content/uploads/2018/12/Australia-TPNW-12-12-18-FINAL.pdf; ICRC, *Millennials on War*, 25 November 2019, www.icrc.org/sites/default/files/wysiwyg/campaign/millennials-on-war/icrc-millennials-on-war_full-report.pdf.

Adoption of the TPNW has coincided with several developments that are beyond Canberra's control, but which increase Canberra's communication challenges: the collapse of nuclear arms control agreements and resurgence of nuclear tensions among the great powers; a rise in the salience of nuclear weapons in US–China relations; a renewed focus on nuclear deterrence in the US alliance; and declining confidence in any nuclear-armed state's capacity to prevent nuclear catastrophe, especially in the context of escalatory pressures and new technologies that could undermine command and control.[3] These developments make deterrence and disarmament even harder to reconcile, exposing the extreme fragility of Australia's policy balance. It is becoming harder to deny that Australia's position within the US alliance and reliance on extended deterrence place Canberra in the role of nuclear enabler and disarmament laggard, regardless of whether it actively contributes to nuclear risks or supports the ongoing shift towards increased nuclear salience.

Disarmament, Deterrence and Public Persuasion

Amid these developments, nuclear disarmament advocates have a distinct public communication advantage over government, despite the former's limited resources. This is partly because vivid stories about the risks of catastrophic nuclear war are more compelling than abstract discussion about the role of nuclear deterrence in promoting strategic stability.[4] Equally significant is the fact that pro-disarmament, pro-TPNW storytellers can more easily claim the moral high ground than their pro-deterrence counterparts, even though some of the ethical questions surrounding nuclear deterrence

---

3   Joseph D. Becker, 'Strategy in the New Era of Tactical Nuclear Weapons', *Strategic Studies Quarterly* 14(1), 2020, 117–40, www.airuniversity.af.edu/Portals/10/SSQ/documents/Volume-14_Issue-1/Becker.pdf; John Borrie, *Strategic Technologies*, Nuclear Risk Reduction Policy Brief No. 2 (Geneva: UNIDIR, 2020), doi.org/10.37559/WMD/20/NRR/03; Erik Gartzke and Jon R. Lindsay, eds, *Cross-Domain Deterrence: Strategy in an Era of Complexity* (Oxford: Oxford University Press, 2019), doi.org/10.1093/oso/9780190908645.001.0001; James Johnson, 'Deterrence in the Age of Artificial Intelligence and Autonomy: A Paradigm Shift in Nuclear Deterrence Theory and Practice?', *Defence and Security Analysis* 36(4), 2020, 422–48, doi.org/10.1080/14751798.2020.1857911; Brad Roberts, 'On Adapting Nuclear Deterrence to Reduce Nuclear Risk', *Daedalus* 149(2), 2020, 69–83, doi.org/10.1162/daed_a_01790.
4   Moreover, the risks of a disarmed world are speculative, while the failure modes and risks of nuclear deterrence 'stand out sharply from past crises and behaviour'. Lewis A. Dunn, *Some Reflections on UNIDIR's Disarmament, Deterrence, and Strategic Arms Control Dialogue—Looking Ahead* (Geneva: UNIDIR, 14 January 2021).

and disarmament are far from black and white.[5] Disarmament advocacy groups in Australia and overseas are aware of this phenomenon, which has helped them rally public support behind the TPNW and mobilise a younger demographic of potential disarmament activists. Indeed, a recent survey by the International Committee of the Red Cross (ICRC) (which has driven much of the global debate on the humanitarian consequences of nuclear weapons), has highlighted the strengths of communication strategies that frame disarmament advocacy around the use of nuclear weapons rather than their possession. Based on the views of 16,000 young adults aged from 20 to 35 in 16 countries, including Australia, the ICRC's 'Millennials on War' survey found that millennials are overwhelmingly opposed to the use of nuclear weapons, with more than eight out of 10 respondents believing that it is 'never acceptable'.[6]

The ICRC's recent findings are significant for those trying to manage public communication on nuclear deterrence and disarmament. The approach of Australia's Liberal-National Coalition (in government since 2013) has been to criticise the TPNW on the basis that it 'has not engaged any state that possesses nuclear weapons', 'will not eliminate a single nuclear weapon … ignores the realities of the global security environment … has weaker safeguards provisions than the existing NPT framework' and is 'inconsistent with [Australia's] US alliance obligations'.[7] None of these arguments directly addresses public concerns about the risks and consequences of nuclear use, and thus does not lend itself to persuasive messaging let alone compelling storytelling. Instead, such arguments echo US denouncements of the treaty, which are unlikely to be persuasive to the Australian non-expert.

Recent studies exploring opinion on nuclear disarmament and deterrence among other US allies and partners reveal that these communication challenges are not unique to Australia.[8] A recent survey conducted

---

5   Tanya Ogilvie-White, *The Logic of Nuclear Deterrence: Assessments, Assumptions, Uncertainties and Failure Modes* (Geneva: UNIDIR, 25 November 2020), doi.org/10.37559/WMD/20/DDAC/03.

6   Magnus Lovold, 'Lessons from the ICRC's Millennials on War Survey for Communication and Advocacy on Nuclear Weapons', *Journal for Peace and Nuclear Disarmament* 4(2), 2020, 410–17. doi.org/10.1080/25751654.2020.1859216.

7   Department of Foreign Affairs and Trade, 'Nuclear Issues', 20 September 2021, www.dfat.gov.au/international-relations/security/non-proliferation-disarmament-arms-control/nuclear-issues/treaties#tpnw.

8   See, for example: Manuel Lafont Rapnouil, Tara Varma and Nick Witney, 'Eyes Tight Shut: European Attitudes to Nuclear Deterrence', European Council on Foreign Relations, 19 December 2018, ecfr.eu/special/eyes_tight_shut_european_attitudes_towards_nuclear_deterrence/.

in Japan is particularly illuminating, providing insight into Japanese attitudes to the TPNW and the extent to which those attitudes can be influenced.[9] First, pollsters asked respondents from a cross-section of Japanese society (N=1333) whether they wanted their prime minister to sign, and Diet to ratify, the TPNW. The results of this initial survey question mirrored the November 2018 Ipsos poll on Australian attitudes, with 75 per cent of Japanese respondents supporting joining the TPNW, 17.7 per cent opposing it and 7.3 per cent undecided. Having gauged a baseline of support, respondents were then shown three real-world criticisms of the treaty to test whether they could be persuaded to change their opinion, based on: 1) claims the treaty would undermine the nuclear umbrella that protects Japan's security, 2) a warning that the treaty is weak because it lacks verification mechanisms and 3) assertions that the TPNW undermines the Treaty on the Non-Proliferation of Nuclear Weapons (NPT). They were also tested to see whether their TPNW support could be weakened in response to peer pressure. Interestingly, respondents' attitudes did not shift significantly in response to any of the criticisms or in response to peer pressure. These findings provided a striking contrast to those from a parallel US study, which found American public support for the treaty declined in response to each argument, and especially security-centric criticisms. No studies of this kind have been conducted in Australia, but the robustness of the Australian public's views on the TPNW may well be closer to Japan's, having developed its own version of the Japanese 'nuclear allergy'.[10]

Australia's Vague Nuclear Assurances

Some of the difficulties of reconciling deterrence and disarmament in public communication strategies are particular to Australia. Whereas other US allies can balance public support for nuclear disarmament against a formal pledge of US nuclear assurances, Australia cannot. This weakens Canberra's security arguments in support of nuclear extended deterrence

---

9   Jonathan Baron, Rebecca Davis Gibbons and Stephen Herzog, 'Japanese Public Opinion, Political Persuasion, and the Treaty on the Prohibition of Nuclear Weapons', *Journal of Peace and Nuclear Disarmament* 3(2), 2020, 299–309, doi.org/10.1080/25751654.2020.1834961.
10   Tanya Ogilvie-White, 'Australia's Rocky Nuclear Past and Uncertain Future', *Bulletin of the Atomic Scientists*, 1 September 2015, doi.org/10.1177%2F0096340215599783; Parliament of Victoria, *Inquiry into Nuclear Prohibition*, November 2020, www.parliament.vic.gov.au/images/stories/committees/SCEP/Inquiry_into_Nuclear_Prohibition_Inquiry_/Report/LCEPC_59-03_Inquiry_into_Nuclear_prohibition.pdf.

and against the TPNW. Having never received an explicit, public promise of nuclear assurance from Washington, despite stating its own expectations in successive white papers since 1994, Australia now finds itself in a position whereby it is becoming a more credible nuclear target (partly due to its joint facilities and their role in US targeting), with only the vaguest of commitment from the US to intervene on Canberra's behalf should the need arise. Putting aside the point that even a formal nuclear pledge would not guarantee US assistance, from the perspective of public communication, this situation poses a serious problem. A communication strategy that presents nuclear weapons as security providers (and the TPNW as a threat to that security) lacks credibility if it cannot be backed up with evidence of a firm commitment—and even more so in the face of Australia's increasing exposure to nuclear risks. This point has not been lost on Australia's expert community, which has become more vocal in its criticisms of official policy, with some calling for more robust nuclear assurances,[11] others arguing that it is time for Australia to revisit developing an independent nuclear capability[12] and still others pushing for the abandonment of nuclear deterrence altogether.[13]

These developments help explain why Canberra's decades-old bipartisan consensus on deterrence and disarmament is coming to an end, raising the stakes in future public communication efforts.[14] As the issue becomes more politicised, the legitimacy issue will come increasingly to the fore. The TPNW and the question of US extended deterrence could well become a major election issue, which could prove highly divisive and, depending on how it is managed, strategically risky. For example,

11 Fiona S. Cunningham, 'Managing US–China Nuclear Risks: A Guide for Australia', United States Studies Centre, 29 September 2020, www.ussc.edu.au/analysis/managing-us-china-nuclear-risks-a-guide-for-australia; Stephen Frühling, Andrew O'Neil and David Santoro, 'Escalating Cooperation: Nuclear Deterrence and the US–Australia Alliance', United States Studies Centre Deterrence Brief, November 2019, www.ussc.edu.au/analysis/escalating-cooperation-nuclear-deterrence-and-the-us-australia-alliance; Ashley Townshend and Brendan Thomas-Noone with Matilda Steward, 'Averting Crisis: American Strategy, Military Spending and Collective Defence in the Indo-Pacific', United States Studies Centre, August 2019, www.ussc.edu.au/analysis/averting-crisis-american-strategy-military-spending-and-collective-defence-in-the-indo-pacific.

12 Sam Roggeveen, 'Maintaining Australia's Security as American Power Recedes', Lowy Institute, interactives.lowyinstitute.org/features/covid-recovery/issues/security/.

13 Marianne Hanson, 'Where Will Australia Stand on Banning Weapons of Mass Destruction?', The Interpreter, 27 October 2020, www.lowyinstitute.org/the-interpreter/where-will-australia-stand-banning-weapons-mass-destruction.

14 Anthony Albanese (leader of the Australian Labor Party), 'Moving Support for the Nuclear Weapon Ban Treaty', Speech to the 48th National Conference of the Australian Labor Party, Adelaide Convention Centre, 18 December 2018, anthonyalbanese.com.au/speech-moving-support-for-the-nuclear-weapon-ban-treaty-tuesday-18-december-2018.

a government determined to retain a role for nuclear weapons in Australia's security architecture, through the US alliance or other arrangements, might attempt to justify the Australian public's exposure to increased nuclear risk by exaggerating threats and mobilising public opinion against adversaries.[15] Although this might be seen by some as a tempting election tactic, it could inflame and empower nationalist and xenophobic sentiment—a dangerous game, especially in the age of social media and fake news. Equally, once in government, a political leader who campaigned on a pro-TPNW platform could find themselves under public pressure to follow through on disarmament commitments that could undermine the US alliance, with implications for conventional deterrence.[16] Although this would not be an inevitable outcome of Australia signing and ratifying the TPNW, military dependence on the alliance (combined with Washington's willingness to punish allies that step out of line) makes it a credible scenario that should not be dismissed.[17]

Reframing the Discussion

The above scenarios highlight the importance of managing Australia's deterrence and disarmament dilemma in a way that rebuilds political consensus and that brings the public along. The past decade has seen some serious missteps in this regard, as successive governments, often under intense US diplomatic pressure, have tried and failed to reconcile diverging deterrence and disarmament goals. To be fair, every road ahead is strewn with political and strategic risk. With no obvious

---

15 Australian political leaders are not immune to this temptation. In launching the *2020 Defence Strategic Update*, Prime Minister Scott Morrison drew parallels between the current strategic environment in the Asia-Pacific and 'similar times many years ago in the 1930s'. Prime Minister of Australia, 'Address—Launch of the 2020 Defence Strategic Update', 1 July 2020, www.pm.gov.au/media/address-launch-2020-defence-strategic-update.

16 This is a possibility if the TPNW becomes a major election issue in Australia. The leadership of the Labor Party is currently divided on the merits of Australia signing the TPNW (some key figures oppose it and even the Labor leader's support for it appears to be carefully qualified). If, however, the party decides a disarmament platform could be part of a successful election strategy, it might unite behind the TPNW and find itself with a mandate to radically overhaul Australia's defence and security policy.

17 For two perspectives, see Tanya Ogilvie-White, 'Australia and Extended Nuclear Assurance', in *Perspectives on Nuclear Deterrence in the 21st Century*, ed. Beyza Unal, Yasmin Afina and Patricia Lewis (London: Chatham House, 2020), www.chathamhouse.org/sites/default/files/2020-04-20-nuclear-deterrence-unal-et-al.pdf; International Human Rights Commission, 'Australia and the Treaty on the Prohibition of Nuclear Weapons'; Richard Tanter, 'An Australian Pathway through Pine Gap to the Nuclear Ban Treaty', *Pearls and Irritations*, 5 August 2019, johnmenadue.com/richard-tanter-an-australian-pathway-through-pine-gap-to-the-nuclear-ban-treaty/.

alternative, Australia's approach has been to try to maintain the status quo. But growing awareness of the potential for deterrence breakdown and escalation, combined with Australian public support for the TPNW and the collapse of the bipartisan consensus, means a new approach is needed. As others have argued, leaders cannot hide from the TPNW, however hard they try.[18]

Australia needs to address this problem in a way that allows it to preserve the US alliance, acknowledge escalatory risks and demonstrate constructive leadership on nuclear disarmament. To do this, it needs to reframe the debate. The first step is to acknowledge that the TPNW is an important part of the longer-term goal of nuclear elimination—a significant international achievement that, over time and if fleshed out sufficiently, has the potential to help create a more secure world. There is nothing to be gained by continuing with a policy of TPNW-bashing, which is jarring for so many and, in any case, undermines international law now that the TPNW has entered into force. Instead, the Australian Government could explain its holdout status as a temporary position, to be reassessed if the treaty is strengthened and strategic circumstances change. This position, expressed in positive and forward-looking language, but without making a formal pledge, has more authenticity and legitimacy than the current policy, and while it will require careful handling within the alliance context, more closely aligns with Australian values.

The second step is to address the subject of nuclear deterrence with more openness in national conversations, policy documents and strategic dialogues—a significant departure from the closed-door policy that Australia has maintained over so many years. This would need to include discussion of what Australia is doing to reduce nuclear risks, including its efforts to prevent nuclear war. Indications are that the Australian public would be open to this discussion, given that those who support the TPNW do so because they do not believe the use of nuclear weapons can be justified under any circumstances (in common with publics in other alliance states, Australians are willing to accept nuclear possession, but

18 Baron et al., 'Japanese Public Opinion', 305; George Perkovich, 'Living with the Nuclear Prohibition Treaty: First, Do No Harm', CEIP Commentary, 10 November 2020, carnegieendowment. org/2020/11/10/living-with-nuclear-prohibition-treaty-first-do-no-harm-pub-83198.

not use).[19] Effective communication could generate support for a strategy of continuing to hold out from the TPNW for now, while other, more immediate nuclear risk-reduction and disarmament measures are pursued.

The success of the second step is dependent on Australia showing genuine leadership on nuclear risk reduction and disarmament and using its influence within the US alliance to that end. This calls for a bold initiative. One idea is to kickstart discussions on a no-first-use (NFU) treaty—a formal, negotiated commitment by all nuclear-armed states not to be the first to use nuclear weapons—or a broader NFU dialogue, which includes some of the most destabilising non-nuclear weapons in the discussion. This has several advantages in the current strategic climate:

1. It would reduce the chance of a surprise nuclear attack by encouraging states that have NFU doctrines to maintain them, and those that do not to commit to them as a confidence-building measure.

2. It would be strongly supported by the Australian public (and publics in other alliance states), which supports nuclear possession but not use.

3. It would help Australia demonstrate its commitment to the NPT, which calls for a reduction in the salience of nuclear weapons in strategic doctrines.

4. It would find support among like-minded states (including members of the Stockholm Initiative), which could be leveraged to advance an NFU proposal in the UN First Committee or other diplomatic fora.

5. It has a reasonable chance of being taken seriously by the Biden administration, which has assembled a strong arms control team and is likely to prioritise nuclear risk reduction.[20]

6. It would coincide with the launch of a global NFU campaign, led by influential non-governmental organisations and civil society groups in Europe and the Asia-Pacific.

---

19 Lovold, 'Lessons from the ICRC's Millennials on War Survey'.
20 The stage has already been set for this debate in the US. In January 2019, Senator Warren and Representative Smith introduced the *No First Use Act*, which states: 'It is the policy of the United States to not use nuclear weapons first'.

There are many criticisms that can be levelled against NFU doctrines,[21] including strategic arguments over the credibility of nuclear threats, which some deterrers argue rely on an adversary signalling its ability and willingness to strike first (to the extent that some believe nuclear weapons should be kept ready for prompt launch, as is the case with US and Russian arsenals).[22] But other strategic thinkers question these assumptions, based on uncertainties stemming from a combination of aggressive doctrines and postures, and uncertainties surrounding new technologies and domains of warfare, all of which are heightening threat perceptions and increasing the risks of escalation and nuclear use.[23] NFU commitments would not eliminate these risks, but they could help reduce them, especially if they are adopted as part of a wider package of confidence-building measures. Further, actively championing NFU commitments at the international level would be an example of ambitious and principled disarmament diplomacy—something Australia was respected for in the past and could be known for again.

---

21 William A. Chambers, Caroline R. Milne, Rhiannon T. Hutton and Heather W. Williams, *No-First Use of Nuclear Weapons: A Policy Assessment*, IDA Paper P-20513, January 2021, www.ida.org/-/media/feature/publications/n/no/no-first-use-of-nuclear-weapons-a-policy-assessment/p-20513.ashx.

22 The strategic objections against NFU and sole purpose do have some validity in the context of the US alliance, but they could be overcome if the US demonstrated to allies that it was significantly improving its conventional capabilities and strengthening alliance cohesion, resilience and defence and security cooperation. See George Perkovich and Pranay Vaddi, *Proportionate Deterrence: A Model Nuclear Posture Review* (Washington: CEIP, 2021), carnegieendowment.org/files/Perkovich_Vaddi_NPR_full.pdf.

23 See, for example: Steve Fetter and John Wolfsthal, 'No First Use and Credible Deterrence', *Journal for Peace and Nuclear Disarmament* 1(1), 2018, 102–14, doi.org/10.1080/25751654.2018.1454257; John P. Holdren, 'The Overwhelming Case for No First Use', *Bulletin of the Atomic Scientists* 76(1), 2020, 3–7, doi.org/10.1080/00963402.2019.1701277; Johnson, 'Deterrence in the Age of Artificial Intelligence'.

17

On 'Campaigning' for Nuclear Deterrence

Brad Roberts

In his famous 1964 film *Dr Strangelove*, Stanley Kubrick used farce to try to make sense of the dilemmas of the nuclear era. Film history buffs will recall the film's subtitle: *How I Learned to Stop Worrying and Love the Bomb*. Kubrick's purpose was in part to illuminate the absurdity of loving the instrument of humankind's possible annihilation. There is a natural public yearning to be free of the long shadow cast by nuclear weapons. But that is much easier said than done. So far, at least, it has proven impossible to create the conditions that would make those protected by nuclear deterrents feel safer disarmed than armed. So long as nuclear weapons remain, there will be a need to ensure that the taboo on their use, now seven decades old, also remains. This implies a continuing role for nuclear deterrence, among other things. Those concerned with nuclear dangers face a true moral dilemma with the twin obligations to work to remove the long shadow and to work to ensure that deterrence is effective for the problems for which it is relevant so long as nuclear weapons remain.[1]

1   The views expressed here are those of the author and should not be attributed to Lawrence Livermore National Laboratory or its sponsors. The author is grateful to Lauren Borja, Jessica Cox, Lewis Dunn, Jacek Durkalec, Madison Hissom, Rod Lyon, Anna Peczeli and Michael Rühle for valuable comments on an early draft of this essay.

For politicians and policymakers, this is challenging terrain. It is difficult to know how to orient oneself within this political minefield. Lawrence Freedman, in writing about deterrence, has captured the essence of the challenge as follows:

> A doctrine that is so associated with continuity and the status quo, which occupies a middle ground between appeasement and aggression, celebrates caution above all else, and for that property alone is beloved by officials and diplomats, was never likely to inspire a popular following. Campaigners might march behind banners demanding peace and disarmament, the media might get excited by talk of war and conflict, but successful deterrence, marked by nothing much happening, is unlikely to get the pulse racing. It has no natural political constituency.[2]

Confronted with the need to engage politically and publicly on these issues, many politicians and policymakers shy away. The disincentives are numerous. The subject matter is inherently complex and arcane. The learning curve is steep. There is no 'natural political constituency' for deterrence to be mobilised. In contrast, the opponents of nuclear deterrence stand by, ready to deploy exquisitely honed arguments and to mobilise their ample constituency.

But silence is counterproductive. It undermines the political foundations of existing policies, calling into question the viability of very long-term projects such as nuclear modernisation cycles spanning decades. It impedes the testing of new thinking against new circumstances. It leaves the attentive public, and their elected representatives, exposed to only one side of the issues. It assumes that the major policy debates have been 'won' and that policies will not be reversed. It fuels the perception of the attentive public that the advocates of deterrence do not have the courage of their convictions—and thus must not believe the policies they choose not to defend. And it leaves the public space on these matters entirely to those with competing agendas. This now includes not just disarmament campaigners but also Russia and China, whose 'information confrontation' strategies aggressively use all of the means available to them to shape the narratives, perceptions and judgements of targeted publics and elites.

---

2   Lawrence Freedman, *Deterrence* (Cambridge: Polity Press, 2004), 25.

The failure to build and maintain a constituency for nuclear deterrence may have even more troubling implications. Not all nuclear-armed states require the consent of the governed to maintain their nuclear deterrents. If the nuclear-armed democracies lose their political will to maintain effective nuclear deterrence so long as nuclear weapons remain, the nuclear-armed authoritarian states stand to gain. The failures of political leaders in the democracies of the 1930s to maintain constituencies for (pre-nuclear) deterrence contributed significantly to the formation of the belief in Berlin and Tokyo that the democracies lacked the resolve to defend their interest. Of course, this proved to be a catastrophic misjudgement, as the democracies proved willing to defend themselves. But to do so, they paid a price they might well have avoided had they been mindful of the messages of weakness they sent.[3]

Thus, for both domestic and international political reasons, politicians and policymakers should not give in to the impulse to shy away.[4] How then should they navigate this difficult terrain? How should they think about the task of advocating for nuclear deterrence without being dismissed as the farcical Dr Strangelove? My experience as a one-time official involved at a senior level in the making of US nuclear deterrence policy and subsequently as the author of a book making the case for nuclear weapons points to the following key lessons.[5]

Five Lessons

First, the interested public, like the interested politician, is fundamentally ambivalent about nuclear deterrence. It has not learned to love the bomb and is worried about life with the bomb—and also about what life without it might mean. The citizens with whom I interact would generally like to be free of nuclear danger, but they do not want to be free of nuclear deterrence prematurely. Public opinion polling bears out these

---

3   This historical analogy is explored more fully in Brad Roberts, 'Nuclear Ethics and the Ban Treaty', in *Nuclear Disarmament: A Critical Assessment*, ed. Brad Nikolas vik Steen and Olav Njolstad (Oslo: Norwegian Nobel Institute, 2019).
4   The debate about how much public discussion of nuclear deterrence policy to encourage stretches back decades. See Harold Brown, 'Domestic Consensus and Nuclear Deterrence', in *Defence and Consensus: The Domestic Aspects of Western Security, Part II,* Adelphi Paper No. 183 (London: International Institute for Strategic Studies, 1983), 22–27; Richard K. Betts, 'Nuclear Weapons', in *The Making of America's Soviet Policy,* ed. Joseph S. Nye (New Haven: Yale University Press, 1984), 125–26.
5   Brad Roberts, *The Case for US Nuclear Weapons in the 21st Century* (Stanford: Stanford University Press, 2015), doi.org/10.1515/9780804797153.

observations. Asked whether they support the Treaty on the Prohibition of Nuclear Weapons (TPNW), respondents are heavily in favour.[6] Asked whether they support unilateral disarmament, respondents are heavily opposed.[7] This ambivalence is deep-seated and stretches back to the 1950s.[8]

This implies that the public interest that can be engaged by advocates of nuclear deterrence is the interest in being better informed. It is not an interest in being recruited to join the nuclear deterrence constituency. In my experience, an ambivalent public seeks opportunities to learn about nuclear deterrence primarily because it is curious about the changing security environment and changing thinking within government about how to respond and shape that environment. The interested public engages on these issues to gain more insight and not to change its mind. Advocates of nuclear deterrence should set their objectives and expectations accordingly.

Second, there are many stakeholders in nuclear deterrence policy and the political discourse is well served by engaging broadly with them. These include the general public, general public policy experts in universities and think tanks, nuclear policy experts, nuclear policy advocacy groups and journalists. Additionally, within the US Government, there are numerous constituencies: policymakers, policy implementers, budget makers, congressional authorisers and appropriators, and their staffs. Within the US military, there are still others with equities on these topics: the Joint Staff, US Strategic Command, the geographic combatant commands with nuclear-relevant threats in their areas of responsibility and the services charged with providing deterrent forces. From a US perspective, there are also important stakeholders in the capitals of allied countries (and in their embassies in Washington, DC), both inside and outside government. Further, many other countries not allied with the US take a strong interest in disarmament diplomacy and in actions by the US and powerful states that affect global nuclear risk.

---

6   See the analysis on polling in Tanya Ogilvie-White's chapter in this volume.
7   Ernie Regehr, 'Nuclear Disarmament or Nuclear Ambivalence?', survey conducted by the Simons Foundation and the Angus Reid Strategies Corporation, 2007, ploughshares.ca/wp-content/uploads/2007/10/brf074.pdf.
8   David S. Yost, 'The Delegitimization of Nuclear Deterrence', *Armed Forces and Society* 16(4), 1990, 487–508, doi.org/10.1177/0095327X9001600401.

This implies the need for a practice of nuclear deterrence advocacy that reaches well beyond the interested public and thus a need to tailor the message to the audience, based on its level of expertise and particular equities. There is some risk of going beyond tailoring to changing the message to suit the interests of different audiences—something that quickly strips away the credibility of the messenger. This second lesson also implies that nuclear deterrence advocacy must be sustained on a nearly continuous basis. After all, regular staff turnover is common to all these institutions.

Third, to tell a good story to these various stakeholders, it is obviously essential to have a good story. Government cannot explain and defend its thinking about nuclear weapons if it has not done any thinking. Having done its homework, it must then be transparent about both the results and the thinking behind the policies.

What makes a story good? I have watched many audiences react badly to official descriptions of nuclear policy that are entirely self-referential. That is, they address only nuclear threats, nuclear deterrence strategy and nuclear weapons. Few stakeholders see the world in such simple terms. Most bring context of some kind, as must the advocates of nuclear deterrence. A good story begins at the beginning: in this case, with a view of that moral dilemma as embedded in a view of the security environment. A good story goes on to explain the place of nuclear deterrence in broader defence and deterrence strategy. It should also include a vision of how to finally escape the dilemmas of nuclear deterrence, however remote that possibility may seem, as well as a well-reasoned case for what steps can and cannot be taken safely to reduce nuclear dangers. A good story refrains from jargon, hyperbole and rhetorical attacks on contrary views.

This implies that government needs the time and means to get its thinking together on these topics. In the US, this has been done through the reviews of nuclear posture and policy conducted by each new presidential administration since 1994. The resulting reports are intended to inform both the executive-legislative discussion of specific policies and programs and the broader public discourse. They have served these purposes well. But to have an enduring impact, they must be seen as the starting point of a continuing public dialogue, not the last word.

This also implies that government needs the requisite expertise—technical, military and political. US Nuclear Posture Reviews (NPRs) draw on the policy expertise of the functional and regional bureaus in the Office of the Secretary of Defense; the military expertise of the Joint Staff, armed services and combatant commands; the technical expertise of the Department of Energy; the diplomatic expertise of the Department of State; the specialised knowledge of the intelligence community; the perspectives of US allies; and the knowledge and advocacy of non-governmental experts. The cast of stakeholders is large, but its actual expertise is quite thin. The US Government's overall capacity for nuclear policy development is heavily constrained by the loss of focus on nuclear deterrence in the two decades after the Cold War and the atrophy of the institutions and investments that underwrote US strategic thought in the first few decades of the nuclear era.

Fourth, expect dissent. As argued above, the public space is contested. The disarmament 'campaigners' have effectively mobilised their 'natural public constituency'. But let's reject their claim that there are two mutually opposed camps of disarmers and deterrers. The disarmament community is in fact many sub-communities (as is the deterrence community). Some see disarmament as a near-term goal, while others see it as a very long-term goal. To be sure, some reject outright the historical, military and moral claims of the nuclear deterrence community and seek only to vanquish a despised political foe. But many others embrace the moral dilemma described in the opening of this essay. I have also found a third group: those who think they disagree with nuclear deterrence policy but do not, in fact, once they understand it.

This implies a value in engaging forthrightly with these different communities but with expectations matched to each. With those who embrace the moral dilemma, expect some progress in building bridges where interests converge (e.g. on measures to reduce and, where possible, eliminate nuclear dangers and risks). With those who do not, expect to change no minds. With those who think they disagree but may not, minds might be changed.

Fifth, the moral debate about nuclear weapons is inescapable and thus should be joined forthrightly. In my experience, the interested public expects and wants engagement on moral issues in addition to military and political ones. The moral case against nuclear weapons is made with passion and conviction. In contrast, the moral case for nuclear weapons is rarely if ever made. For the interested public, this raises important questions about the legitimacy of nuclear deterrence policy. One case is far easier to make than the other. The moral case against nuclear weapons is built on a single powerful image: the devastation of Hiroshima and Nagasaki and the suffering of the survivors of the bombing. The moral case for nuclear weapons is built on a montage of historical experience, military strategy and political theory. That is, the moral case involves judgements about the causes of war and peace, the requirements of operational and strategic success in war and opportunities to affect an adversary's decision calculus.

This is a challenge for which government is not well equipped. Its ranks are not filled with skilled moral philosophers. But this does not relieve the advocates of nuclear deterrence of the moral obligation to make their case. This implies a more ample discourse about the role of nuclear deterrence in US grand strategy than has so far been developed in periodic NPRs. The moral case for nuclear deterrence begins with the responsibility to protect. The moral case for extended deterrence begins with recognition of the fact that the responsibility to protect does not stop at national borders.[9]

Campaigning for Nuclear Deterrence

This catalogue of lessons attests to the breadth and depth of the necessary communication by the policymaker to stakeholders. Much more than a single document or speech is needed. In the US, the reports of the NPR are the starting point for the needed public discourse, not the last word. This suggests that it is useful to borrow from the advocates of disarmament the notion of campaigning.

Disarmament campaigning has been under way for decades. The Campaign for Nuclear Disarmament, founded in 1957 and based in the UK, helped launch the broader international Campaign to Abolish Nuclear Weapons. Campaigning for disarmament involves sustained advocacy by civil society actors, sometimes in partnership with like-minded international organisations and governments, to establish new norms and legal mechanisms and to impact national decision-making for disarmament purposes by states possessing nuclear weapons or dependent

---

9   Points of reference include Michael Quinlan, *Thinking About Nuclear Weapons: Principles, Problems, and Prospects* (Oxford: Oxford University Press, 2009), doi.org/10.1093/acprof:oso/9780199563944.001.0001. See also Roberts, 'Nuclear Ethics and the Ban Treaty'.

on nuclear protection by another.[10] As John Borrie of the UN Institute for Disarmament Research has argued, campaigning is also about 'changing the discourse—the manner in which things are talked about, including which questions are asked and answered'.[11] This campaign has enjoyed significant success in working with like-minded states to create and bring into force the TPNW. Its impact earned it a Nobel Peace Prize in 2017.

Nuclear deterrence campaigning would entail some of the same approaches: sustained advocacy in critical national capitals and media markets, partnerships with stakeholder institutions, the defence of existing norms and mechanisms and efforts to change the discourse by asking the right questions—all aimed at sustaining the political foundations for nuclear deterrence in states possessing nuclear weapons or dependent on nuclear protection by another. As Freedman's analysis suggests, prizes will not be handed out and there is no 'natural constituency' to mobilise for a parade. But public service often does not generate public acclaim.

Inherent to the notion of a campaign is acceptance that the objective is long term. In this case, the debate about the utility and morality of nuclear weapons is never likely to be settled. So long as nuclear weapons remain, these matters will remain in contention.

Given the passions that attach to nuclear policy debates, it is hardly surprising that it has been tainted by the broader decline of public debate in the US. Rather than stick to the issues in a manner that informs public discourse about the substance of the matters in dispute, policy advocates often resort to *ad hominem* attacks, apparently with the belief that demonising the other side in the public policy debate will persuade an undecided public. This has plagued both 'sides' in the nuclear debate. There is no better example of this malady than a prominent 2020 book on nuclear deterrence policy in which the authors attack the people who make policy judgements with which they disagree. They blame a faceless 'nuclear bureaucracy' whose views are 'so entrenched' that its core ideas are 'never questioned'. They cynically impute a motive for self-enrichment with the argument that this faceless bureaucracy 'if left to itself … will keep the contracts and the money flowing'. They chastise the military for 'a long

---

10   Rebecca Johnson, 'Arms Control and Disarmament Diplomacy', in *The Oxford Handbook of Modern Diplomacy* (Oxford: Oxford University Press, 2013), doi.org/10.1093/oxfordhb/97801995 88862.013.0033.

11   John Borrie, 'Changing the Discourse on Nuclear Weapons: What it Means and Why it's Important', accessed online 6 June 2018 (site discontinued).

tradition of military opposition to nuclear diplomacy'. They characterise some policymakers as 'delusional'. They accuse 'the president's own team' (in this case, Barack Obama's) of being 'the biggest roadblock' to the implementation of his policies.[12]

Such demonisation serves public understanding poorly. In his January 2021 inaugural address, President Joe Biden argued that 'politics need not be a raging fire destroying everything in its path. Every disagreement doesn't have to be a cause for total war'. Everyone has a responsibility to restore some civility to our national and international policy debates. It is possible to engage purposefully and passionately in the debates about nuclear deterrence and disarmament while also raising the quality of debate. Tempting though it may be, personal criticism of others must be avoided, even while disagreeing with what they think or the policies they advocate. Speak to the issues, not the personalities. Defend nuclear deterrence from first principles of history, politics and morality and not by attacking the advocates of disarmament, even when they exercise no such restraint. Do not paper over differences; respectfully illuminate them and thereby inform the debate.

US Allies and Nuclear Deterrence Advocacy

These lessons and arguments are crafted from my experience as a policymaker and analyst in the US. Our particular national history as the sole user of nuclear weapons imparts a special obligation on the US for leadership in debates about nuclear deterrence and disarmament. Our historical role as a leader of the international effort to promote international nuclear order also obliges the US to play a constructive role in dealing with twenty-first-century nuclear dangers. Our longstanding role as a security guarantor to others brings with it the expectation of leadership in strategy and policy development. Our aspiration to serve as a model of our values and way of governance creates an additional obligation to tend to the requirements of an informed electorate on these matters.

---

12 William J. Perry and Tom Z. Collina, *The Button: The New Nuclear Arms Race and Presidential Power from Truman to Trump* (Dallas: Ben Bella Books, 2020).

US allies face a similar but not identical set of imperatives and equities. As democratic states, they too must promote an informed electorate. As nations seeking safety under the US nuclear umbrella, they must also help to ensure that US strategy is credible and that US policy is effective. As beneficiaries of a nuclear-backed US security guarantee, they must make a public case for extended deterrence. To do so, they must convey a clear understanding of the role of that umbrella in the current security environment, and of how US nuclear strategy balances near-term deterrence requirements with medium-term risk-reduction goals and long-term disarmament objectives. In Europe, there are some additional imperatives and equities, as some allies there also play a particular role in the practice of US extended nuclear deterrence. They do so by participating in NATO's nuclear-sharing arrangements and dual-capable aircraft (DCA) mission (i.e. they own and operate DCA and host on their territories the US nuclear weapons that could be delivered by those aircraft in a time of war). The withdrawal of any one country from the mission could cause the complete collapse of the alliance's unique sharing arrangements—at a time when alliance leaders have repeatedly expressed a commitment to maintain and, if possible, strengthen them. Thus, US allies too would be well served by joining the campaign for nuclear deterrence.

But confronted with the need to engage politically and publicly on these issues, politicians and policymakers in countries allied with the US appear even more reticent than their US counterparts. Their history of engagement is limited and, in some cases, non-existent. In many allied countries, the disarmament constituency is strong and the nuclear deterrence constituency non-existent. In many countries allied with the US, the nuclear debate is mostly a debate about US nuclear policy, which is inadequate.

It is therefore not surprising that most messaging about nuclear policies and nuclear deterrence emanates from alliance mechanisms rather than allied capitals. NATO has had a lot more to say about these matters over the years than most of its member states. Summit communiqués have been especially useful as a mechanism for deterrence messaging, in both Europe and Asia. These are valuable starting points but fall short of effective campaigning.

Allied governments interested in 'upping their game' on deterrence campaigning face many of the same challenges faced by the US, but even more. They do not have even a thin layer of experts sprinkled across the stakeholder institutions, nor have they invested the resources outside government to enable informed discourse with a deterrence expert community. Finally, they do not have the requirements to conduct policy and posture reviews as they relate to nuclear deterrence.

As a near-term remedy, the US could do more to draw its allies into its own policy and posture reviews. Consultations with allies are now a standard part of US NPRs. But consultation could become substantive collaboration on certain aspects of these reviews. It could also be more purposeful in using formal dialogue mechanisms with allies to advance the development of expertise both inside and outside allied governments.

Over the longer term, however, there can be no substitute for actions by US allies to bolster their capacities for deterrence campaigning. They would be well served by instituting regularised reviews and statements. NATO, for example, could commit to periodic reviews of its deterrence and defence posture, building on the initial (and, so far, only) review conducted in 2012; this would lend continuity of purpose to the alliance's effort to adapt and strengthen its posture in the context of a changing security environment, while also improving the public discourse. It could also commit to a more visible leadership role in the transatlantic deterrence discourse—an approach urged upon it in 2020 by an advisory group on NATO's future commissioned by the alliance's secretary general. Their report urged NATO to:

> Better communicate on the key role of nuclear deterrence policy
> in ensuring the security of the Allies and their populations …
> [and] systematically reach out to, and seek to inform, the expert
> community and civil society.[13]

US alliances in the Indo-Pacific should not wait upon the advice of a future commission to communicate and reach out. At the very least, their defence white papers should set out clearly and concisely the roles of nuclear deterrence and of the US nuclear umbrella in reducing the risk of attack on their most vital interests.

---

13 The 'reflection group' appointed by the NATO secretary general issued a report in November 2020 recommending (among many other items) that 'NATO should continue and revitalise the nuclear-sharing arrangements … The political value of this commitment is as important as the military value it brings'. See *NATO 2030: United for a New Era, Analysis and Recommendations of the Reflection Group Appointed by the NATO Secretary General*, November 2020, www.nato.int/nato_static_fl2014/assets/pdf/2020/12/pdf/201201-Reflection-Group-Final-Report-Uni.pdf.

* * *

Neither the interested publics in the US and allied countries nor their elected officials will soon 'learn to love the bomb'. But the public debate about nuclear strategy and policy can be joined and raised in many useful ways. The point of departure must be a thoughtful and comprehensive review of nuclear policy and posture in the context of a broader review of national security strategy and national defence strategy. But much more is required. The case for nuclear deterrence must be made on historical, military and moral terms.

Above all, policymakers seeking to advance a campaign for nuclear deterrence must have reasonable expectations. They can expect to raise the level of debate and to build support for policy. But the debate cannot be 'won'; the debate about nuclear disarmament and nuclear deterrence will not be settled until nuclear weapons are shoved into 'the dustbin of history' (to quote Ronald Reagan), which implies it will be with the US for a long time to come.

Conclusions

18

Managing Deterrence in the 21st Century

Stephan Frühling and Andrew O'Neil

The introductory chapter to this volume opened with the premise that US allies in Europe and the Indo-Pacific need to become more embedded in, and proficient with, discussions with Washington over escalation and nuclear deterrence. In the Indo-Pacific, long gone are the days when the US and its allies were content with a division of labour that saw Washington manage the risk of great power conflict with little input from its allies. Extended deterrence consultations with Japan and South Korea have created an expectation of greater transparency from Washington over when, where and under what circumstances the US would employ nuclear weapons. But despite this, alliances in the Indo-Pacific remain far from the mature political and military discussions that can provide a common basis for deterrence communication, alignment of force structure and posture, crisis management, as well as managing enduring differences between allies about how they engage their respective populations.

Great Power Competition, Alliances and Deterrence

The scale of strategic and geopolitical challenges facing Australia, the US and other allies in the Indo-Pacific is daunting. For the first time since before Australia signed its security treaty with the US three-quarters of a century ago, the possibility exists that a hostile peer competitor might be able to force the US out of the Indo-Pacific in a great power conflict. Given the stakes involved, a conflict between China and the US and its allies over Taiwan is the most likely contingency that could see such a cataclysmic geopolitical outcome. And China is more likely today than in the past to be successful in such an undertaking—or at least to perceive the odds of forced reunification as favourable enough to try.

Depending on the political and military context at the time, there may be incentives for China to rapidly escalate such a conflict—including to the threat or use of nuclear weapons. As China is most likely to escalate in this manner in the event that it confronts defeat or has its core territory threatened in a conventional conflict, it is not sufficient for the US and its allies to prepare to 'win' through improved conventional capabilities alone. Increased risks of conflict and growing escalation pathways thus challenge US alliances just as improved alliance capabilities and political unity become more important for strengthening the credibility of deterrence. And to mitigate the risk of inadvertent or accidental escalation, improving the prospects for crisis management through prior confidence-building measures that promote transparency is more relevant than traditional arms control. Not only does the latter have a mixed record of success, but also any US attempt to forge arms control with China today would require Washington to engage with Beijing in a way that raises challenges for reassuring Japan, and potentially South Korea and Australia.

For Australia, the resurgence of great power competition underscores established challenges that arise from its geographical location. Given the ongoing focus of the US–South Korea alliance on the threat from North Korea, Australia and Japan are the key US allies in the Indo-Pacific with major (albeit different) roles and capabilities in helping to deter Beijing and, if necessary, assisting the US in fighting a war to defend Taiwan. Such a role carries political and military risk for Australia, which Canberra has long sought to 'manage' by avoiding any of the firm commitments (such as stationing a permanent US force presence on its soil) that would help underpin deterrence at the alliance level. But if deterrence fails and Taiwan is lost, Australia might, as Elbridge Colby points out in this volume, confront the same dilemmas regarding what commitments it would be willing to make to stem further Chinese expansion into the Philippines and maritime South-East Asia. And when increasingly long-range precision strike capabilities reduce the geographic value of Australia for the US, the alliance could itself come into question in the long term.

The institutional complexion of the alliances discussed in this volume varies significantly, and these differences exert a strong influence over the way they are adapting to the new environment. But there is also a certain convergence that may make these differences less stark now than during the Cold War. This, in itself, changes expectations and poses its own challenges. In the US – Republic of Korea case, the heavily operational focus of alliance cooperation that was forged in the 1970s at a time when South Korea was an authoritarian state is not especially well suited to addressing the political challenges of managing competition with China. In Japan, unequal alliance arrangements rooted in the experience of the Pacific War are increasingly challenged by closer cooperation, the ambitions and implicit assumptions of which may risk outpacing the constraints arising from the pacifist sentiment that remains strongly rooted domestically among Japanese citizens.

In general, the gap between what is required to manage the stresses that escalation—through deterrence and in war—imposes on alliances and the current political-military frameworks to control these remains significant. While NATO's institutional legacy from the Cold War provides an enticing blueprint for managing deterrence with Russia, even here the disappearance of the Warsaw Pact buffer between NATO Europe and Russia means that the dynamics of escalation would today be much faster and, as a consequence, harder to control. Sten Rynning points out that while NATO has found it easier to address the challenges of escalation at the military rather than political level, the theatre-wide approach informing its military strategy raises its own political challenges. At the level of US alliances in the Indo-Pacific, no equivalent concept has yet emerged. Greater cognisance of the need for shared understanding of the dynamics of escalation, if not necessarily shared operational planning for various scenarios, is a common theme that emerges from all the chapters in this volume on these alliances. A conflict over Taiwan may present a geographical focal point for such work that has eluded NATO, but different political constraints remain major obstacles in all three of the US's Indo-Pacific alliances.

A major theme that emerges from the volume, then, is the importance of political unity—as an enabler of closer operational integration but also as something that can be challenged by it. As Michael Rühle writes in his contribution, political unity more so than military power is the glue that binds security alliances together. The prospect of allied involvement against any Russian or Chinese attempt to use force over the specific issue at stake, such as Taiwan, serves as a deterrent because it brings into play not just additional force structure and basing locations, but also uncertainty on the part of any aggressor over its capacity to control the scope and level of conflict. As Jeffrey Larsen observes in this volume, deterrence is ultimately psychological and is contingent on adversary perceptions.

Communication of deterrence is, first and foremost, about the affirmation of alliance unity and, as Alexander Mattelaer points out in the case of NATO, engagement of all allies in planning renders the posture of deterrence materially more credible. As was the case during the Cold War, there will be debate and disagreement between those who perceive a preference on the part of China (or Russia) to use force, prioritise immediate deterrence and hence seek to improve military options even at the cost of increasing political tensions on the one hand, and those who see the choice of conflict as a more remote prospect, hence preferring general deterrence to maintain political unity among allies even at the cost of military effectiveness on the other.[1] But these are trade-offs that occur within an overall alliance deterrence posture that seeks to push the boundaries of what is politically feasible in *reducing* the perception that allies would not stand with each other—not from an approach to alliances that seeks to *preserve* the option of doing so, which has been Australia's traditional approach.

The nuclear aspects of deterrence have always been challenging in this regard, and the absence of any notion of nuclear 'burden sharing' as exists in NATO makes this even more so, both politically and practically, for US allies in the Indo-Pacific. However, the silver lining that emerges from this volume regarding nuclear weapons is how much they remain in the background of strategic competition in the Indo-Pacific. Escalation to the use of nuclear weapons against the US homeland by China is most likely if China is losing a conventional conflict. But, like the US, Beijing will have options other than nuclear weapons to target allied homelands with effect (such an unrestrained cyber attacks) as it moves up the escalation ladder. China has no realistic ability to undermine US nuclear retaliatory capabilities, and in general has little incentive to increase the prominence of nuclear forces that could only undermine its scope for conventional primacy in the Indo-Pacific. Moreover, as Oriana

---

1   On the NATO Cold War experience, see Ivo Daalder, *The Nature and Practice of Flexible Response: NATO Strategy and Theatre Nuclear Forces Since 1967* (New York: Columbia University Press, 1991), doi.org/10.7312/daal92104.

Skylar Mastro notes in her chapter, Beijing has no obvious incentives to use nuclear weapons against US allies in the Indo-Pacific because of the need to preserve its limited stockpile for use against US targets, as well as China's no-first-use declaration.

Besides the need to deter Chinese (or Russian) escalation to nuclear use to terminate a conflict, the general possibility that US nuclear forces might come into play in the case of catastrophic losses remains an important element of managing escalation—and deterring threats to US allies—in this new era of great power conflict. However, neither in Europe nor in the Indo-Pacific can nuclear weapons carry the main burden of deterrence as they did during the Cold War. NATO is explicit about the use of nuclear weapons changing the nature of a conflict but not in articulating the detail of escalation below (or above) that level. Nuclear weapons have a crucial but limited overall role in a strategy that ultimately rests on the ability to deter, fight and prevail through conventional means. In this context, it is also notable that NATO deliberately responded to Russia's violation of the Intermediate-Range Nuclear Forces (INF) Treaty not with the introduction of new nuclear intermediate-range missiles of its own, but through adjustments to its conventional forces and existing, limited nuclear forces.[2]

Societal aversion to nuclear weapons remains strong in Japan as well as Australia, and politically separating nuclear from any conventional elements of deterrence is thus paramount in the Indo-Pacific, as well as in NATO Europe. But even the overall rather minor adaptations to US nuclear forces in the 2018 NPR might raise political difficulties thought long gone in relation to US Navy ship visits, as well as questions about how they fit into the management of escalation in the Indo-Pacific that allies are yet to address. But—and at this point the dark cloud re-emerges more sharply into focus—this relatively minor role of nuclear weapons for alliances is also partly due to the lack of a common understanding of the concept of escalation in general.

In Australia's case, deterrence has emerged as a prominent concept in the country's *2020 Defence Strategic Update*.[3] Yet, the underlying concept remains highly abstract and focused on capabilities rather than the

---

2   'Remarks', by NATO Secretary General Jens Stoltenberg at the Brussels Forum, NATO, 23 June 2020, www.nato.int/cps/en/natohq/opinions_176715.htm.
3   Department of Defence, *2020 Defence Strategic Update*, www1.defence.gov.au/sites/default/files/2020-11/2020_Defence_Strategic_Update.pdf.

political credibility or circumstances underlying how these capabilities would be used; the *2020 Defence Strategic Update* has done little to specify how (conventional) deterrence articulates with the broader US posture in the region. Indeed, recapitulation in the *2020 Defence Strategic Update* of Australia's well-worn formula that 'only the nuclear and conventional capabilities of the United States can offer effective deterrence against the possibility of nuclear threats against Australia'[4] reaffirms a sole-purpose approach to nuclear weapons that is at odds with US nuclear policy.

Even in the highly institutionalised US–South Korea alliance, Seukhoon Paul Choi concludes in this volume that Washington and Seoul are yet to reach a shared understanding of escalation dynamics and the role of deterrence in the evolving strategic environment. However, almost all contributions to this book underscore the importance of such a shared concept, whether as the basis of political unity as an element of deterrence; to manage the political implications of nuclear weapons; to manage the extreme compression of time for decision-making in crisis management; to reduce the risk of technological surprise resulting from new, non-nuclear capabilities; to create a shared basis for interpreting signals implicit in force movements and 'hardware' cooperation; or because it is simply 'inadequate', as Brad Roberts points out, that among many US allies the outer limits of their own nuclear debate only reach as far as discussing US policy.

Importantly, a shared understanding of escalation does not mean agreement on all relevant choices. As Michael Rühle points out in this volume, it is ultimately impossible to resolve all differences of interests between those allies extending guarantees of support and those receiving them. But the Cold War NATO example demonstrates that it is possible to find compromises that enable cooperation to proceed or, as Paul Schulte once phrased it, to 'politically manage' such differences 'by creating a common *deterrence culture* … within which joint planning … could be conducted and normalized'.[5] While questions of when and how to initiate the use of nuclear weapons are today less of a focal point for such debates than they were during the Cold War, different interests remain, not least regarding the desirable scope for escalation, including in the case

---

4   Ibid., para 2.22.
5   Paul Schulte, 'Tactical Nuclear Weapons in NATO and Beyond: A Historical and Thematic Examination', in *Tactical Nuclear Weapons and NATO*, ed. Tom Nichols, Douglas Stuart and Jeffrey McClausland (Carlisle Barracks: Strategic Studies Institute, US Army War College, 2012), 25 (emphasis in original).

of 'minor' deterrence failures like those that strained the US–South Korea alliance in 2010, the speed of escalation or the desirability of horizontal escalation in major conflict.

Implications of the Book's Analysis

How can US alliances in the Indo-Pacific start building this common understanding and common deterrence culture? Three distinct, but closely related areas emerge from the contributions to this volume.

First, there is a need to move from *consultation* about US nuclear posture and deterrence, which can often entail the US simply informing allies of what has happened, to a more genuine *joint development* of assessments, concepts and planning for deterrence.[6] Even if deterrence dialogues and committees established in the US–Japan and US–South Korea alliances a decade ago have, to borrow a NATO colloquialism, helped to 'raise the nuclear IQ' in these alliances, the contributions in this volume also point to the limitations, if not divisive aspects, that can arise from constrained formats that remain narrowly focused on the North Korean threat, or include a perception of the US 'educating' its allies. As Brad Roberts points out, there is an opportunity for consultation evolving into substantive *collaboration* on some aspects of the Biden administration's forthcoming Nuclear Posture Review. This could have the added beneficial effect of reinforcing the credibility of US extended nuclear deterrence after a period of alliance anxiety under the Trump administration. Indeed, there are strong parallels with the way that the US in the 1960s tried to find new, more cooperative ways of engaging its non-nuclear allies on the practical and political challenges of deterrence, which moved from increased access to information on US policy towards joint analysis and political agreement on basic principles.[7] Because Australia has not been receptive to even the relatively limited dialogues that commenced in North-East Asia in 2011 in its own alliance relationship with the US, the learning curve and political significance of such cooperation would be considerable.

---

6   For recent discussion of this theme through the lens of non-proliferation, see Ivo Daalder, Chuck Hegel, Malcolm Rifkind and Kevin Rudd, 'Preventing Nuclear Proliferation and Reassuring America's Allies', The Chicago Council on Global Affairs, 10 February 2021, www.thechicagocouncil.org/research/report/preventing-nuclear-proliferation-and-reassuring-americas-allies.
7   Paul Buteux, *The Politics of Nuclear Consultation in NATO: 1965–1980* (Cambridge: Cambridge University Press, 1983).

Second, there is a need for Indo-Pacific allies to address more systematically their own force structure and 'hardware' cooperation aspects of deterrence in their alliances. In Australia's case, new conventional long-range strike capabilities are emerging, yet thinking about their use and effect remains nascent and focused on the tactical level. In the Japanese and, in particular, South Korean cases, conventional strike capabilities that did not exist in the past now provide these allies with greater options for direct influence on the dynamics of escalation. At the same time, the political and strategic limits of a US nuclear posture in the Indo-Pacific whose visible elements today rest solely on nuclear-capable aircraft based outside the region are also coming into sharper relief, through the increasing vulnerability of such forces, the overuse of strategic bombers for signalling and the lack of any significant adjustment (even in the face of momentous strategic shifts since US nuclear weapons were withdrawn from the region in 1992). As Michito Tsuruoka points out in his chapter, there is scope for thinking about closer practical cooperation beyond escorting US strategic bombers passing through the region. In fact, doing so would not just make an important contribution to demonstrating political unity of alliances, but also may help catalyse closer and more enduring institutionalised cooperation at the operational level, even in the US–Australia alliance.

The third strong theme emerging from the volume is the need for governments to actively engage populations about the issues canvassed in this book. A key lesson from NATO's travails of the 1970s and 1980s is that agreeing on and implementing changes to force structure and posture to improve deterrence capabilities and operational effectiveness are insufficient if these measures fail to reassure allies' own populations. Like deterrence, reassurance is ultimately psychological, but there is a reluctance today in many countries to publicly address requirements for deterrence and escalation management, or even arms control. The argument that there is a binary choice between seeking nuclear (and general) disarmament on the one hand, and relying on deterrence on the other is a false one, as it ignores that the ultimate goal of increased security depends on the broader strategic environment in which it is sought. As Tanya Ogilvie-White argues in this volume, restricted engagement of the public on nuclear matters has ultimately backfired and strengthened the hand of disarmament advocates whose case is already a more compelling one to make.

Statements by NATO governments highlight that they recognise 'that progress on arms control and disarmament must take into account the prevailing international security environment', that they 'regret that the conditions for achieving disarmament are not favourable today'[8] and that the Treaty on the Prohibition of Nuclear Weapons 'does not reflect the increasingly challenging international security environment'.[9] In contrast, the Australian Government continues to discuss disarmament with no reference to the security and deterrent value of nuclear weapons.[10] Indeed, the joint communiqués following annual Australia–US ministerial meetings lack *any* reference to the strategic role of nuclear weapons in allies' security. If allies are to continue to share the benefits from US nuclear deterrence, making the case—or, in Brad Roberts's words, 'campaigning'—for it in the prevailing strategic circumstances must be a shared responsibility. As Alexander Mattelaer points out in this volume:

> The fundamental willingness to engage in nuclear deterrence is perhaps the hardest question of all. Yet without such political willingness on the part of US allies, it is equally fair to ask whether the US extended deterrence commitment can be fully relied upon. Simply put, can one ask one's ally to do what one is not as a matter of principle willing to do for oneself?

***

In the end, developing a shared understanding of escalation dynamics, maintaining political unity about a shared approach to deterrence, moving from consultation to joint assessment, policy and planning, alliance reviews of force structure and posture implications for escalation, and public campaigning for the importance of nuclear deterrence are all mutually supporting. Together, these measures would be transformative for US alliances in the Indo-Pacific because they involve accepting a degree of heightened strategic risk that many allies have so far eschewed. Yet, while the risks of entrapment will always be a factor in the calculations of any ally, failing to clarify expectations and commitments in relation

---

8 'Warsaw Summit Communiqué', NATO, 8–9 July 2016, para 65, www.nato.int/cps/en/natohq/official_texts_133169.htm.
9 'North Atlantic Council Statement as the Treaty on the Prohibition of Nuclear Weapons Enters Into Force', Press Release, NATO, 20 December 2020, para 1, www.nato.int/cps/en/natohq/news_180087.htm.
10 Department of Foreign Affairs and Trade, 'Towards a Nuclear Weapons Free World', www.dfat.gov.au/international-relations/security/non-proliferation-disarmament-arms-control/nuclear-issues.

to deterrence and escalation pathways runs the risk of the US and its allies not being able to take unified action during crises—indeed, of not deterring them from arising in the first place. The adverse implications for the future of alliances in the Indo-Pacific that would inevitably flow from this should be enough to energise policymakers in all alliance capitals to strive for closer cooperation on deterrence and escalation.

Author Biographies

Seukhoon Paul Choi is a principal at StratWays Group, a geopolitical risk advisory in Seoul. He specialises in political-military affairs, international security and strategy design. Until 2018, he worked as a strategist and international relations specialist at the United Nations Command, ROK–US Combined Forces Command and US Forces Korea, in both the Commander's Strategic Initiatives Group and the Directorate for Strategy, Policy, Plans and Strategic Communications. Previously, he worked as a research associate at the Council on Foreign Relations, was a visiting scholar at Fudan University, a faculty lecturer at the Korea Military Academy and an officer in the Republic of Korea Army.

Elbridge Colby is a principal at the Marathon Initiative. He served as Deputy Assistant Secretary of Defense for Strategy and Force Development in 2017–18, during which he led the development of the 2018 National Defense Strategy. He is the author of *The Strategy of Denial: American Defense in an Age of Great Power Conflict* (New Haven: Yale University Press, 2021).

Andrew Davies is a senior fellow at the Australian Strategic Policy Institute. He holds a PhD in physics and worked as a research scientist in the Department of Defence before moving into capability analysis and signals intelligence. He has lectured in intelligence and defence force structuring at The Australian National University.

Stephan Frühling is Associate Dean, Partnerships and Engagement in the College of Asia and the Pacific at The Australian National University, where he researches and teaches in the Strategic and Defence Studies Centre. He was the Fulbright professional fellow in Australia–US Alliance Studies at Georgetown University, Washington, in 2017. He worked as a 'Partner across the Globe' research fellow in the research division of the NATO Defense College in Rome in 2015, and was a member of the Australian Government's external panel of experts on the development of the *2016 Defence White Paper*.

Łukasz Kulesa is Deputy Head of Research at the Warsaw-based Polish Institute of International Affairs. His research interests include deterrence, arms control, NATO, Russian security policy and non-proliferation of weapons of mass destruction. His recent publications include 'Operationalizing the "Polish Fangs": Poland and Long-Range Precision Strike', *The Nonproliferation Review*, 2020; *Dilemmas of Arms Control: Meeting the Interests of NATO's North-Eastern Flank* (ICDS, 2020); and 'The Future of Conventional Arms Control in Europe', *Survival*, 2018. Between 2014 and 2019, Łukasz was research director at the European Leadership Network. From 2010 to 2012, he worked at the National Security Bureau.

Jeffrey A. Larsen is a research professor in the Department of National Security Affairs, US Naval Postgraduate School, Monterey, California, and President of Larsen Consulting Group in Colorado Springs, Colorado. A retired US Air Force pilot, he was director of the research division at the NATO Defense College, Rome, from 2013 to 2018. He holds a PhD in politics from Princeton University. He is co-editor of *On Limited Nuclear War in the 21st Century* (Stanford: Stanford University Press, 2014).

Oriana Skylar Mastro is a centre fellow at the Freeman Spogli Institute for International Studies, Stanford University, where her research focuses on Chinese military and security policy, Asia-Pacific security issues, war termination and coercive diplomacy. She is also a senior non-resident fellow at the American Enterprise Institute and serves as an officer in the US Air Force Reserve. For her contributions to US strategy in Asia, she won the Individual Reservist of the Year Award in 2016. She has published widely, including in *Foreign Affairs*, *International Security*, *International Studies Review*, *Journal of Strategic Studies*, *Washington Quarterly* and *Survival*. Her book, *The Costs of Conversation: Obstacles to Peace Talks in Wartime* (Ithaca: Cornell University Press, 2019), won the 2020 American Political Science Association International Security Section Best Book by an Untenured Faculty Member. She holds a BA in East Asian studies from Stanford University and an MA and PhD in politics from Princeton University.

Alexander Mattelaer is Vice Dean for Research and an Associate Professor in International Security at the VUB Brussels School of Governance. He is also a senior research fellow at Egmont – The Royal Institute for International Relations, and a member of the scientific committee of the Belgian Royal Higher Institute for Defence. As a Fulbright Schuman fellow, he visited Harvard University and the National Defense University. His research interests include deterrence and defence planning, transatlantic relations and NATO, and the politics of European integration.

Masashi Murano is Japan Chair Fellow at the Hudson Institute. His research areas include US–Japan defence cooperation and nuclear/conventional deterrence analysis. Prior to joining Hudson, he was a research fellow at the Okazaki Institute (a Tokyo-based think tank). In addition to these experiences, he has been involved in research, analysis, tabletop exercises and facilitation of numerous classified products related to strategic intelligence assessment and policy planning for the Japanese Government. His recent publications include 'The Modality of Japan's Long-Range Strike Options', *Texas National Security Review*, 1 October 2020.

Andrew O'Neil is Acting Dean of the Graduate Research School and Professor of Political Science at Griffith University. Prior to entering academia full-time, and after completing his PhD, he worked as a Commonwealth public servant with Australia's Department of Defence. He is a member of the Australian Research Council's College of Experts and is a former member of the National Consultative Committee on National Security Issues.

Brad Roberts has served as Director of the Center for Global Security Research at Lawrence Livermore National Laboratory since September 2015. From 2009 to 2013, he was Deputy Assistant Secretary of Defense for Nuclear and Missile Defense Policy. In this role, he served as policy director of the Obama administration's Nuclear Posture Review and Ballistic Missile Defense Review and led their implementation. Roberts also serves as a member of US Strategic Command's Strategic Advisory Group. Prior to entering government service, he was a research fellow at the Institute for Defense Analyses and the Center for Strategic and International Studies, editor of the *Washington Quarterly* and an adjunct professor at George Washington University. Between leaving the Office of the Secretary of Defense in 2013 and assuming his current responsibilities, he was a consulting professor at Stanford University and William Perry fellow at the Center for International Security and Cooperation. While there, he authored *The Case for US Nuclear Weapons in the 21st Century*, which won the Choice Award for Outstanding Academic Title in 2016.

Michael Rühle is head of the Hybrid Challenges and Energy Security Section in NATO's Emerging Security Challenges Division. Previously he was head of speechwriting in the NATO Political Affairs Division, and senior political adviser in NATO's Secretary General's Policy Planning Unit. Before joining NATO's International Staff in 1991, Rühle was a Volkswagen fellow at the Konrad Adenauer Foundation in Germany and a visiting fellow at the Center for Strategic and International Studies, Washington. He has published widely on international security issues.

Sten Rynning is Professor and Vice Dean for Research at the Faculty of Business and Social Sciences, the University of Southern Denmark, where he founded the Center for War Studies in 2011 and headed it until 2019. He is a non-resident fellow of the NATO Defense College and a senior fellow of the Danish Institute for Advanced Studies. He is the author of numerous books and articles on NATO and modern war.

Brendan Sargeant is Professor of Practice in Defence and Strategic Studies and head of the Strategic and Defence Studies Centre, Coral Bell School of Asia Pacific Affairs, The Australian National University. From September 2013 to October 2017, he was the associate secretary of the Australian Department of Defence. Prior to that appointment, he was the Deputy Secretary Strategy. As associate secretary, he was responsible for oversight of the implementation of the First Principles Review, a major reform of defence organisation and enterprise governance, planning, performance and risk management. He was principal author of the *2013 Defence White Paper*.

Tomohiko Satake is a senior fellow in the Defence Policy Division at the National Institute for Defence Studies, Tokyo. His research interests include alliance studies, Indo-Pacific security and Japanese security policy. Between 2013 and 2014, he served as a deputy director for international security at the International Policy Division of Japan's Ministry of Defense. His publications include 'Japan–Australia Security Cooperation in the Bilateral and Multilateral Contexts' (co-authored with John

Hemmings), *International Affairs*, 2018. He earned a BA and MA from Keio University, and a PhD in international relations from The Australian National University.

Michito Tsuruoka is an Associate Professor at Keio University, Japan. Until 2017, he was a senior research fellow at the National Institute for Defense Studies. Tsuruoka served as a visiting fellow at the Royal United Services Institute (2013–14), deputy director of the International Policy Division, Ministry of Defense (2012–13), and adviser for NATO at the Embassy of Japan in Belgium (2005–08). He studied politics and international relations at Keio University and Georgetown University and received a PhD from King's College London. He has published on international security, contemporary European politics and Japan's foreign and security policy.

Heather Williams is a senior lecturer at King's College London in the Centre for Science and Security Studies and in the Defence Studies Department. During the 2020–21 academic year, she will be a visiting fellow at the Managing the Atom Project in the Belfer Center at the Harvard Kennedy School, and from 2020–21 she was a Stanton Nuclear Security fellow in the Security Studies Program at Massachusetts Institute of Technology. She currently leads projects on emerging technology, the future of arms control and the Treaty on the Non-Proliferation of Nuclear Weapons. She is a non-resident senior associate with the Project on Nuclear Issues at the Center for Strategic and International Studies, an associate fellow at the Royal United Services Institute and a senior associate fellow with the European Leadership Network. She previously worked at Chatham House and was a specialist adviser to an inquiry by the House of Lords into nuclear disarmament. Williams completed her PhD in the Department of War Studies at King's College London, has a BA in international relations and Russian studies from Boston University and an MA in security policy studies from George Washington University.

Tanya Ogilvie-White is Research Adviser to the Asia-Pacific Leadership Network; Director of the Global Security Programme at the New Zealand Centre for Global Studies; and a senior fellow at the Coral Bell School of Asia Pacific Affairs, The Australian National University. Previously, she was research director of the Centre for Nuclear Nonproliferation and Disarmament, Crawford School of Public Policy; senior analyst at the

Australian Strategic Policy Institute, Canberra; Stanton Nuclear Security fellow at the International Institute for Strategic Studies, UK; and senior lecturer in international relations, University of Canterbury, New Zealand.

Index

Note: Page numbers with 'n' indicate footnotes.

www.ingramcontent.com/pod-product-compliance
Lightning Source LLC
Chambersburg PA
CBHW050808270326
41926CB00026B/4639